Homeland Security

Recent Titles in the
CONTEMPORARY WORLD ISSUES
Series

Books in the **Contemporary World Issues** series address vital issues in today's society such as genetic engineering, pollution, and biodiversity. Written by professional writers, scholars, and nonacademic experts, these books are authoritative, clearly written, up-to-date, and objective. They provide a good starting point for research by high school and college students, scholars, and general readers as well as by legislators, businesspeople, activists, and others.

Each book, carefully organized and easy to use, contains an overview of the subject, a detailed chronology, biographical sketches, facts and data and/or documents and other primary source material, a forum of authoritative perspective essays, annotated lists of print and nonprint resources, and an index.

Readers of books in the Contemporary World Issues series will find the information they need in order to have a better understanding of the social, political, environmental, and economic issues facing the world today.

Homeland Security

A REFERENCE HANDBOOK

Michael C. LeMay

ABC-CLIO ™

An Imprint of ABC-CLIO, LLC

Santa Barbara, California • Denver, Colorado

Library of Congress Cataloging-in-Publication Data

Names: LeMay, Michael C., 1941-, author.
Title: Homeland security : a reference handbook / Michael C. LeMay.
Description: Santa Barbara, California : ABC-CLIO, [2018] | Series: Contemporary world issues | Includes bibliographical references and index.
Identifiers: LCCN 2018014179 (print) | LCCN 2018015116 (ebook) | ISBN 9781440854101 (ebook) | ISBN 9781440854095 (alk. paper)
Subjects: LCSH: National security—Law and legislation—United States. | Internal security—United States. | Civil defense—Law and legislation—United States. | United States. Department of Homeland Security—History. | Terrorism—United States—Prevention. | Security, International—United States.
Classification: LCC KF4850 (ebook) | LCC KF4850 .L46 2018 (print) | DDC 344.7305/34—dc23
LC record available at https://lccn.loc.gov/2018014179

ISBN: 978-1-4408-5409-5 (print)
       978-1-4408-5410-1 (ebook)

22 21 20 19 18   1 2 3 4 5

This book is also available as an eBook.

ABC-CLIO
An Imprint of ABC-CLIO, LLC

ABC-CLIO, LLC
130 Cremona Drive, P.O. Box 1911
Santa Barbara, California 93116-1911
www.abc-clio.com

This book is printed on acid-free paper ∞

Manufactured in the United States of America

vii

5   DATA AND DOCUMENTS, 243

Homeland Security: A Reference Handbook defines the term and concept of homeland security, which came into the lexicon of American politics and government following the terrorist attacks of September 11, 2001. In the founding period of the American republic, such policy came under the rubric of "domestic tranquility" and "internal affairs." The horrific international terrorist attacks of September 11, 2001, shook the American psyche as did no other event since the devastating attack on Pearl Harbor on December 7, 1941. The killing of nearly 3,000 persons (not all of whom were Americans) in the single-day attacks that downed the World Trade Center Twin Tower buildings in New York City, severely damaged the Pentagon in Washington, D.C., and downed the plane that crashed into a Pennsylvania farm field only because of the heroic sacrifice of the plane's innocent passengers who prevented it from reaching its intended target (the capitol building in Washington, D.C.) forever changed how Americans thought about international terrorism. No longer was it something tragic that happened "over there," in Europe or the Middle East or Asia.

The political and governmental policy-making responses to 9/11 were profound and, as will be seen herein, impacted many aspects of U.S. civil rights and liberties, culture, economy, federal, state, and local government relations and organization, immigration policy, national security policy, public policy making, politics, privacy rights, and expectations, in short, virtually the entire array of American policy issues. It contributed to the growing polarization of American politics.

It deeply affected how Americans view their government and how well—or badly—the government is protecting its citizens from terror, both domestic and international.

As do all books in the Contemporary World Issues series, *Homeland Security* approaches its subject in a straightforward and objective manner. It illuminates the complexity of homeland security issues and the ongoing struggle by policy makers to secure the homeland while balancing a number of American values and concerns that are inherently conflicted. Current American politics struggles with the issue. The book examines the historical background to better understand the approach governments—federal, state, and local—have taken to achieve security. It discusses the extensive discourse in our scholarly literature that explains or advocates government policy concerning homeland security. It focuses primarily on the government policy response since 2001. It offers answers to essential questions about national and homeland security concerns and issues that are inherently interconnected. It tries to make that discourse accessible to high school students, undergraduate students, and general readers who have become interested in this complex topic that spans immigration policy, border control and security, and complex human rights issues that are intertwined with homeland security policy. It examines the history and background and explores the myriad problems and controversies raised by the attempt to secure the nation from terrorism while grappling with human rights, civil and privacy rights, the interrelations of minority groups and the majority society, the right to religious beliefs and freedoms balanced with the need to protect the safety of citizens facing a threat that is so often perceived as coming from a "foreign religion."

A perspective chapter offers a broad range of voices from all sides of the issue. They add crucial and diverse perspectives to that of the author's expertise and come from other established scholars of the topic, from beginning scholars approaching the issues with state-of-the-art analyses, and from stakeholders affected by and therefore involved in the complex politics of the homeland security debate. It introduces the reader to the concept of "groupthink" behavior in decision making and how that affected the creation of the Department of Homeland Security. It covers management problems arising from merging so many diverse agencies and programs into one huge department of government. It introduces the reader to the concept of cyberattacks and warfare and how they affect internal security. It examines the problem of trying to balance the need for greater safety and security with the cherished American values of civil liberty and privacy rights. It shows why immigration reform— inherently linked to security issues—is so complex and difficult to achieve, enact, and implement. It examines climate change and how the political debate over climate change and policy designed to mitigate it meet political opposition despite the increasing frequency and intensity of climate-related natural disasters. It reviews the scandals that shook the Secret Service, an agency now housed within the Department of Homeland Security. It covers the controversy associated with President Trump's use of executive orders to impose a travel ban on visitors to the United States from Muslim-majority countries. It explores the needs of American business and the economy that have been adversely impacted by policy designed to secure the homeland by tightening controls of the visa application and visitors' visa program. It illustrates the rich complexity of the federal system of government and how the three levels of government impact homeland security policy making. It covers how migration to the United States had contributed to a positive (for the U.S. economy and society) brain drain and how current policy to ensure greater security has adversely affected that brain-drain trend. It examines how the Social Security program is affected by the crackdown on immigration and more restrictive immigration policy.

Chapter 1 discusses the history and background of homeland security lawmaking. It covers some of the precursor laws that comprised federal policy before the 9/11 attacks. It provides a thorough examination of the economic, political, and social contexts surrounding the nation's sense of security and how they were so deeply shaken by the 9/11 and subsequent terrorist incidents. The historical background chapter is designed to provide the context through which the reader can better understand current events. It presents that discussion in a comprehensive and unbiased manner, allowing readers to form their own judgments on the issue.

Chapter 2 outlines some of the most problematic concerns related to homeland security policy making and why those issues pose such difficulty for effective policy making to ensure homeland security. It addresses efforts taken at all levels of government to cope with these problems, detailing specific actions taken to date, and discussing some proposed solutions to the problems that are now on the agenda of government, particularly at the national level.

Chapter 3 is comprised of nine original essays by scholars and stakeholders involved in the homeland security issue. The chapter brings together voices from diverse disciplinary perspectives to examine many sides of the issue and to enrich the perspective that the primary author is able to provide.

Chapter 4 describes the key organizations and people involved as stakeholders in the homeland security discourse. It profiles hundreds of organizations and both government and nongovernment actors who advocate for or against various policy proposals to cope with the problems inherently involved in homeland security. They are the participants who are involved in solutions to the problems raised by the need to better secure the safety of the American people and the homeland.

Chapter 5 offers some key data and documents gathered from government sources. They are presented in graphs (line, bar, and pie charts), tables, and excerpts and summaries of primary-source documents.

Chapter 6 is a resource chapter. It comprises a list of annotated books on the subject, scholarly journals that are also annotated, and films and videos as nonprint sources. Together they give the reader a fairly comprehensive review of the discourse on homeland security and will hopefully direct the reader to further research on the topic.

A chronology of key moments in the history of homeland security is then provided. These have occurred mostly since 2001, but a few precursor events are also listed and described.

Finally, a glossary provides easy access to definitions of the key terms used in the homeland security debate. These terms define the key concepts and explain any jargon associated with the topic, some of which will undoubtedly be unfamiliar to many readers. The glossary is followed by a comprehensive index.

Homeland Security

Introduction: Precursor Events to the Homeland Security Act

A mere year and two weeks after the tragic terrorist attacks of September 11, 2001, on November 25, 2002, President George W. Bush signed into law the nearly 500-page bill establishing the Department of Homeland Security (DHS; S. 4901 and HR 5005; P.L. 107–296). The law was enacted by a vote of 73–26 in the U.S. Senate, and a vote of 295–132 in the House of Representatives (see also www.dhs.gov/homeland-security-act-2002). The law initiated the largest federal government reorganization of the executive branch since the establishment of the Department of Defense in 1949. Congress had replaced the War Department in 1947 with the National Military Establishment, and then, in 1949, merged the army, navy, and air force into the cabinet-level Department of Defense, headed by a secretary of defense appointed by the president and confirmed by the U.S. Senate (https://www.defense.gov/About; see also LeMay 2006: 208).

With its establishment in 2002, the new DHS became the third largest of the federal executive branch departments, after the Department of Defense and the Department of Veteran Affairs. It merged 22 agencies and more than 190,000 employees. According to President Bush's statement on signing

---

The hijacked airplane attacks on the Twin Towers on September 11, 2001, sent the strongest psychological shock to American politics since the 1941 Pearl Harbor attack. Within a year, Congress enacted the USA Patriot Act and the Homeland Security Act. (Kentannenbaum/Dreamstime.com)

HR 5005 into law, the new department's primary mission "was to help prevent, protect against, and respond to acts of terrorism on U.S. soil" (http://www.dhs.gov/dhspublic/display?content-191). The act sailed through Congress with remarkable alacrity, passed by bipartisan votes in both chambers and by margins seldom seen since. To better understand why that was the case, it is helpful to review a number of precursor events that paved the way for enactment of the DHS Act (see Alden 2008; Brader, Valentino, and Suhay 2008, Clarke 2004; Enders and Sandler 2005; Lansford 2003; Motomura 2014; Roots 2003; Rosenblum 2011; Torr 2004; Zolberg 2008).

The Immigration and Nationality Act of 1965

The 1965 Act (79 Stat. 911) ended the national origins quota system and replaced it with a preference system that had seven goals:

1. to preserve family unity and reunite separated families,
2. to meet the need for some highly skilled immigrants,
3. to ease problems created by emergencies, such as political upheavals and natural disasters,
4. to assist cross-national exchange programs,
5. to bar immigrants who might present problems of adjustment due to their physical or mental health, past criminal history, dependency, or for national security reasons (what in today's terminology would be homeland security),
6. to standardize admission procedures, and
7. to establish limits for the Americas (see the bill excerpted and summarized in LeMay and Barkan 1999: 256–261).

The 1965 Act became the prevailing policy approach for legal immigration to the United States and is the fundamental immigration law to this day, only amended at the margins by subsequent legislation.

However, there was an unanticipated consequence of the 1965 Act that was especially associated with the seventh goal, to limit legal immigration from the Americas. It set off an exponential growth in unauthorized (aka "illegal") immigration. That surge in unauthorized immigration, particularly in undocumented immigration across the southern border with Mexico, resulted, by 2000, in an estimated 11–12 million unauthorized immigrants residing in the United States. Prior to the 1965 law, South and Central American countries had no quotas. In addition, because of the Bracero Program (1942–1964), Mexico had been sending annually more than 300,000 temporary workers (legally allowed to stay for nine months) to America. The Bracero Program was begun by executive order in 1942 but was subsequently approved and funded by Congress in 1944 (Act of February 14, 1944: Supply and Distribution of Farm Labor, 58 Stat. 11; 50 U.S.C., App. 1351, summarized in LeMay and Barkan 1999: 197–198). This program, lasting more than two decades, established the networks of migration from Mexico that became the steady stream of exponential growth in unauthorized immigration after 1970.

The 1965 law limited legal immigrants to 20,000 annually from each country. The Congress amended the 1965 Act by the Act of October 20, 1976. The 1976 law attempted to better control immigration from the Western Hemisphere and to reduce the ever-lengthening waiting period for legal immigrants (LeMay and Barkan 1999: 270–272). Despite this effort, however, unauthorized immigration continued its exponential growth, and conservative Republicans continued to attack unauthorized immigration, with fears of terrorists entering the country across the borders heightened by the September 11 attacks.

The Immigration Reform and Control Act of 1986 (IRCA)

With the election of conservative Republican president Ronald Reagan, in 1980, Congress again addressed the issue of the illegal immigration flow. Congress passed and President Reagan signed into law the Act of November 6, 1986 (100 Stat. 3360, excerpted and summarized in LeMay and Barkan

1999: 282–288; for a book-length and detailed analysis of IRCA, see LeMay 1994). IRCA attempted to demagnetize the pull that the U.S. economy had on Mexico and Central American countries by imposing employer sanction penalties on U.S. employers who knowingly hired unauthorized, undocumented immigrants. The law did produce a decline in the unauthorized flow, at least as measured by apprehensions at the southern border, but that decline was quite short-lived. Within two years of passage of IRCA, the border apprehension rate rose again to pre-1986 heights, and by 1991, exceeded them (LeMay 1994: 113). An unanticipated consequence of IRCA was a huge spike in the fraudulent documents industry. By showing counterfeit documents, the illegal immigrant could be hired, and the employer could evade punishment by claiming it had not "knowingly" hired an unauthorized worker. There was no secure and effective way that an employer could check the validity of the documents and the "green card" (right-to-work authorization) of the prospective employee.

In 1990, Congress moved to enact reforms of the legal immigration law and processes. By passing the Act of November 29, 1990 (IMMACT, 104 Stat. 4981) Congress modified certain provisions within IRCA, placing new ceilings for a worldwide level of immigration. It redefined the preference system with respect to family reunification and to employment and added a new preference category called diversity immigrants that had been introduced in IRCA as a temporary measure. It established a Commission on Legal Immigration Reform and provided for a temporary stay of deportation for certain immigrants to maintain family unity or who had temporary protected status (LeMay and Barkan 1999: 288–295).

Proposition 187, Al Qaeda's Probing Acts of Terrorism, and the 1996 Immigration-Related Reform Acts

Deeply upset over the failure of the federal government to control the nation's borders, the state of California joined Florida and Texas in filing law suits against the federal government asking for the estimated billions of dollars they had to bear and that they claimed they had to spend on costs related to illegal immigrants and their children. Then, in November 1994, California passed an initiative measure to send a message to Congress: the "Save Our State" initiative, more commonly known as Proposition 187 (for summary excerpt, see LeMay and Barkan 1999: 296–299).

What should have been another red flag for national government policy makers that went unnoticed because the various intelligence agencies were not communicating well with each other and failed to "connect the dots" was the development of international terrorism and the ideology of radical Islam, especially the organization known as *Al Qaeda*—meaning "the base." Al Qaeda was devoted to killing other humans and especially to kill noncombatants (Miniter 2011: 7). In February 1998, Osama bin Laden signed a fatwa declaring war on the West and Israel and soon after released a video declaring war on the United States. Al Qaeda was behind a thwarted 2000 millennium attack plot that included the attempted bombing of Los Angeles International Airport (LAX). On October 12, 2000, Al Qaeda terrorists attacked the U.S.S. *Cole* in the port of Yemen. That attack killed 17 U.S. navy sailors.

The strategic planner of international terrorism plots was Khalid Sheikh Mohammad (hereafter, KSM), who, until his capture by the United States in 2003, was for 15 years at the center of every major Al Qaeda plot including (1) the 1993 bombing of the World Trade Center in New York City, that took six lives; (2) the bombing of two night clubs in Bali, killing six; (3) the 2001 attempted airline bombing by the "shoe" bomber, Richard Reid, that had it been successful would have killed the hundreds of passengers and crew on the flight; (4) a plan to crash airplanes into the U.S. Bank Tower in Los Angeles; (5) the September 11 attacks that did kill nearly 3,000 persons; (6) a plot to bomb London's Heathrow Airport and the Empire State Building, where about 1,000 people work; (7)

plots to bomb skyscrapers in Los Angeles, Seattle, Chicago, and to bomb the Panama Canal; (8) a plot to assassinate President Bill Clinton, Pope John Paul II, and the prime minister of Pakistan; and (9) the personal beheading of the *Wall Street Journal* reporter Daniel Pearl in Karachi, Pakistan (Miniter 2011: 2–3).

KSM joined the Muslim Brotherhood sometime in the mid-1970s. The Brotherhood had been founded by al-Banna in 1928. The Muslim Brotherhood's intellectual leader was Sayyid Qutb, who preached "armed jihad," or holy war, that later became the intellectual source for Al Qaeda (Miniter 2011: 16–31). That concept also inspired and was preached by the Wahhabi School of Sunni Islam and its puritanical "salafis"— a fundamentalist group associated with Wahhabism. International terrorism took an institutional and state-based root with the Iranian revolution of 1979. The revolution created the first radical Islam terror state. It is likely that KSM met Osama bin Laden in Tora Bora, Afghanistan's White Mountains, in 1995, and began planning the 9/11 attacks with Osama bin Laden and other terrorists in Al Qaeda, like Mohammad Atef, the head of Al Qaeda's military wing, in Kandahar, Afghanistan, in 1998. They carried out dry runs of hijackings to test their ability to get box cutters on board U.S. airplanes. They sent several of the perpetrators of the 9/11 attacks to Jones Aviation, a Sarasota, Florida, pilot training school (Miniter 2011: 111–128). U.S. policy makers were slow to react to international terrorism, overconfident of the ability to thwart such plots from happening in the United States. Until 9/11, international terrorism was too often and too pervasively perceived as something that happened "over there"—in Europe or the Middle East, rather than in the American homeland (Clarke 2004).

The California law was immediately challenged in federal district court, and many of its provisions were declared unconstitutional (*LULAC et al. v. Wilson et al.*, 1995). Although the law was overturned by the Supreme Court, it succeeded in its goal of sending a message to Congress (the *LULAC* decision is summarized in LeMay and Barkan 1999: 300–301).

Congress received California's Proposition 187 message. In 1996 Congress passed two laws that essentially enacted at the federal level the provisions in Proposition 187. It did so by folding its provisions into the omnibus 1997 spending bill (H.R. 3610, P.L. 104–208), which President William Clinton signed into law in 1996: the Personal Responsibility and Work Opportunity Act of August 22, 1996. It was a broader welfare reform measure that contained new restrictions on both legal and illegal immigrants (summarized in LeMay and Barkan 1999: 301–304).

Congress followed that law with another one in September 1996: the Illegal Immigration Reform and Immigrant Responsibility Act of September 30, 1996 (LeMay 2006: 196–198; LeMay and Barkan 1999: 304–310). The latter law contained many provisions designed to crack down on illegal immigration at the borders, several of which are briefly described here. It authorized an increase in the number of Border Patrol agents from 5,000 to 10,000, funded an additional 900 Immigration and Naturalization Service (INS) agents to investigate and prosecute cases of smuggling illegal immigrants and 300 agents to investigate visa overstayers. It authorized the building of a border fence, issued biometric identifiers into Border Crossing Cards, increased the penalty for the attempted fleeing through checkpoints by up to five years in prison and the deportation of those so convicted. It authorized creation of an entry-exit system database for the INS to keep better track of visa overstayers. It allowed wiretaps to investigate immigration document fraud and increased penalties for immigrant smuggling, authorized 25 additional prosecutors to prosecute cases of immigrant smuggling and document fraud, and increased the penalty for such fraud from five to ten years, and up to 25 years for those involving terrorism. It allowed the seizure of boats, airplanes, and real estate if they were used in the commission of a crime or were assessed as profits from the proceeds of a crime. It expanded the power and streamlined the proceedings to detain and deport unauthorized immigrants. It expanded the employment verification system, establishing a basic pilot program for employers to contact the INS to verify a job applicant's eligibility to work. It banned illegal immigrants from virtually all public benefit (welfare) programs and limited the use of parole by the INS of detainees to facilitate mass immigration. It stipulated national standards for several state-issued documents: birth certificates, driver's licenses, and other identification documents. Despite such increasingly strong attempts at a "border control" approach to cope with illegal immigration, the number of unauthorized immigrants in the United States continued to rise. These presidential and congressional actions and provisions set the stage for enactments that followed the 9/11 attacks, including the law to establish the DHS.

In 1998, Congress established a 14-member, bipartisan Defense-Department chartered commission on national security, known as the Hart-Rudman Commission after its cochairs, Senators Gary Hart (D-CO) and Warren Rudman (R-NH). It issued its final report, "Road Map for National Security: Imperative for Change," on January 31, 2001 (http://fas.org/irp/threat/nssg .pdf). It called for sweeping changes in structure and policy for national security. The new Bush administration, however, largely ignored the recommendations (many of which would seem especially prescient just months later, after the 9/11 attacks). Among their many recommendations, they called for more coordination of the various intelligence agencies to deal with the problem of "stovepiping," in which information is transmitted directly through levels of a hierarchy while bypassing intervening levels, or related separate agencies, that remain uninformed about this information (Alden 2008: 33–41; http://www.freedictionary. com/stovepiping). An example would be the CIA or the FBI failing to alert the State Department or the DHS of intelligence that might put an individual on a terrorist watch-list.

The Making of Fortress America in Response to International Terrorism

When the 19 terrorists flew their four hijacked planes into the World Trade Center in New York City and the Pentagon building in Washington, D.C., and the plane that crashed in a field near Shanksville, Pennsylvania, killed a total of 2,977 innocents plus the 19 hijackers, Congress reacted and the president took executive actions with nearly unprecedented speed and sweeping powers. President Bush vowed the perpetrators and planners of the attacks would be hunted down and brought to justice. The administration changed immigration policy making and implementation. The disarray, ineffectiveness, and inefficiency at the INS was exposed by the 9/11 attacks. One of the first reactions to the attacks was the closing of the Statue of Liberty Island national park:

> After jet planes crashed into the World Trade Center and the Pentagon, the Statue of Liberty closed to visitors. The policy was intended to protect an enduring symbol of American ideals. Yet the closing of Lady Liberty was emblematic of the damage that had already been done to the image of America as a country that welcomed foreigners and of the shift in America's attitude toward strangers. (Wucker 2006: 139)

On September 14, 2001, Congress passed, and President Bush signed into law on September 18, the Authorization for Use of Military Force against Terrorists, approving the law under Section 5 (b) of the 1973 War Powers Resolution. This became the fundamental legal authorization for all subsequent "War on Terror" policy actions. Two days later, President Bush delivered an ultimatum to the Taliban government of Afghanistan, known as the Islamic Emirate of Afghanistan, to turn over Osama bin Laden and all other Al Qaeda leaders then based in Kandahar, Afghanistan. The U.N. Security Council had also demanded that the Taliban turn over Osama bin Laden. The Taliban refused to comply, and on October 7, 2001, U.S. forces, along with United Kingdom and several other coalition forces, began "Operation Enduring Freedom," the invasion of Afghanistan. The invasion began with an aerial bombardment of Taliban and Al Qaeda installations in Kabul, Kandahar, Jalalabad, Konduz, and Mazar-i-Sharif. It was the opening salvo of the War on Terrorism in response to the 9/11 attacks (http://www.history.com/this-day-in-history/u-s-led-attack-on-Afghanistan-begins).

A basic tenet of national security is survival of the state (Rudolf 2006). Within hours of the 9/11 attacks, President Bush made prevention of another attack the single, unequivocal, overriding priority of his presidency. The administration prioritized national security and the prevention of another terrorist attack over reforming border relations with Mexico, by enacting a program that the Bush administration called "compassionate conservatism." It allowed unfettered study and research by foreign students, and ensured the privacy of personal life and communication. Attorney General John Ashcroft stated in testimony before the 107th Congress: "Our fight against terrorism is not merely or primarily a criminal justice endeavor. It is defense of our nation and its citizens. We cannot wait for terrorists to strike to begin investigations and to take action. The death tolls are too high, the consequences too great. We must prevent the first. We must prosecute the second" (107 Congress 2001).

Ashcroft ordered the strict enforcement of an INS rule requiring foreign visitors to file change of address forms supposedly being used by the federal government to keep track of visitors entering the United States with temporary visas. The system was not computerized, and the INS had a backlog of some 2 million paper documents unprocessed and piled up in boxes and stored in a Kansas City warehouse. After Attorney General Ashcroft's order, the INS was inundated with change of address forms at a rate of 30,000 per day, and the unprocessed backlog soon mounted to 4 million. The INS estimated that there were some 4 million "overstayers," foreigners who were in the country with expired visas. They are persons who entered the United States legally, with temporary visas, who then stayed beyond the time specified in their visas at which time they are to voluntarily depart the United States. By overstaying their visas their status becomes unauthorized (i.e., illegal).

Even more shocking, the INS sent a letter to the Jones Aviation, Sarasota, Florida, flight school approving the student visas of two of the September 11 attackers. The decision to approve them had been made prior to the attack, but the paperwork to notify the flight school had been backlogged for months and was not actually sent to the flight school until some months after the attack. The INS agency received a D in overall management in the 2002 Federal Performance Report—in sharp contrast, for example, to the A rating given the coast guard in that report. The INS was broadly considered to be among the worst federal agencies, with its investigators viewed as undertrained, overworked, and overstressed. There was widespread and bipartisan support in Congress for a major restructuring of the INS (LeMay 2006: 204).

Nineteen hijackers executed the 9/11 attacks. All had come to the United States on temporary visas—as students, tourists, or on business. They entered the country among the more than 30 million annual visitors, a number impossibly too large to effectively screen out all possible terrorists crossing the open borders by using such temporary visas. Indeed, in 2001, U.S. Customs and Border Patrol's 19,000 employees monitored $1 trillion in goods and about 500 million vehicles and people who crossed through more than 7,500 miles of U.S. land borders, and nearly 130 international airports and seaports— a truly monumental task. On the Canadian border alone, 334 INS agents had to screen 300,000 crossings each day! In August 2001, the passengers in U.S. air traffic numbered 65.4 million travelers that month. In October 2001, it fell by 24 percent, and in two years after 9/11, the number of arrivals to the United States from Canada and Mexico had fallen from 51 million to 41 million (Alden 2008: 26, 43–48).

The perpetrators of the attacks were almost immediately and publicly identified as Islamic terrorists, acknowledged by Osama bin Laden as Al Qaeda "holy warriors" who were implementing his "fatwa" to pursue "jihad." In a mere three days following the attack, the Council on American-Islamic

Relations received more than 300 reports of hate crimes and harassment, about half the number reported for the entire year 2000 (Wucker 2006: 140–141).

On October 8, 2001, President Bush issued Executive Order 13228. It established the Office of Homeland Security and the Homeland Security Council within the Executive Office of the President (Birkland 2004: 179–180; Broder 2002: 4; Crotty 2003: 457; *The Press Enterprise* 2002: A-l; LeMay 2015: 24; Relyea 2003: 613; see also Clarke 2004; Flynn 2004; Jones 2001; Lansford 2003; O'Hanlon et al. 2002; Walcott and Holt 2003). President Bush appointed former Pennsylvania governor Tom Ridge to head the office.

Critics in Congress, citing the recommendations of the final report of the National Commission on Terrorist Attacks in the United States, felt the executive order did not go far enough. Senator Joseph Lieberman (D-CT) introduced a proposal to establish a DHS as a cabinet-level department (S. 1534). Senator Lieberman and Representative Mac Thornberry (R-TX) then introduced a more elaborate version, in May 2002 (S. 2452, H.R. 4660). President Bush initially opposed the idea of creating a new department, as he had opposed the Hart-Commission Report, but ultimately responded to political pressure to do more than what the executive order could accomplish. He had an administration team, consisting of Mitchell Daniels, Jr., director of the Office of Management and Budget (OMB); Andrew Card, Jr., the White House chief of staff, and White House counsel at the time; Alberto Gonzalez, draft the administration's departmental plan, introduced as HR 5005 on June 24, 2002 (Relyea 2003: 617). Two laws that were passed quickly in response to the 9/11 attacks best characterize and symbolize the policy to build "Fortress America."

The USA Patriot Act of October 26, 2001

Within six weeks of the 9/11 attacks, a jittery Congress was exiled from its offices by an anthrax contamination incident widely viewed as another terrorist attack and confronted by warnings that likely more terrorist attacks were soon to come. The Bush administration responded by proposing a new arsenal of antiterrorism weapons. While there were only five deaths among the 21 persons who contracted anthrax, the psychological impact from the incident far exceeded the actual damage. An already-shaky economy took a hit, as did the U.S. postal system, and the public's confidence that such incidents of terrorism "can't happen here" (Yount 2004: 9). Congress passed the USA Patriot Act by a vote of 357–66 in the House of Representatives, and by 98–1 in the Senate, without public hearings or a committee report. President Bush signed the bill into law on October 26, 2001 (Crotty 2003: 457; LeMay 2015: 248; Torr 2004: 43–44; Wucker 2006: 141; it is also discussed in Alden 2008; Clarke 2004).

The USA Patriot Act bill was written largely by Assistant Attorney General Viet Dinh, who had been born in Saigon during the Vietnam War and came to America as a refugee. In practice, many of the act's consequences contributed to the discrimination it purported to condemn. It had few, if any, checks and balances to protect anyone who was tagged in error, even unintentionally. Attorney General Ashcroft gutted the immigration appeals board, removing five members who had been most sympathetic to immigrants. It required immigrants to register and be finger-printed. Of the 82,000 who complied and registered, 13,000 were told to leave the country, often on minor technicalities that were not the fault of the immigrants but of the slow-turning wheels of the immigration bureaucracy (Alden 2008: 141–144). "The new terrorism policy [sent] the message that immigrants of certain nationalities should be viewed as potential terror suspects first and welcomed as newcomers second, if at all" (Tumlin 2004: 1177).

Proponents argued that the USA Patriot Act was needed to catch terrorists and deter further terrorist attacks. They praised its provisions for enhanced interrogation of suspected terrorists and to control enemy "sleeper-cells," and its sweeping new powers to penetrate Al Qaeda cells: expanded surveillance, the use of informants, revisions to search and seizure procedures, the use of wiretaps, arrests, and the detentions of suspected terrorists. Proponents maintained that the law would take the handcuffs off law enforcement officials in dealing with the terrorist threat (LeMay 2006: 205; Torr 2004: 29).

The USA Patriot Act reaffirmed the computerized tracking system known as the Student and Exchange Visitor Information System (SEVIS). It required regular reporting by educational institutions on the enrollment status of their international students (LeMay 2013, Vol. 3: 82; Mittlestadt et al. 2011). Almost immediately there were long delays in visa approvals, particularly for students from Muslim-dominant countries. Thousands of students felt the full effects of the new law. Those coming from some 20 plus Muslim-dominant countries, as well as students coming from Egypt, Pakistan, Indonesia, China, and Russia, soon were so delayed in getting approval that they had to drop out of the process. Approval of student visas for people coming from the "Axis of Evil" countries (Iran, Iraq, Libya, Sudan, Syria, and North Korea) ground to a halt. From October 1, 2002, to August 1, 2003, the State Department received 270,000 student visa applications in all, and approved 175,000. That was 65,000 fewer visas than had been approved in 2002 (Alden 2008: 197–212). And many already in the country voluntarily deported themselves. Michele Wucker notes: "Assessing the new mood in America, Arabs and Muslims simply left the country rather than risk being detained with no notice to their families" (2006: 145).

Soon after the enactment of the Patriot Act, the Department of Justice (DOJ) announced it had broken up terrorist cells in Portland, Detroit, and Buffalo, charging 17 individuals with terrorist-related activities. The DOJ began targeting the financing operations of such reputed cells.

Critics decried the law as too sweeping and too dangerous an intrusion on civil liberty protections and as a threat to constitutional checks and balances, to open government, and to the rule of law. They argued that it evaded the Fourth Amendment by enabling federal agents to conduct "sneak and peek" searches, covert searches of a person's home or office without notice and with a striking lack of judicial oversight. The American Civil Liberties Union (ACLU) filed a legal challenge against Section 215 of the act, arguing that the law allowed the FBI to violate First Amendment rights, Fourth Amendment rights, and the right of due process.

As one such critic, David Cole, noted:

> It appears the greatest threat to our freedoms is posed not by the terrorists themselves, but by our government's response. . . . Administration supporters argue that the magnitude of the new threat requires a new paradigm. But so far we have seen only the repetition of the old paradigm—broad incursions on liberties, largely targeted at unpopular noncitizens and minorities, in the name of fighting a war. What is new is that this war has no end in sight, and only a vaguely defined enemy, so its incursions are likely to be permanent. (cited in Torr 2004: 12)

And in fact, the nonterrorists most affected by the Patriot Act in the months following 9/11, some 1,200 immigrants, were mostly Muslims, rounded up by police and immigration officials across the nation. Some were held for months without access to a lawyer or even having charges brought against them before an immigration judge. Only a few were deported, and even fewer were ever charged with any crime. Most were subsequently released as wholly innocent persons swept up in the post-attack hysteria. Fear of international terrorism was palpable and widespread (Lehrer 2004: 71). An estimated 1,500 to 2,000 individuals were detained under the act. Their number could only be estimated as the government stopped issuing daily numbers after November 2001, when it was at 1,182. None of those detained were ever charged with involvement in the September 11 attacks and most were cleared by the FBI of any involvement in terrorism (Etzioni and Marsh 2003: 37–38; see also Alden 2008; Salehyan 2009; Torr 2004). "According to a report released in June 2003, by Inspector General Glenn A. Fine, 762 illegal immigrants were detained for months after 9/11. None of them were charged with terrorism. Fine chastised the government for holding many immigrants for months without access to lawyers, on dubious evidence of terrorist ties" (Wucker 2006: 147).

The 9/11 attacks struck the death knell for the INS. The INS came to life in 1864, first called the Bureau of Immigration. It was enacted by Congress at the request of President Abraham Lincoln to address the acute Civil War–era labor shortage. The Immigration Act of 1891 (26 Stat. 1084, U.S.C. 101) revised it amid the first comprehensive national immigration law, which established the Office of Superintendent of Immigration, increased penalties for landing an illegal immigrant, strengthened enforcement processes, and centralized immigration policy under the aegis of the national level of government and giving it the decisive role in immigration affairs (Alden 2008: 63; summarized in LeMay and Barkan 1999: 66–70). In the decade prior to 9/11, the INS grew substantially. From 1990 to 2000, its budget increased from $1.2 billion to support a staff of 17,000 to a budget of $6.2 billion and a staff of 37,000. Despite that increase, the INS was notoriously ineffective. In 2000, as noted, the backlog of applications increased 400 percent from 1994 to 2000, to reach 4 million. When the terrorists struck, on September 11, 2001, 250,000 applications had been sitting with the INS for more than 21 months just waiting to be processed (Alden 2008: 65–66). After the attacks, President George W. Bush declared a war on terrorism, "a war largely waged through anti-immigrant measures" (David Cole, cited in Alden 2008: 94). Jim Ziglar, head of the INS on 9/11, noted that "after the night of 9/11. . . I was a person non-grata from then on, because I was not tough enough in the crisis" (cited in Alden 2008: 87). Within the Bush administration the question was how broadly and aggressively should the war on global terrorism be fought using immigration and border enforcement as weapons in the new war?

As in all other times of war, the federal government manipulated the discourse of patriotism to rally political support and to limit dissent. The USA Patriot Act was passed after only two days of debate and amid the atmosphere of national hysteria (HR 3162, PL 107–56; Platt and O'Leary 2003: 7). Attorney General John Ashcroft put it as follows: "Aggressive detention of lawbreakers and material witnesses is vital to preventing, disrupting, or delaying new attacks. It is difficult for a person in jail or under detention to murder innocent people or to aid and abet in terrorism" (cited in Alden 2008: 89).

Jim Ziglar was suspected by the attorney general and his inner circle as too soft on terrorism. "In the Justice Department, in that era, you were either with us 100 percent or you're against us 100 percent. If your friends are my enemies, you're my enemy. It was really a very poisoned sort of atmosphere" (cited in Alden 2008: 97). Under pressure from the leadership of the DOJ, Ziglar resigned in August 2002 (Alden 2008: 184).

The DOJ began an immediate, and some would call it a hysterical, campaign of detention. "Of the 762 people detained in the months after 9/11 on immigration violations, more than 200 would spend 51 to 100 days in jail, while another 175 would spend up to 150 days in jail. More than 125 would be held longer, some for a year or more. And not a single one of the detainees was ever charged with terrorism or a terrorist-related offense" (Alden 2008: 98). The mood in the public and especially in Congress clearly portended the demise of the INS.

Dissolving the INS and Creating the DHS

When the 36,000 employees of the INS were absorbed into the new DHS, they left behind the only entity within it that was abolished. The September 11 attacks and their aftermath provided the "coup de grace" to the INS, a finale to the long-standing efforts in Congress to dissolve the agency hampered by notorious mismanagement, a string of failures, backlogs of millions of applications for naturalization, the all-too-apparent failure to keep track of the 4 million foreigners in the country with expired visas, and the approval of student visas for two of the hijackers six months after the hijacking (September 11 Commission Report n.d.: 80–82).

The failure of the INS to control the borders was considered a major factor in the attacks, and the agency was blamed for letting in the hijackers. The student visa application process was clearly a massive INS failure, especially in tracking students after their arrival. But it should be noted that the INS had to cope with enormous numbers. From 1980 to 2000, students studying in the United States grew from 50,000 to 600,000. By 2000, nearly 40 percent of the doctorates in science and engineering and 30 percent of master's degrees were held by foreign-born students. In mathematics, computer science, and physical and life sciences, 60 percent of postdoctoral students doing research were foreign-born. And the United States benefited greatly from this "brain drain." One-third of American Nobel Prize winners were foreign-born, and between 1990 and 2001, 50 percent were foreign-born (Alden 2008: 188–189).

The INS was among the agencies merged into the new department. Twenty-two agencies were merged into a federal behemoth entailing many administrative problems and unanticipated consequences for policy implementation. The DHS described its mission as follows:

The mission of the Department of Homeland Security is to prevent terrorist attacks within the United States, reduce America's vulnerability to terrorism, and minimize the damage and recovery efforts from attacks that occur. DHS is also dedicated to protecting the rights of American citizens and enhancing public services, such as natural disaster assistance and citizenship services. (http://www.dhs.gov/home)

Title IV, Section 402 of the Homeland Security Act transfers responsibilities from the INS in the DOJ to the DHS into two Bureaus: the Bureau of Citizenship and Immigration Services (BCIS), responsible for processing visas and petitions for naturalization, asylum, and refugee status; and the Bureau of Immigration and Customs Enforcement (referred to as the Bureau of Border Security in the act), responsible for immigration enforcement (ICE) (https://www.dhs.gov/xlibrary/assets/NIPP_plan.pdf; LeMay 2006: 211–212).

The DHS Act moved 190,000 employees to the new department, and the Congressional Budget Office (CBO) determined the number of affected workers at 225,000 and pegged the cost of creating the new department at $3 billion. That would cover just the cost of the reorganization itself, not the increased costs of additional security technology, which were significant (LeMay 2006: 216). The DHS was comprised of the following agencies, directorates, and offices: Citizenship and Immigration Services Ombudsman, Office of Civil Rights and Civil Liberties, Domestic Nuclear Detection Office, Federal Law Enforcement Training Center, Office of Intelligence and Analysis, Office of the General Counsel, Office of Health Affairs, Office of the Inspector General, Office of Legislative Affairs, Office of Public Affairs, Office of Partnership and Engagement, Office of Operations Coordination, Office of Policy, Privacy Office, Science and Technology Directorate, Management Directorate, U.S. Customs and Border Protection (CBP), Federal Emergency Management Agency (FEMA), U.S. Immigration and Customs Enforcement, National Protection and Programs Directorate, Transportation Security Administration, U.S. Citizenship and Immigration Services, U.S. Secret Service, U.S. Coast Guard (http://www.dhs.gov/organization).

Congress perceived the post-9/11 situation to be an emergency. Emergencies often cry out for drastic and expensive changes in public policy that on reflection seem ill-conceived (Roots 2003: 503). The rushed and little-debated law exhibited "groupthink" behavior. Groupthink is a social psychological term referring to the phenomenon in so striving for consensus within a group that people set aside their personal beliefs to adopt the opinion of the rest of the group. People holding opinions that oppose the overriding opinion of the group remain quiet to keep peace rather than disrupt the uniformity of the group. As a result, decisions made under groupthink conditions almost always are poor decisions with more than usual unanticipated consequences (Janis 1982; Sneider 2004).

In addition to creating the DHS, the president and Congress engaged in a number of other policies intended to increase homeland security. For example, in November 2001, the administration announced that a U.S. drone attacked and killed the military head of Al Qaeda, Mohammad Atef (Miniter 2011: 119). In 2002, the "Terrorist Financing Tracking Program" was established under the authority of the USA Patriot Act. It authorized the National Security Agency (NSA) to monitor the movement of terrorist financial resources and further electronic surveillance programs. It approved a Total Information Awareness program established as the Defense Advanced Research Project Agency (DARPA). Also in 2002, the National Security Entry-Exit Registration System (NSEERS) was implemented (Alden 2008: 110–116; 222–223). It broadened the scope of preexisting nationality-based registration requirements by mandating noncitizens from 25 countries, 24 of which were Muslim-majority nations, to register with a federal program (LeMay 2006: 84). It began to implement the SEVIS that Congress had authorized in 1996 but never implemented it until after the 9/11 attacks (http://www.memphis.edu/iei/pdfs/sevis/pdf; http://www. studyinthestates.dhs.gov/sevis). By December 2003, Secretary Ridge was able to do away with N-SEERS, the Muslim registration system, and replace it with US-VISIT, a system unpopular abroad for its finger-printing aspect, but US-VISIT did identify visa overstayers and was considered Ridge's signature accomplishment at DHS (Alden 2008: 248–254).

One of the DHS's earliest, and arguably its most derided, programs was promotion of what it called the Homeland Security Advisory System, a color-coded, five-level scale of threat: low, guarded, elevated, high, and severe. It was vague as to the criteria for each level, and even more vague as to what state and local governments were supposed to do as the threat level changed. It quickly became a source of jokes and ridicule. In early 2002 the United States opened the Guantanamo Bay Detention camp, more commonly known as Gitmo, located on the Guantanamo Bay Naval Base in southeastern Cuba. It was used to house Muslim militants and suspected terrorists captured by U.S. forces in Afghanistan, Iraq, and elsewhere. The camp began receiving suspected terrorist members of Al Qaeda, fighters for the Taliban, and eventually hundreds of prisoners from various countries brought to the camp without charges and without the legal means to challenge their detentions, many from covert ("black") secret prisons that the United States had begun operating abroad (Burke 2004). President Bush maintained that the United States was neither obliged to grant basic constitutional protections to the prisoners since the base was outside U.S. territory nor required to observe the Geneva Conventions regarding the treatment of prisoners of war and civilians during wartime, arguing the conventions did not apply to "unlawful enemy combatants" (http://www .britannica.com/print/article/1503067).

KSM's right-hand man in the 9/11 attacks, Ramzi bin al Shibh, was captured in Karachi in 2003, and his capture and files and laptops seized then led to the capture of KSM, who was interrogated between March 2003 and September 2006 at several black sites, and then transferred to Guantanamo Bay where he was subjected to "enhanced interrogation" (i.e., water boarding). After breaking KSM with water boarding, subsequent debriefing by his de-briefer, Deuce Martinez, uncovered plots to use planes to attack London's Heathrow Airport, the Paris-Dakar Rally, and a Singapore bombing plot (Miniter 2011: 175–180).

In 2003, in order to improve procedures to increase coordination and cooperation between the FBI, the Department of Energy, the Department of Commerce, and the DHS, the independent Terrorist Threat Integration Center was established as a joint venture between the CIA and the DHS. The center was housed in CIA headquarters. The establishment of the center was in part a response to the merger of so many agencies and units into the DHS that made management of so many tasks more difficult to do efficiently (LeMay 2015: 61). (This critique of the management problems of the DHS is made in Birkland 2004; Broder 2002; Halperin 2003; Jacobson 2003; Kemp 2003; Lehrer 2004; Light 2002).

Tom Ridge was nominated and approved by the Senate as the new secretary of the DHS (serving from 2003 to 2005). President George W. Bush authorized the creation of the U.S. Northern Command to provide integrated homeland defense and coordinated Pentagon support to federal, state, and local governments. The 2005 budget increased by 780 percent the funding to support first-responders. He signed into law Project Bioshield, a $5.6 billion program to develop vaccines and other medical responses to biological, chemical, nuclear, and radiological weapons, and invested more than $7 billion in all aspects of biodefense. Aviation security was improved by hardened cockpit doors, training flight crews in handguns, and deploying thousands of air marshals. To protect seaports, Congress passed the Container Security Initiative in 2005 (http://www.cbp.gov/border-security/ports-entry/cargo-security/csi/; LeMay 2006: 228–230; 2013, vol. 3: 84–85).

The National Container Security Act allowed U.S. inspectors to screen high-risk shipping containers at major ports abroad before they are loaded in ships bound for U.S. ports. About 90 percent of the world's total cargo moves by container, and 46 percent of all U.S. imports arrive by oceangoing cargo containers. The Container Security Initiative (CSI) is an umbrella term for security initiatives such as the Customs-Trade Partnership Against Terrorism (C-TPAT), the 24-hour advance notification rule requiring shippers to transmit by electronic means manifest information to customs 24 hours before the shipment leaves the foreign port. CSI refers to the specific port-to-port shipping element, and C-TPAT is the customs-to-business element. There are four key elements of CSI: identifying high-risk containers; prescreening containers before they are shipped; technology to prescreen high-risk containers; and using smarter, more secure containers (LeMay 2006: 228–229).

In 2004, another measure was introduced in Congress. It amended the Maritime Transportation Security Act by directing the DHS to evaluate the effectiveness of the systems used by U.S. Customs to identify high-risk shipments and amended shipping laws to grant U.S. district courts to restrain violations of certain port security requirements. It authorizes the secretary of Transportation to refuse or revoke port clearance of any owner, agent, master, officer, or person in charge of a vessel that is liable for a penalty or fine for violation of such requirements. It directs the secretary to require un-cleared, un-laden imported goods remaining on a wharf for more than a few calendar days to be removed and placed in public storage or general warehouse for inspection, and imposes a penalty of $5,000 on the consignee for each bill of lading remaining on the wharf or pier in violation of the requirement. It directs the DHS to report to specified congressional committees recommendations to develop a timeline for implementation of a Transportation Worker Identification Credential in seaports, and to report to congressional oversight committees on the security of ships and facilities used in the cruise line industry. It directs the undersecretary of Homeland Security for Border and Transportation Security to establish a maritime transportation security plan grant program to help fund compliance with federal security plans among port authorities, facility operators, and state and local agencies required to provide security devices (LeMay 2006: 230).

In December 2004 President Bush signed into law the Intelligence Reform and Terrorism Prevention Act (PL-108–458).

It created a director of national intelligence (DNI) to oversee 15 government agencies involved in intelligence, and established a National Counter Terrorism Center (NCTC). President Bush appointed John Negroponte, the U.S. ambassador to Iraq, as the first DNI. The law includes several antiterrorism provisions, such as adding 2,000 additional Border Patrol agents each year for five years, improving baggage screening procedures, and imposes new standards on information that must be contained in drivers' licenses, making it easier to track suspected terrorists not tied to known terrorist groups (LeMay 2006: 231; 2015: 349).

The aim of the NCTC is to get the government to think about intelligence more strategically than operationally. It extends the model to weapons of mass destruction by establishing a National Counter Proliferation Center, and gives the DNI authority to establish other such intelligence centers (e.g., bioterrorism, chemical). Critics of the DNI position decry its use of what they called the "czar approach," an overreliance of a single bureaucrat to coordinate the various intelligence centers, and the failure to make structural changes in the collection process. The latest change grants the government broader authority to spy on anyone who is a noncitizen and suspected of being a threat even if he or she not tied to a terrorist group (the so-called lone-wolf terrorist, inspired by but not associated with groups like Al Qaeda and ISIS).

The Bush administration requested a budget of $50 billion over five years to fund a Comprehensive National Cybersecurity Initiative (CNCI) (Clarke and Knake 2010: 114–115).

The 1996 Illegal Immigration Reform and Immigrant Responsibility Act had established a pilot program for a partnership between the federal government and local law enforcement agencies to screen individuals who are engaged in police operations on their immigration status. The program was not implemented until the DHS was established and ICE was created. It was called the Secure Communities program, and under it individuals who were imprisoned in local jails and are suspected of being out of status (i.e., unauthorized immigrants) are finger-printed and entered into a federal database. The biometric record-keeping is similar to the finger-printing and photographing requirements of the US-VISIT tracking program (LeMay 2006: 86).

Also in 2005, the House of Representatives passed the Border Protection, Anti-Terrorism and Illegal Immigration Control Act, which was enrolled and agreed to by both the House and the Senate (H.R. 1268) (summarized in LeMay 2015: 256–262). It imposed federal standards on state governments for the issuance of driver's licenses or other state-issued identification cards. It mandated that the states require applicants for such documents to provide valid documents to prove they were citizens; were lawfully admitted for permanent resident status; were approved for asylum; had valid, unexpired non-immigrant visa status; had approved deferred action status; or had a pending application for adjustment to permanent resident status. The law required a photo-id and to display the expiration date of the temporary driver's license or temporary identification card. It required the state to verify the validity of the documents the applicant provided, to employ technology to capture a digital image of the identity source of documents for electronic storage and transfer, and to store paper copies for ten years. The states were to establish fraudulent document recognition training programs for all employees engaged in the issuance of driver's licenses or identification cards.

Further Homeland Security Measures in the Bush Years

In 2005, Tom Ridge stepped down as secretary of Homeland Security. Richard Clarke, a key White House national security intelligence advisor, was critical of Tom Ridge as secretary of Homeland Security. He felt Ridge, as a politician with no security background, was simply not up to the task of effectively managing the DHS. In a book published after Clarke left the administration, he faults the Bush administration for invading Iraq; taking their attention off the Al Qaeda, the Taliban, Afghanistan; the attempt to capture and bring to justice Osama bin Laden; and fighting what he called the wrong war—squandering the opportunity to eliminate Al Qaeda, which fled Afghanistan for the remote tribal areas of neighboring Pakistan. Al Qaeda emerged and grew stronger because of the inaction of the Bush administration. Clarke especially faults the administration for failure to take seriously the need to create and upgrade the capacity of the United States to use cyber warfare against the asymmetrical international terrorists groups, like Al Qaeda, its West African affiliate, Boko Haram, and other such international terrorist groups (Clarke 2004: 247; http://www.history.com/this-day-in-history/u-s-led-attack-on-afghanistan-begins; see also www.bbc.com/news/world/africa http://www.cfr.org/backgrounder/boko-haram).

In its first three years of existence, under Secretary Ridge, the DHS filed immigration charges against a staggering 814,000 people, but of those, only a dozen cases made a claim of terrorism (Alden 2008: 278).

President Bush nominated and on February 15, 2005, the Senate confirmed Michael Chertoff as the new secretary of Homeland Security by a vote of 98–0 (Alden 2008: 265). Chertoff was a federal judge on the U.S. Court of Appeals for the Third Circuit, and as a former federal prosecutor, he had prosecuted terrorism cases, including the 9/11 attacks. Chertoff appointed Michael Jackson as his deputy secretary, and they reorganized the 31 programs in the DHS to report directly to Jackson. Chertoff's policy chief was Steward Baker, the former general counsel at the NSA (Alden 2008: 267–268).

During his term as secretary of Homeland Security, Chertoff worked to strengthen border control, intelligence analysis, and infrastructure protection, becoming the chief proponent of the "secure the borders" approach (Alden 2008: 285). He pledged that by 2008, the DHS would field 18,000 Border Patrol agents and would complete the construction of 370 miles of border fence. By December 2005, Congress approved 700 miles of double-layered border fence (Alden 2008: 271–275). Chertoff unveiled the Secure Border Initiative (SBI) with electronic devices to serve as "virtual fences," and in 2006 Congress passed the Border Fence bill (the Secure Fence Act of 2006, H.R. 6061; Alden 2008: 273–274; act excerpted and summarized in LeMay 2015: 264–267).

About six months after Chertoff took the helm of the DHS, Hurricane Katrina struck, on August 29, 2005. It ranks as the third-most intense and the fifth-deadliest hurricane in U.S. history. The Federal Emergency Management Agency (FEMA), the section of DHS that was in charge of responding to Hurricane Katrina, performed badly, but the coast guard performed admirably by rescuing some 34,000 people in New Orleans alone. In the storm, 1,245 people died, and the property damage was estimated at $108 billion (http://www.history.com/topics/hurricane-katrina). Following Hurricane Katrina, Chertoff worked hard to improve the effectiveness of FEMA.

Secretary Chertoff oversaw a considerable expansion of DHS's border patrol. By 2008, DHS had fielded 18,000 Border Patrol agents and oversaw the construction of 370 miles of border fence (Alden 2008: 275). Under Secretary Chertoff, DHS expanded the number of deportation officers from 650 to 15,600; attorneys from 770 to 1,440; and detention beds from 21,107 in 2002 to 33,000 in 2008 (Alden 2008: 297). As of 2008, increased border and interior enforcement spending by DHS had reached $10 billion per year, most of that for Border Patrol agents (Alden 2008: 301). By 2008 year's end, DHS had ten-point fingerprint readers at all border checkpoints (Alden 2008: 268).

By February 2008, the pilot program Secure Border Initiative was assessed a failure. Its technology malfunctioned. Its radar system failed in bad weather. Its motion detection-activated cameras were ineffective (Alden 2008: 286).

Intelligence gathered from interrogations at Gitmo enabled DHS to thwart several terrorist plots before those plots could be operationalized. In 2006, they stopped a Sears Tower plot. In 2007, they stopped two attack plots: one targeting Fort Dix and the other John F. Kennedy International Airport. Guantanamo Bay's "enhanced interrogation techniques," which included "water boarding" and "walling," however, were considered torture by many. Torture is defined as "an irreversible, permanent, and negative change in a person's well-being" (Miniter 2011: 182). Senator John McCain (R-AZ), who had been tortured as a prisoner-of-war in Vietnam, held it ineffective, and he introduced the Detainee Treatment Act of 2005, which forbade its use. It was passed by Congress and signed into law by President Bush on December 30, 2005. It incorporated both the McCain Amendment and the Lindsey Graham (R-SC)-Carl Levin (D-MI) Amendments (Miniter 2011: 188).

On March 9, 2006, President Bush signed into law the bill commonly referred to as Patriot Act II. It amended the USA Patriot Act; its minor amendments aimed at civil liberty concerns (https://georgewbush-whitehouse.archives.gov/infocus/patriot-act/). Critics, however, maintained that its provisions still led to privacy and civil liberties abuses (Clarke and Knake 2010: 134).

Also in June 2006, the Supreme Court ruled in *Hamdan v. Rumsfeld* (548 U.S. 557) that the White House needed congressional approval before trying Al Qaeda detainees before military tribunals. The CIA director Michael Hayden and Secretary of State Condoleezza Rice agreed to transfer Al Qaeda prisoners held at black sites to Guantanamo Bay (Miniter 2011: 189–190).

Secretary of Homeland Security Michael Chertoff served for the remainder of President Bush's second term, until January 21, 2009 (https://www.dhs.gov/michael-chertoff).

Homeland Security Actions during the Obama Administration

In the 2008 election, President Barack Obama campaigned on promises to overturn what he characterized as abuses of power regarding civil rights and liberties in the government's antiterrorism policy. In particular, President Obama shifted significantly several approaches of the DHS. One might characterize the shift as a 180 degree change. His Republican critics attacked him as being "soft" on terrorism and predicted new attacks on the homeland by international terrorists along the lines of the 9/11 attacks. In point of fact, however, no such attacks occurred during the entire eight years of his two-term presidency. And where President Bush's antiterrorist team failed to catch Osama bin Laden, President Obama's did catch and kill Osama bin Laden, as well as a host of other leaders of Al Qaeda. During his campaign, President Obama had promised to close the Guantanamo Bay prison. Upon taking office, he signed an executive order to that effect, but its implementation was blocked by Congress.

To oversee the DHS and change its approach, he nominated Janet Napolitano, the former Democratic governor of Arizona (2003–2009), a former chair of the National Governors Association (NGA; the first woman to serve), as secretary of DHS. While chair of the NGA she created its Public Safety Task Force and the Homeland Security Advisors Council. She had an extensive security background, having served as attorney general of Arizona, where she helped write the law to break up human smuggling rings, and as U.S. attorney for the District of Arizona, she led the investigation into the Oklahoma City Bombing. As governor of Arizona, she opened the first state counterterrorism center, spearheaded efforts to transform immigration enforcement, and had presided over large-scale disaster relief efforts and readiness exercises to craft emergency plans (https://www.dhs.gov/archive/person/janet-napolitano; she served as secretary of DHS from January 21, 2009, to September 6, 2013, leaving the office to serve as the president of the University of California [http://www.ucop.edu/president/about/index.html]).

In 2009, the DHS created a system to scan cyber traffic to and from federal agencies looking for malware (e.g., viruses and worms). The system was named the Einstein System, which had three aspects: Einstein 1 to monitor cyber traffic flow; Einstein 2 to do deep intrusion analysis to detect malware; and Einstein 3, which attempts to block Internet packets that appear to be malware (Clarke and Knake 2010: 120–121). Malware is an abbreviated term meaning "malicious software" that is designed to gain access to or damage a computer without the knowledge of the owner. It includes spyware, keyloggers, true viruses, worms, or malicious codes that infiltrate a computer and, through it, possibly a computer system or network (https://us.norton.com/internetsecurity-malware.html). The system was part of a cyber security defense triad: (1) deep packet inspection, (2) a secure power grid, and (3) the Department of Defense systems to ferret out and protect against cyber "logic bombs" (Clarke and Knake 2010: 166–178, 254–266).

The DHS was charged with defense against cyber warfare. "Cyber warfare is that unauthorized penetration by, or on behalf of, or in support of, a government into another nation's computer system or network, or any other activity affecting a computer system, in which the purpose is to add, alter, or falsify data, or cause the disruption of or damage to a computer or network device, or the objects a computer system controls" (Clarke and Knake 2010: 228). The definition fits the events that eventually happened in 2015–2016—the Russian hacking and cyberattack on the 2016 U.S. elections.

As secretary of the DHS, Napolitano led its 230,000-employee global workforce. She pushed three cross-cutting initiatives: (1) increasing cooperation among federal, state, local, private sector, and international partners; (2) deploying the latest science and technology to support the mission of DHS, including beefed-up cyber security; and (3) maximizing efficiency in operations across the DHS. She forged new global partnerships to share information, facilitate scientific research, and coordinate law enforcement efforts; opened a new DHS-led coordinated cyber security watch and warning center; and created a new Fusion Center Program Management Office.

In 2008 and in 2009, the Center for Strategic and International Studies (CSIS) and the National Academy of Science Commission, respectively, were established. Both warned of the need to increase cyber security and the dangers of cyber war. To expand its computer capacity faster and at less cost, DHS adopted commercial, off-the-shelf software. Although less expensive, the flip side is that such software is highly vulnerable (Clarke and Knake 2010: 135–140).

Secretary Napolitano continued Secretary Chertoff's policy to deploy additional personnel and technology to the Southwest border. Under her leadership, DHS increased coordination with federal, state, local, and Mexican law enforcement as part of the Obama administration's Southwest Border Initiative. She implemented the Western Hemisphere Travel Initiative for land and sea travel to the United States. She also expanded a pilot program, known as Global Entry, to streamline the screening process at airports for trusted travelers through biometric identification.

DHS entered into new partnerships with international counterparts to crack down on drug and firearms trafficking. She began implementation of the Obama administration's "smart and effective" enforcement of immigration laws. When she took office, six years after the establishment of the department, she found that the personnel system still had a temporary feel to it (Clarke and Knake 2010: 120). She instituted a new, comprehensive worksite enforcement strategy to reduce demand for illegal employment and protect employment opportunities for the country's legal workforce; initiated reforms to the country's immigration detention system to enhance security and efficiency by prioritizing the health and safety of detainees; and expanded the Secure Communities program that employed biometric information to target criminal immigrants incarcerated in U.S. correctional facilities to over 100 jurisdictions across the country.

One could well argue that cyber warfare began to develop during July-August 2008 when Russia launched a cyberattack on the Republic of Georgia, formerly a part of the Soviet Union. Georgia had gained its independence and broke away from Russia after the Soviet Union's collapse. The Russian cyberattack on Georgia elections had many parallels to those used against the United States in 2016. As would be the case in 2016, in the 2008 attack on Georgia, Vladimir Putin's government claimed patriotic Russians not connected to the government might have been behind the cyberattacks, which used a cyber "weapon" known as distributed denial of service (DDOS) and Botnet (the capturing and use of "robot" computers linked into a network or system to flood the attacked country's Internet system with an overwhelming number of demands or messages that essentially cause the country's system to breakdown [Clarke and Knake 2010: 18–21]).

North Korea launched a similar DDOS attack on South Korea and the United States in July 2009. U.S. websites were hit by nearly 1 million requests per second, blocking the servers of the Treasury, Secret Service, Federal Trade Commission, and Department of Transportation. They also attempted to do so to the White House, but that attack failed because a system was in place to divert requests to over 20,000 servers around the country. In a second wave, North Korean cyber warriors attacked South Korean banks and government agencies (Clarke and Knake 2010: 24–25).

Five takeaways are demonstrated by the 2008–2009 attacks: (1) cyber war is real; (2) cyber war happens at the speed of light; (3) cyber war is global; (4) cyber war skips the kinetic battlefield; and (5) cyber war has begun (Clarke 2010: 30–31). "Cyberspace is defined as all of the computer networks in the world and everything they connect and control" (70). Richard Clarke was special advisor to the president (Bush) for cyber security (112–113).

The NSA became the world's leading center of cyber space expertise. In 2008, the director of national intelligence was Mike McConnell. His successor was Air Force General Ken Minihan. President Obama's Secretary of Defense Bob Gates

was a former CIA officer and member of the National Security
Council. He organized what became known as the U.S. Cyber
Command. The director of the NSA would have the rank of a
four-star general. A three-star general headed the U.S. Cyber
Defense Information System, headquartered at Fort Mead,
which housed America's defensive and offensive cyber war
forces, comprising the 29th Air Force of 6,000 to 8,000 cyber
warriors. The navy's cyber war command is the 10th Fleet,
NetWarCom (Naval Network Warfare Command), and it was
based at Fort Huachuca, Arizona, growing out of the 9th Sig-
nal Command to become the Network Enterprise Technology
Command. The army's manager of the Land War Net was its
Global Network Operations and Security Center (NGNOSC).
These cyber forces, however, were focused on offensive capability. As Mike McConnell, then DNI, noted: "All the offensive
cyber capacity the U.S. can muster won't matter if no one is
defending the nation from cyber attack" (Clarke and Knake
2010: 43). Both McConnell and Minihan believe that the
cyber defensive mission should be handled by the DHS, which
defends all non-Department of Defense government agencies
(44, 143).

In an effort to foster fiscal discipline, Napolitano initiated
a department-wide efficiency review designed to cut costs and
streamline operations by eliminating nonmission critical travel,
and by purchasing enterprise licenses for commonly used software (known as off-the-shelf), estimated to save hundreds of
millions of dollars in cost avoidance. As noted, however, such
commercial, off-the-shelf software is much more vulnerable to
cyberattack.

What DHS had to defend against was the offensive cyber
capability of countries like Israel, France, United Kingdom,
Taiwan, Iran, Australia, South Korea, India, Pakistan, several
NATO states, and most importantly, Russia (Clarke and Knake
2010: 64). Moscow's equivalent to the NSA is its Federal Commission for Government Communications and Information
(FAPSI), headquartered in the city of Voronezh. As Clarke

notes, "FAPSI (now called the Service of Special Communications and Information) runs what might be the largest, and certainly one of the best, hacker schools in the world. By now, of course, they are calling themselves cyber warriors" (Clarke and Knake 2010: 63–64).

What makes cyber war possible are three flaws: (1) flaws in the design of the Internet, (2) flaws in both hardware and software, and (3) the move to put more and more critical systems online (ibid.: 73–74). DHS, moreover, was slow to respond to cyber war possibilities, in part because it had such many and varied responsibilities and missions divided among its 22 agencies.

One such competing DHS mission is disaster relief, headed by the FEMA. In the aftermath of the 2005 hurricanes Katrina and Rita, DHS awarded more than $2.1 billion to Louisiana and Mississippi for recovery and rebuilding. DHS established two joint public assistance teams and a new arbitration process to resolve long-standing issues over public assistance funding. DHS partnered with the Department of Housing and Urban Development (HUD) to provide long-term housing to more than 11,000 families displaced by Hurricane Gustav (2008), and offered families remaining in temporary housing the option to buy their mobile homes and park models.

In 2010, DHS helped thwart a bombing plot aimed at the New York City subway system and a car bombing plot targeting Times Square. DHS participated, on May 2, 2011, in the Obama administration's most successful national security operation—the capture and killing of Osama bin Laden (OBL). Osama bin Laden, as noted, was the mastermind of the 9/11 attacks and the world's most wanted international terrorist. A raid by 23 Navy Seals descended on a compound in Abbottabad, a tourist and military center a few miles north of Pakistan's capital, Islamabad. The daring and covert raid took 40 minutes. The team killed five terrorists, including Osama bin Laden and his adult son. No Americans were injured in the attack. Osama bin Laden's body was positively identified by DNA, and buried at sea. President Obama announced to the nation in a special television address that "justice has been done." Computer files collected during the raid showed that Osama bin Laden had been planning to assassinate President Obama and planned to carry out another 9/11 style attack on its anniversary. As noted previously, Osama bin Laden had escaped the caves of the Tora Bora region in Afghanistan and eluded U.S. authorities for five years. U.S. cyber warriors in the CIA had finally tracked him to the Abbottabad compound in August 2010, although they could not be positive that he would be in the compound until the raid. The Seal team raid occurred without warning to the Pakistan military, and given that Osama bin Laden had spent the last five years of his life in the well-populated area that was less than a mile from the Pakistan military academy, U.S. officials suspected Pakistan authorities of helping to shelter Osama bin Laden in Abbottabad (http://www.history.com/this-day-in-history/osama-bin-laden-killed-by-u-s-forces).

The 9/11 attacks not only raised fears of international terrorists entering the United States that produced public anxieties toward Arabs and Muslims; they exacerbated tensions around Mexican immigration, particularly the undocumented flow that influenced every administration since 2001 (LeMay 2015: 95–96; Rodriquez 2008). A 2009 report by the Government Accountability Office (GAO) found that identification priorities were not being met and could result in an unmanageable number of low-priority illegal immigrants being reported to ICE, and the misuse of authority by local officials (Aizenman 2009; LeMay 2015: 96). In June, 2011, DHS director John Morton issued two memoranda stating that all deportation orders—some 300,000—then in process were to be reviewed to identify only the high-priority removal cases to consider certain circumstances surrounding an individual's unauthorized presence in the United States prior to enforcing deportation proceedings. Critics charged that "prosecutorial discretion" was not being consistently implemented nationwide, and that judicial backlogs were not being remedied as planned. But in October 2011, DHS announced that in 2010 ICE had deported the largest number of individuals in the agency's history. Of the 400,000 persons removed, 55 percent were removed for felonies or misdemeanors, and 37 percent of those were arrested and deported for drug-related or traffic offenses. In terms of protecting against homeland security threats, such cases were hardly demonstrative of the need for effective prosecutorial discretion in deportation cases (LeMay 2015: 96–97).

Among the most controversial and arguably most significant policy changes of the Obama administration that affected DHS and USCIS was the Deferred Action for Childhood Arrivals (DACA), initiated by executive action on June 15, 2012. The proposal to offer a pathway to permanent residency for unauthorized immigrant minor children goes back to what is called the Dream Act (for Development, Relief, and Education for Alien Minors). The various Dream Act bills proposed to enact a multiphase process by which illegal immigrant minors would first be granted conditional residency and upon fulfilling further qualifications, permanent residency. The first Dream Act bill was proposed in the U.S. Senate in August 2001, sponsored by Senators Dick Durban (D-IL) and Orrin Hatch (R-Utah), and in the House by Representative Luis Gutierrez (D-IL). It failed to pass and has been reintroduced numerous times since then (2006, 2007, 2009, 2010, 2011, 2012), each time failing to overcome Republican-backed filibusters. At one time or another, various Dream Act bills have been cosponsored by 128 representatives and 39 senators. The Dream Act bills have been supported by almost every Democrat, and by a small group of Republicans. Proponents of the bill have been unable to overcome the need for a 60-vote majority in the Senate (a veto-proof, filibuster-breaking majority). Frustrated by the inability to get a Dream Act bill passed in Congress, President Obama issued his executive order, the Deferred Action for Childhood Arrivals (DACA) on June 15, 2012 (https://www.dhs.gov/archive/deferred-action-childhood-arrivals; https://www.uscis.gov/humanitarian/consideration-deferred-action-childhood-arrivals-daca; LeMay

2015: 361). By executive action, he undertook to implement many of the ideas and provisions of the various Dream Act bills.

The Congressional Budget Office (CBO) estimated that, if enacted, the Dream Act would reduce deficits by $1.4 billion over 2011–2020, and increase government revenues by a projected $2.3 billion over a decade. A University of California Los Angeles study estimated that, if enacted, the Dream Act would generate between $1.4 trillion and $3.6 trillion in taxable income over a 40-year period (LeMay 2015: 32). One would reasonably expect that those levels of deficit reduction and government revenue increases, and the associated economic growth potential, would normally have attracted Republican Party support. But the congressional and national party leadership had decided to adamantly oppose any and every bill proposed by President Obama and, using the filibuster process, managed to kill Dream Act bills each time they were introduced.

The frustrated president decided to use his executive actions powers, which were vulnerable to being overturned by the next president, but had the virtue of bypassing the recalcitrant Republican opposition in Congress. DACA shifted the focus of USCIS and DHS enforcement resources (ICE) on the removal of individuals who pose a danger to national security or a risk to public safety, including persons convicted of violent, felony, or repeat offender crimes. DHS would exercise prosecutorial discretion as appropriate to ensure that law enforcement resources were not expended on low-priority cases—namely, children who came to the United States as minors who also met other key guidelines. DACA registered individuals could request consideration for deferred action for a period of two years, subject to renewal, and may be eligible for employment authorization (in the vernacular, issued "green cards"). The requirements were:

1. Persons under the age of 31 as of June 15, 2012;
2. Persons who had arrived in the United States before reaching age 16;

3. Persons who had continuously resided in the United States since June 15, 2007;

4. Persons who were physically present in the United States on June 15, 2012, and at the time of making the request for DACA consideration with USCIS;

5. Persons who entered without inspection before June 15, 2012, or who had lawful immigration status expired as of June 15, 2012;

6. Persons who are currently in school, have graduated from a U.S. high school, or have obtained a certificate of completion or obtained a general education development (GED) certificate, or are an honorably discharged veteran of the coast guard or armed forces of the United States; and

7. Persons who have not been convicted of a felony, significant misdemeanor, three or more other misdemeanors and do not otherwise pose a threat to national security or public safety (https://www.dhs.gov/archive/deferred-action-childhood-arrivals; see also LeMay 2015: 277–278, 351).

Extension of DACA and Issuance of DAPA

Upon Janet Napolitano's resignation in 2013, President Obama nominated and the Senate confirmed Jeh Johnson as secretary of Homeland Security, the position he held until the end of President Obama's second term, in 2017. He was sworn in as secretary of Homeland Security on December 23, 2013. As noted, he assumed charge of the third-largest department of the executive branch. He took charge of a workforce of 229,000 employees. Among its 22 constituent units are the Transportation Security Administration, CBP, Immigration and Customs Enforcement, U.S. Citizenship and Immigration Services, FEMA, the Coast Guard, and the Secret Service.

DHS is responsible for counterterrorism; cyber security; aviation security; border security; port security; maritime security; administration and enforcement of immigration laws; protection of national leaders (the Secret Service); protection of critical infrastructure; detection of and protection against chemical, biological, and nuclear threats to the homeland; and responses to disasters (www.dhs.gov/archive/person/jeh-johnson).

President Obama extended DACA in 2014. The new executive action extended the deferred action period and employment authorization provisions from two to three years, changed the effective date for having to have lived continuously in the United States from January 1, 2010, rather than the prior requirement of 2007, are of any age (removing the requirement of having been born since June 15, 1981), and met all other DACA guidelines (http://www.uscis.gov/immigrationaction; LeMay 2015: 33).

The 2014 action also established the Deferred Action for Parental Accountability (DAPA). This program was intended to cover undocumented persons living in the United States who are the parent of a U.S. citizen or lawful permanent resident meeting the following guidelines: (1) have lived in the United States continuously since January 1, 2010; (2) had, on November 20, 2014, a son or daughter who is a U.S. citizen or lawful permanent resident; (3) are not an enforcement priority for removal from the United States, under the November 20, 2014 action. The order issued provisional waivers for unlawful presence to undocumented individuals who have resided unlawfully in the United States for at least 180 days and who are the sons and daughters of U.S. citizens, or the spouse and sons or daughters of lawful permanent residents. This expanded a provisional waiver program first announced in 2013 and clarified the meaning of the "extreme hardship" standard that must be met to obtain a waiver (LeMay 2015: 33).

Republicans scoffed at President Obama for being soft on illegal immigrants and endangering the nation's security by being so. But in point of fact, between 2009 and 2015, President Obama's administration had removed more than 2.5 million people through immigration orders. That total does not include those who "self-deported" or those turned away at the borders by CBP. Liberal critics of President Obama labeled him "the Deporter-in-Chief," as the numbers of deportations of unauthorized immigrants were more than those of any other presidential administration in history, and in fact, more than the sum of all presidents of the 20th century (http://abcnews.go.com/Politics/obama-deportation-policy-numbers/story?id=41715661).

Implementation of the extension of DACA and of DAPA was halted by an injunction. On Monday, February 16, 2015, Judge Andrew S. Hanen of the U.S. District Court for the Southern District of Texas issued a preliminary injunction to temporarily halt DHS from implementing DAPA and extended DACA programs. Secretary Jeh Johnson announced that pending an appeal of the injunction, DHS would not accept requests for the expansion of DACA or the plan to accept requests for DAPA   (http://www.cmsny.org/federal-court-halts-dapa-and-expanded-daca-programs). The injunction did not affect the 740,000 persons who had registered through DACA prior to Judge Hanen's decision (Warren 2014).

Homeland Security Actions and Issues during the Trump Administration

If President Obama, on assuming office, initiated a 180 degree change in policy from that of the Bush administration, Present Trump, in his first six months in office, initiated a 270 degree change in policies from that of the Obama administration. President Trump, moreover, did so exclusively through executive orders and his presidential appointment power, despite the fact that congressional Republicans had excoriated President Obama for "over-using" his executive orders power.

On January 21, 2017, President Trump's nominees for secretary of Defense and for secretary of Homeland Security were sworn into office. Secretary of Defense Jim Mattis is a retired Marine Corps general who had previously commanded U.S. Joint Forces Command, NATO's Supreme Allied Command for Transformation, and U.S. Central Command where he directed military operations of more than 200,000 soldiers, sailors, airman, coast guardsmen, marines, and allied forces across the Middle East. After retirement from the marine corps in 2013, he served as visiting fellow at the Hoover Institute at Stanford University where he specialized in the study of leadership, national security, strategy, innovation, and the effective use of military force. In 2016, he coedited the book *Warriors and Citizens: American Views of Our Military* (www.defense.gov/About/Biographies/Biography-View/Article-Jim-Mattis). Secretary of Homeland Security John F. Kelly was also a marine corp general who served as commander of SOUTHCOM where he worked closely with the FBI and DEA, as well as with then secretary of Homeland Security Jeh Johnson. Since he was retired less than a year, the U.S. Senate gave him a special waiver to serve in the Cabinet and confirmed him on January 20, 2017, as the fifth secretary of Homeland Security (https://www.dhs.gov/news/2017/01/20/john-f-kelly-sworn-fifth-secretary-homeland-security).

On January 25, 2017, President Trump issued an executive order to build the wall on the U.S. border with Mexico. The action also ordered the immediate detainment and deportation of unauthorized immigrants and requires state and federal agencies to tally how much foreign aid they are sending to Mexico, and orders the U.S. CBP agency to hire 5,000 additional border patrol agents. Despite his often-made campaign promise, the executive order has U.S. taxpayers footing the bill to construct the wall—at a cost estimated at $18 billion. Since construction of a border wall of hundreds to thousands of miles would need congressional allocation of funding, the executive order is for a "pilot" wall program and is funded by shifting a few million dollars in the existing budget (http://www.whitehouse.gov/the-press-office/2017/01/25/executive-order-border-security-and-immigration-enforcement-improvements).

On January 25, President Trump signed an executive order, titled "Enhancing the Public Safety in the Interior of the United States," cutting funding for "sanctuary cities" (https://www.whitehouse.gov/presidential-actions/executive-order-enhancing-public-safety-interior-united-states/). The city of San Francisco immediately filed a suit in federal court claiming that the order is unconstitutional.

On January 27, President Trump issued the first immigration "travel ban" that targeted seven Muslim-majority nations (Iran, Iraq, Libya, Somalia, Sudan, Syria, and Yemen). The ban blocked entry to the United States of Syrian refugees and temporarily suspended entry to other refugees and citizens from those nations for admission to the United States for 90 days. Ostensibly, the ban was to provide the new administration with sufficient time to develop new "extreme vetting" of immigrants from those seven countries (https://www.whitehouse.gov/presidential-actions/executive-order-protecting-nation-foreign-terrorist-entry-united-states/).

On January 28, 2017, he issued a memorandum reorganizing the National Security Council and the Homeland Security Council adding White House advisor Steve Bannon to them. On April 4, however, he had to remove Steve Bannon from both councils since Bannon lacked appropriate security clearances.

On January 31, 2017, President Trump fired the acting attorney general (AAG), Sally Yates, for refusing to defend in federal court his immigration order. AAG Yates had argued that the ban was unconstitutional and refused to implement the ban. On February 3, 2017, U.S. district judge James Robart of the 9th Circuit Court of Appeals in Seattle, Washington, an appointee of Republican president George W. Bush, ruled the ban was unconstitutional and halted enforcement of the ban by the Trump administration. The travel ban barred hundreds of refugees seeking entrance to the United States (https://www.seattletimes.com/seattle-news/politics/federal-judge-in-seattle-halts-trumps-immigration-order/).

President Trump issued a second immigration travel ban by executive order on March 6, 2017. The second order banned immigrants from six Muslim countries (dropping Iraq from the list) and suspended all refugees for 120 days. The revised order cut the number of refugees that would be accepted in 2017 by more than half—from 110,000 to 50,000. Refugees from Syria were no longer banned indefinitely. The new ban revised language that favored religious minorities, which President Trump had stated would apply to persecuted Christians from the Middle East.

On March 15, U.S. district court Judge Derrick Watson, of Hawaii, put an emergency hold on the ban. Hours later, U.S. district court Judge Theodore Chuang, of Maryland, issued a nationwide preliminary injunction prohibiting the revised travel ban from taking effect. The ban stipulated guidance for agencies to implement the new travel ban. With the judicial ruling placing an injunction of the ban, President Trump vowed to appeal the decision to the U.S. Supreme Court (http://www.npr.org/sections/thetwo-way/2017/03/15/520171478/trump-travel-ban-blocked-nationwide-by-federal-judges-in-hawaii-and-maryland; https://www.wsj.com/articles/trump-appeals-latest-travel-ban-ruling-1500072777?mod=cx_picks&cx_navSource=cx_picks&).

On April 12, 2017, President Trump issued a memorandum delegating terrorist report requests to the then FBI director, James Comey.

In May, President Trump's DHS established an office called the Victims of Immigration Crime Enforcement (VOICE).

In June, the administration struggled with language to legally define what exactly constitutes a "sanctuary city" that would thereby be denied federal funds.

On June 21, 2017, the Supreme Court partially upheld Trump's second executive order travel ban and announced it would hold full oral arguments on the ban in the fall session, 2017. However, the ruling exempted from the ban persons with previously approved visas. It exempted persons with a "bona fide" connection (e.g., "close family member") to a U.S. citizen, or permanent resident immigrant (green-card holder) (https://www.jdsupra.com/legalnews/muslim-country-travel-ban-upheld-in-part-70428/).

Immediately after the Supreme Court ruling, the Trump administration issued guidelines as to what constituted "close family ties," which excluded grandmothers and other extended family relatives. In July, a Hawaii judge ruled that grandparents could not be excluded. On July 15, 2017, U.S. district judge Derrick Watson issued an order on interpreting the Supreme Court's June 21 decision. Judge Watson stated: "Common sense, for instance, dictates that close family members may be defined to include grandparents. Indeed, grandparents are the epitome of close family members." State Department counselor officials had early reversed their first guideline that had excluded fiancés, now allowing them to obtain visas. Attorney General Jeff Sessions stated that the Justice Department would reluctantly return again to the Supreme Court and filed a "notice of appeal" (https://www.washingtonpost.com/world/national-security/judge-rejects-hawaii-bid-to-exempt-grandparents-from-trumps-travel-ban/2017/07/06/8e3a3252-625d-11e7-8adc-fea80e32bf47_story.html?utm_term=.c898718a55a4).

Conclusion

In 15 years since the establishment of the DHS, national policy makers have struggled with how best to implement policy to protect the nation while balancing that policy approach with concerns for civil liberties of citizens. Five secretaries of Homeland Security have attempted to cope with managing a huge and complex department that often proved difficult to manage. They struggled to craft and implement policy in relationship with other federal departments, such as the CIA, State Department, Department of Justice, Department of Commerce, Department of Energy, Department of Interior, and with state bureaucracies including state and local police, first-responder agencies, state agencies of DHS, and other outside of government stakeholders in security issues. DHS has experienced challenges from the judiciary, including federal courts and state supreme courts.

Homeland Security policy has struggled to defend against the development of cyber warfare technology and subsequent cyberattacks on the nation, particularly against the 2016 elections. DHS has oscillated between approaches about how best to manage against security threats from the Bush administration to the Obama administration, and back again with the Trump administration. That struggle will undoubtedly continue into the future. The next chapter discusses problems, issues associated with homeland security matters, and some proposed solutions to those problems.

References

Aizenman, N. C. 2009. *GAO Report Says 287(g) Illegal Immigration Program Lacks Key Internal Controls.* http://www.washingtonpost.com/wp- dyn/content/article/2009/03/03/AR20090304231.html.

Alden, Edward. 2008. *The Closing of the American Border: Terrorism, Immigration, and Security since 9/11.* New York: HarperCollins Perennial.

Birkland, Thomas. 2004. "The World Changed Today: Agenda-Setting and Policy Change in the Wake of the 9/11 Terrorist Attacks," *The Review of Policy Research,* March, 21(2): 179–201.

Brader, Ted, Nicholas Valentino, and Elizabeth Suhay. 2008. "What Triggers Public Opposition to Immigration: Anxiety, Group Clues, and Immigration Threat," *American Journal of Political Science,* 52 (4): 959–978.

Broder, David. 2002. "Security in the Homeland," *The Washington Post National Weekly Edition,* September 2–8: 4.

Burke, Jason. 2004. "Secret World of U.S. Jails," *The Guardian,* London, June 13, 28–31. www.theguardian.com/world/2004/jun/13/usa.terrorism.

Clarke, Richard. 2004. *Against All Enemies: Inside America's War on Terror*. New York: Free Press.

Clarke, Richard and Robert Knake. 2010. *Cyber War*. New York: HarperCollins.

Commission Report-9/11. n.d. *Final Report of the National Commission on Terrorist Attacks on the United States*. New York: W. W. Norton.

Crotty, William. 2003. "Presidential Policymaking in Crisis Situations: 9/11 and Its Aftermath," *Policy Studies Journal*, August, 31(3): 457–465.

Enders, Walter, and Todd Sandler. 2005. "Transnational Terrorism, 1968–2000: Thresholds, Persistence, and Forecasts," *Southern Economic Journal*, January, 71(3): 467–483.

Etzioni, Amitai, and Jason H. Marsh, eds. 2003. *Rights v. Public Safety after 9/11: America in the Age of Terrorism*, Lanham, MD: Rowman and Littlefield.

Flynn, Stephen. 2004. *America the Vulnerable: How Our Government Is Failing to Protect Us from Terrorism*. New York: HarperCollins.

Halperin, Morton. 2003. "Safe at Home." *American Prospect*, November, 14 (10): 36–40. http://www.bbc.co.uk/news/world-africa-1380950. Accessed July 8, 2017.

Hamdan v. Rumsfeld, 548 U.S. 557, June 2006.

http://abcnews.go.com/Politics/obama-deportation-policy-numbers/story?id=41715661. Accessed July 14, 2017.

http://www.bbc.co.uk/news/world-africa-380950. Accessed July 8, 2017.

http://www.britannica.com/print/article/1503057. Accessed July 8, 2017.

http://www.cbp.gov/border-security/ports-entry/cargo-security/csi/.

http://www.cfr.org/backgrounder/boko-haram. Accessed July 8, 2017.

http://www.cmsny.org/federal-court-halts-dapa-and-expanded-daca-programs. Accessed July 14, 2017.

http://www.dhs.gov/archive/person/jeh-johnson. Accessed July 11, 2017.

http://www.dhs.gov/dhspublic/display?content-191. Accessed December 9, 2004.

http://www.dhs.gov/home. Accessed July 7, 2017.

http://www.dhs.gov/news/2009/12/15/secretary-napotano-highlights-accomplishments-in-2009. Accessed July 9, 2017.

http://www.dhs.gov/organization. Accessed June 5, 2017.

http://www.fas.org/irp/threat/nssg.pdf. Accessed July 2, 2017.

http://www.freedictionary.com/stovepiping. Accessed July 7, 2017.

http://www.history.com/this-day-in-history/osama-bin-laden-killed-by-u-s-forces. Accessed July 12, 2017.

http://www.history.com/this-day-in-history/us-led-attack-on-afghanistan-begins. Accessed July 9, 2017.

http://www.history.com/topics/hurricane-katrina. Accessed July 7, 2017.

http://www.memphis.edu/iei/pdfs/sevis.pdf. Accessed July 8, 2017.

http://www.npr.org/sections/thetwo-way/2017/03/15/520171478/trump-travel-ban-blocked-nationwide-by-federal-judges-in-hawaii-and-maryland. Accessed July 15, 2017.

http://www.studyinthestates.dhs.gov/sevis. Accessed July 9, 2017.

http://www.ucop.edu/president/about/index.html. Accessed July 10, 2017.

http://www.uscis.gov/immigrationaction. Accessed July 10, 2017.

http://www.us.norton.com/internetsecurity-malware.html. Accessed July 14, 2017.

http://www.whitehouse.gov/presidential-actions/executive-order/border-security-and-immigration-enforcement-improvements. Accessed July 15, 2017.

https://www.defense.gov/About/Biography-View/article-Jim-Mattis. Accessed July 10, 2017.

https://www.dhs.gov/archive/deferred-action-childhood-arrivals. Accessed July 10, 2017.

https://www.dhs.gov/archive/person/janet-napolitano. Accessed July 10, 2017.

https://www.dhs.gov/homeland-security-advisory-system. Accessed May 25, 2017.

https://www.dhs.gov/michael-chertoff. Accessed July 7, 2017.

https://www.dhs.gov/news/2017/01/20/john-f-kelly-sworn-fifth-secretary-homeland-security. Accessed May 25, 2017.

https://www.dhs.gov/xlibrary/assets/NIPP_plan.pdf. Accessed May 25, 2017.

https://www.georgewbush-whitehouse.archives.gov/infocus/patriotact. Accessed July 7, 2017.

https://www.jdsupra.com/legalnews/muslim-country-travel-ban-upheld-in-part-70428/.

Accessed July 15, 2018.

https://www.seattletimes.com/seattle-news/politics/federal-judge-in-seattle-halts-trumps-immigration-order/. Accessed July 15, 2015.

https://www.uscis.gov/humanitarian/consideration-deferred-action-childhood-arrivals-daca. Accessed July 10, 2017.

https://www.washingtonpost.com/world/national-security/judge-rejects-hawaii-bid-to-exempt-grandparents-from-trumps-travel-ban/2017/07/06/8e3a3252-625d-11e7-8adc-fea80e32bf47_story.html?utm_term=.c898718a55a4. Accessed July 15, 2017.

https://www.whitehouse.gov/presidential-actions/executive-order-enhancing-public-safety-interior-united-states/. Accessed July 15, 2017.

https://www.whitehouse.gov/presidential-actions/executive-order-protecting-nation-foreign-terrorist-entry-united-states/. Accessed July 15, 2017.

https://www.wsj.com/articles/trump-appeals-latest-travel-ban-ruling-1500072777?mod=cx_picks&cx_navSource=cx_picks&. Accessed July 15, 2017.

Jacobsen, Gary. 2003. "Terror, Terrain, and Turnout: Exploring the 2002 Midterm Elections," *Political Science Quarterly*, Spring, 118 (1): 1–23.

Janis, Irving. 1982. *Groupthink,* 2nd ed. Boston: Houghton-Mifflin.

Jones, Jeffrey M. 2001. "The Impact of the Attacks on America," Princeton, NJ: Gallup News Service, http://www.gallup.com/poll/4894/impact-attacks-america-Aspx.

Kemp, Roger. 2003. "Homeland Security: Trends in America," *National Civic Review*, Winter, 92 (4): 45–53.

Lansford, Tom. 2003. "Homeland Security from Clinton to Bush: An Assessment," *White House Studies,* Fall, 3 (4): 403–411.

Lehrer, Eli. 2004. "The Homeland Security Bureaucracy," *Public Interest,* Summer: 71– 86.

LeMay, Michael. 1994. *Anatomy of a Public Policy*. New York: Praeger.

LeMay, Michael. 2006. *Guarding the Gates: Immigration and National Security*. Westport, CT: Praeger Security International.

LeMay, Michael. 2013. *Transforming America: Perspectives on U.S. Immigration, vol. 3:* 81–107. Santa Barbara, CA: Praeger Press.

LeMay, Michael. 2015. *Illegal Immigration*, 2nd ed. Santa Barbara, CA: ABC-CLIO.

LeMay, Michael and Elliott Barkan. 1999. *U.S. Immigration and Naturalization Laws and Issues: A Documentary History*. Westport, CT: Greenwood Press.

Light, Paul C. 2002. *Homeland Security Will Be Hard to Manage*. Washington, DC: Brookings Institution Center for Public Service.

LULAC et al. v. Wilson et al., November 20, 1995, 908 F. Supp. 755, C.D. Cal. 1995.

Miniter, Richard. 2011. *Mastermind: The Many Faces of the 9/11 Architect*. New York: Penguin Books.

Mittlestadt, Michelle, Bureke Speaker, Doris Meissner, and Muzaffer A. Chishti. 2011. *Through the Prism of National Security: Major Immigration Policy and Program Changes in the Decade since 9/11*. Washington, DC: Migration Policy Institute. http://www.migrationpolicy.org/pubs/FS23_Post-9- 11policy.pdf. Accessed July 7, 2013.

Motomura, Hiroshi. 2014. *Immigration Outside the Law*. New York: Oxford University Press.

O'Hanlon, Michael E., Peter R. Orszay, Iro H. Daadler, I. M. Destler, David L. Gunter, Robert E. Latan, and James Steinberg, eds. 2002. *Protecting the American Homeland: A Preliminary Analysis*. Washington, DC: The Brookings Institution.

107 Congress. 2001. *Administration's Draft Anti-Terrorism Act of 2001: Hearing before the Committee on the Judiciary House of Representatives*. Washington, DC: U.S. Government Printing Office. http://judiciary.house.gov/legacy/75288.pdf.

Platt, Tony and Cecilia O'Leary. 2003. "Patriot Acts," *Social Justice,* Spring, 30 (1): 5–22.

Relyea, Harold C. 2003. "Organizing for Homeland Security," *Presidential Studies Quarterly,* September, 33 (3): 602–625.

Rodriquez, Robyn. 2008. "Disunity and Diversity in Post 9/11 America," *Sociological Forum*, 23 (2): 379–389.

Roots, Roger. 2003. "Terrorized into Absurdity: The Creation of the Transportation Security Administration," *Independent Review,* Spring, 7(4): 503–518.

Rosenblum, Marc. 2011. *U.S. Immigration Policy since 9/11: Understanding the Stalemate Over Comprehensive Immigration Reform.* Washington, DC: Migration Policy Institute.

Rudolf, Christopher. 2006. *National Security and Immigration Policy Development in the United States and Western Europe since 1945.* Stanford, CA: Stanford University Press.

Salehyan, Idean. 2009. "U.S. Asylum and Refugee Policy toward Muslim Nations since 9/11," in Terri Givens, Gary Freeman, and David Leal, eds. *Immigration Policy and Security: U.S., European and Commonwealth Perspectives,"* 52–65. New York: Routledge.

Sneider, Daniel. 2004. "The Groupthink Failure: A Centralized Bureaucracy Won't Improve Intelligence," *Knight Ridder/Tribune News Service,* September 10, p. 4246.

Torr, James. ed. 2004. *Homeland Security.* San Diego, CA: Greenhaven Press.

Tumlin, Karen C. 2004. "Suspect First: How Terrorism Policy Is Reshaping Immigration Policy," *California Law Review,* 92 (4): 1173–1239.

Walcott, Charles E. and Karen M. Holt, 2003. "The Bush Staff and Cabinet System," *Perspectives on Political Science,* Summer, 32 (3): 150–156.

Warren, Robert. 2014. "Democratizing Data about Unauthorized Research in the United States: Estimates of Public Use Data, 2010 to 2013," *Journal on Migration on Migration and Human Security.* DOI: http://dx.doi/ org/10.14240/jmhs.v2i4.38. Accessed July 14, 2017.

Wucker, Michele. 2006. *Lockout.* New York: Public Affairs/Perseus Publishers.

www.dhs.gov/homeland-security-act-2002. Accessed July 15, 2017.

Yount, Lisa, ed. 2004. *Fighting Bioterrorism.* San Diego, CA: Greenhaven Press.

Zolberg, Aristide. 2008. *A Nation by Design: Immigration Policy in the Fashioning of America.* Cambridge, MA: Russell Sage Foundation, Harvard University Press.

2 Problems, Controversies, and Solutions

Introduction

This chapter focuses on some of the major problems and controversies that developed leading up to the enactment of the Department of Homeland Security (DHS) and then as the department implemented the law and dealt with controversies associated with ensuring homeland security. It covers the concept and impact of "groupthink" problems inherently involved in President George W. Bush administration's efforts to establish, first by executive order, the Office of Homeland Security within the White House and then congressional actions to establish the cabinet-level DHS.

This chapter addresses management problems of the new DHS arising from its mission complexity and the behemoth nature of the department. It focuses on problems of civil liberties and privacy rights of citizens versus the need to protect the nation from external attacks from international terrorist organizations as well as internal threats from "lone-wolf" terrorists radicalized and inspired by them. It discusses problems of technology development and administration approaches to

President George W. Bush signs the USA Patriot Act during a ceremony in the White House on October 26, 2001. The law was passed in response to the terrorist attacks of September 11, 2001, and gives intelligence and law enforcement agencies unprecedented authority to conduct terror investigations. It also led to an anti-Muslim immigrant backlash that raised civil liberties concerns. (The White House)

implement defense against cyberattacks. It examines the need for comprehensive immigration reform and how the stalemate in Congress over legislative action to enact such reform negatively impacts efforts to ensure homeland security. Climate change and the frequency and intensity of natural disasters are looked at, as well as how fiscal constraints impact the Federal Emergency Management Agency's (FEMA) efforts to cope with them, particularly the Hurricane Katrina debacle, contrasting the ineffectiveness of FEMA with the effectiveness of the U.S. Coast Guard facing the impact of Hurricanes Katrina and Rita. It reviews the sex scandals that rocked the Secret Service and the reputation of the agency within the DHS. It examines the political and judicial controversies engendered by President Trump's two executive orders to impose a Muslim travel ban and the federal court challenges of those travel bans.

Problems associated with business needs in the efficient and the timely issuing of visa applications are contrasted with security concerns. These are examined in the context of how the tightening of student and visitor visa applications and the negative impact problems in implementing those applications have caused for the U.S. economy.

The United States is a federal system. Complex relations between the national level of government with state and local governments affect homeland security concerns. How active should state and local communities and bureaucracies be in assisting the national government in immigration enforcement, exemplified by the Secure Communities initiative? And in sharp contrast, why do many local governments choose to embrace the sanctuary movement? Do sanctuary cities and churches pose a threat for homeland security?

For many decades the United States benefited from a "brain-drain" flow in which intellectually gifted and entrepreneurial talented persons migrated from developing nations to the United States. The chapter looks at how that brain drain has been negatively affected by the crackdown of legal immigration that resulted from homeland security concerns.

Finally, the United States has an increasingly aging population and a natural population growth that is close to zero. Future population growth, especially of working-age individuals, is almost entirely dependent on immigration. The chapter focuses on how homeland security concerns have impacted legal immigration and how that in turn is affecting the solvency of the Social Security system.

With each of these issues and controversies, the chapter identifies key stakeholders both within and without the government. Those stakeholder organizations and leaders are profiled in Chapter 4. Chapter 2 discusses proposed solutions to deal with each of those problems. It looks at how in each problem area a balance may be achieved between homeland security policy needs and other policy needs in those politically problematic areas. The problems associated with homeland security controversies and issues inherently entail the need and effort to achieve a balance in public policy addressing them. Solutions to those problems can be reached only through the political process that underlies all public policy making.

Groupthink Problems and the Establishment of the DHS and Homeland Security Policy

As referenced in Chapter 1, the policy-making process that led to the establishment of the cabinet-level DHS exhibits a number of problems identified by groupthink theory (LeMay 2006: 216–219). Groupthink is the term used for a theory extensively developed and popularized by Irving Janis (1972, 1982). It describes faulty decision making that occurs in groups as a result of forces that bring a group together—that is, forces of group cohesion. What Janis describes as typical group decision-making problems notable of groupthink decision making all appear to be present in the process to establish DHS, including the following:

1. Inadequately considering all alternatives in order to maintain unanimity.

2. Poor examination of decision objectives.

3. Failure to properly evaluate the risks of the chosen solution alternative.

4. Insufficient or biased information searches.

5. The desire for group conformity and unanimity essentially overrides the need to decide effectively (http://www. decision-making-solutions.com/group-decision-making-problems-groupthink-theory).

Janis notes several precursors to groupthink behavior and decision making:

1. Organizational faults such as directive leadership, lack of formal procedures, or lack of social diversity in the decision team

2. A challenging decision environment that includes external threats, time pressures, and/or moral dilemmas

In the rush to prevent future attacks, and in the post-9/11 hysteria, conformity between both the administration team developing the homeland security response and the congressional legislative process essentially short-circuited more deliberative decision making. Normal congressional policy processes typically involve several to many committees considering proposed bills, which take months to years when the proposed revision to a law is complex and far-reaching. Hearings are held, with many voices on both sides of an issue being heard. The two political parties typically weigh in on the proposal. Many stakeholders from the government agencies to be affected by the proposed law weigh in, as do lobbyists from a host of nongovernment stakeholders.

The legislative process is typically slow, often excruciatingly complex, and one that gives opponents of change the advantage over those advocating change. Inertia seems to be inherent in the routine legislative policy process. But that very complexity of the normal legislative process tends to ensure compromise in positions, a deeper examination of all the issues and concerns, and a "check and balance" of competing views on the legislation. Such a policy process tends to lessen "unforeseen consequences." Those constraints are absent in the "crisis" mode of decision making, such as the decision that resulted in the establishment of the DHS (Kowert 2002; Roots 2003; Yehiv 2003). As noted, the vote was 90–9 in the Senate and 299–121 in the House. Among Republicans, the vote was 212–6. There was virtually no debate about dissolving the Immigration and Naturalization Service (INS). What comparatively little debate there was concerned unionization and civil service protection, and whether or not the Coast Guard should be moved to the DHS. There was relatively little debate about civil liberty and privacy concerns (LeMay 2006: 218–219).

Management Problems for a Behemoth Department

The decision to merge 22 agencies into one huge department responsible for 190,000 employees, each agency of which had its own prior "bureaucratic culture" and some that were hardly compatible with one another, posed several management problems (LeMay 2006: 219–228). The INS and the Coast Guard, for example, had vastly different cultures, personnel management styles; bureaucratic jargon; and data collection, storage, and analysis capabilities. Critics noted merging them into one department with a new mission and goals would not be easy. As one critic stated:

> The behemoth known as the DHS is less than what it seems. Guided by advisors from the Defense and Justice departments and the CIA, the [Bush] administration ensured that the DHS has quite limited authority. So now, while the DHS oversees a number of areas—everything from federal airline safety to federal responses to hurricanes and floods—it has no authority to oversee the counterterrorism activity and priorities of other agencies. These

include the Defense Department, the Justice Department, and the CIA, the very agencies that are crucial to homeland defense. Instead of streamlining our domestic preparedness strategy, the DHS has simply become another agency added to the mix, equal but not primary. (Kayyem 2003: 46)

Opponents of the merger into such a huge bureaucracy predicted management problems, and the problems soon surfaced. FEMA, U.S. Customs and Border Protection, the Secret Service, and the Transportation Security Administration (TSA) were all criticized for mismanagement. The TSA, for example, grew more bloated, more incompetent, and less accountable. The TSA security screeners at the Minneapolis-St. Paul International Airport, the 16th busiest airport in the country, failed to detect smuggled explosive materials and fake weapons in 17 of 18 attempts by undercover agents of the Inspector General's office—a 95 percent failure rate. Such security systems checks failures have been increasing over time. In 2002 a failure rate of 25 percent was reported. That rate jumped to 75 percent by 2007. Between 2007 and 2015, the TSA increased its screeners by more than 50 percent, from 30,000 to 46,000, and spent $550 million on staff training and new screening equipment but failed to detect mock explosives and banned weapons in 67 of 70 cases in 2015. The Government Accountability Office blasted the TSA for wasting resources on a behavior detection program that had little, if any, scientific basis, and its results were no more than slightly better than pure chance (https://www.gao.gov/products/GAO-16-7071; http://www.gao.gov/newitems/do827r.pdf).

The agenda of the DHS appears to be a compendium of conventional wisdom to beef up preparedness with a limited sense of critical priorities. Critics note that DHS strategy seems to be to try anything and everything. An often-criticized attempt to guide the nation in terrorism response was the color-coded threat scheme. It proved largely unworkable, forcing local jurisdictions to respond to vague threats, allocate police over-time, and wait it out. The scheme was scrapped after a few years (LeMay 2006: 220).

The DHS's four directorates carry out varied missions. The Border and Transportation Directorate is the most visible of the four. Its budget is the largest within the department. It houses the TSA and two border agencies—Immigration and Customs Enforcement (ICE) and Customs and Border Protection (CBP). Roughly half of all DHS employees work in this directorate, most notably the baggage and passenger screeners.

The Emergency Preparedness and Response Directorate is dominated by FEMA. FEMA has four basic functions: funding rebuilding efforts after a disaster, giving expert advice on preparing for disasters, giving operating and capital assistance to local emergency response agencies (known as "first-responders"), and managing secret facilities intended to help the federal government survive a catastrophic attack. FEMA uses an all-hazards approach to emergency management. It helps local first-responder agencies prepare comprehensive plans to cope with a variety of potential hazards, both natural and man-made. It administers a vaccine stockpile program. It manages programs to mitigate nuclear, chemical, and biological attacks transferred to the DHS from the FBI and the Department of Energy. It maintains a First Responders Group that partners with first-responders at all levels of government to identify, validate, and facilitate the fulfillment of needs through the use of existing and emerging technologies, knowledge, products, and standards. It does so to (1) make first-responders safer; (2) help first-responders share data and critical information; (3) help first-responders better communicate through interoperability; and (4) engage, communicate, and partner with first-responders (https://www.dhs.gov/science-and-technology/first-responders).

The Science and Technology Directorate is the smallest in the DHS. It funds university research of various types and manages four laboratories, which develop countermeasures for weapons of mass destruction involving nuclear, chemical, or biological weapons.

Finally, the Information Analysis and Infrastructure Protection Directorate coordinates information about terrorist threats. The directorate combines six separate programs from agencies such as the FBI and the Department of Energy. It was responsible for the much-derided, color-coded scheme for warnings about terrorist threats. It produces daily homeland security briefings for the president by analyzing information from the nominally independent Terrorist Threat Integration Center, created by President Bush in January 2003. The center, a joint venture of the FBI, CIA, and DHS, is housed in CIA headquarters and is largely staffed by the CIA. DHS's top officials are not always privy to the sources and methods used by the center to develop its reports (Kemp 2003: 52; Lehrer 2004).

The merger of so many disparate agencies into such a huge department is more likely to create challenges to a federal government that is more responsive, effective, and efficient—the values underlying the very reason to create the DHS. Elisha Krause details four management problems from the reorganization that simply add additional obstacles to achieving those very values:

1. Mission complexity. DHS monitors annually 6 million containers and 600 million passengers on aircraft boarding or deplaning at 430 major airports and patrols 95,000 miles of coastline. It is responsible for preparing for and preventing terrorist attacks. It coordinates first-responders and monitors intelligence to protect against threats to the homeland.

2. Cultural incompatibility. Major problems arise from trying to combine disparate organizational cultures, competing technologies used in day-to-day operations, such as integrating different infrastructure platforms, software

applications, applications for e-mail databases, network-ing, and security protocols. Maintaining good communi-cation is complicated by doing so internally and externally between a host of federal agencies, and vertically with state and local first-responders and with the general public. DHS merges agencies like the Coast Guard and FEMA that had relatively high ratings in overall management (A and B, respectively), with INS agencies noted for their notoriously poor performance management (D ratings).

3. Task obfuscation. In its early years of operation, the DHS seemed more concerned with making Americans feel safer than with improving the quality of internal security. The very behemoth nature of the DHS results in greater levels of overhead and administrative costs.

4. Symbolic versus real performance results. Creating the DHS tends to foster a false sense of safety—that some-thing is being done. (Krause 2003: 51–58; LeMay 2006: 221–222; see also Haynes 2004; Light 2002).

Wendy Haynes notes:

Each of the twenty-two agencies brings its own array of existing management challenges and program risks to the new mega-department. The U.S. Comptroller General reported that many of the major components merging into the new department, including the TSA, already face considerable problems such as strategic human capital risks, information technology management challenges, and financial management vulnerabilities (GAO 2002). Informed observers fear that neither the president's requested budget . . . for the new department, nor the reorganization plan . . . come anywhere near providing the funds and the foresight to successfully implement the president's National Strategy for Homeland Security (July 2002). . . . Add to the mix the role complexities . . . a bewildering array of congressional oversight and appropriations committees, the challenge of meeting a grueling implementation schedule, and the absence of a culture of cooperation with [the agencies], and a daunting homeland security agenda begins to look more like an impossible and potential catastrophic dream. We will be witness to a mind-boggling demonstration of the complexity of joint action. (Haynes 2004: 369)

Eli Lehrer notes similar problems and concerns:

It is clear that DHS's scope is far smaller than the entire task of homeland security. Given that DHS does not have direct control over much of what it is supposed to do, it comes as no surprise that a number of tasks DHS promised to perform remain undone. A national assessment of critical infrastructure—a disaster mitigation function—may take as long as five years but was promised in one year. A repeated promise to create a single unified terrorist watch list, likewise, may never come to fruition. DHS has decided to build a complex terrorist tracking computer system instead. Access control tasks, which DHS does have more control over, does appear to have proceeded more smoothly: TSA, for example, has met goals to screen every airline passenger and perform X-rays of CTT scans of checked luggage, and Customs and Border Protection will eventually be tracking foreigners visiting the United States, albeit several years behind schedule. . . . Some of these failings stem from the growing pains in starting a new federal agency. But their roots are likely deeper than that. DHS simply does not have the breadth of control necessary to mandate that state and local emergency managers or even other federal agencies do what it says. (Lehrer 2004: 74)

The solutions of the TSA's response to criticisms of its management problems can be characterized, unfortunately, as "more of the same": more employees, more taxpayer money; more pointless harassment of passengers, including enhanced pat-downs and inspections of books and food and making passengers remove their shoes. Such efforts have never caught a terrorist and never foiled a terrorist plot. They have increased government authority by increasing intrusions into citizens' privacy and civil liberties.

The logical solution to problems and controversies arising from the behemoth nature of the DHS is to restructure the department. While that solution is logical, it is politically unlikely at this time. With each year that the department exists and operates, it becomes less likely that it will be restructured in any significant way. The political pressure to do so has eased as the DHS's management problems eased over the 15 years of the agency's existence. The lessening of the management problems, plus the inertia of policy making, and the political support vested in the department accrued over those 15 years, moreover, makes restructuring unlikely. Spinning off a few agencies might be possible and would lessen the behemoth nature of the DHS. Given the Trump administration's emphasis on stopping illegal immigration and reducing legal immigration, there might be a willingness to create a cabinet-level department of immigration, removing those functions from the DHS. Such structural reform would offer the opportunity to streamline immigration bureaucracies (Wucker 2006: 222–226).

Having a cabinet-level department of immigration might enhance programs designed to foster "patriotic assimilation." The Hudson Institute's John Fonte described patriotic assimilation: "Patriotic assimilation does not mean giving up one's ethnic traditions, customs, cuisine, and birth language. It has nothing to do with the food one eats, the religion one practices, the affection one has for the land of one's birth, or the languages one speaks. Patriotic assimilation occurs when a newcomer essentially adopts American civic values and the American heritage as his or her own" (cited in Wucker 2006: 227). Setting up immigration policy implementation in a new department of immigration would enable more resources to be used for civic and English-language education. Currently, such English-language programs for second-language learners meet only 5 percent of the demand. USCIS (U.S. Citizenship and Immigration Services) has a waiting list of 9,000 people for one adult education provider alone. Houston has the capacity to instruct about 35,000 people in English each year, although nearly 1 million need such classes. A new department of immigration is more likely to upgrade and revise tests for citizenship. The current test uses questions that are often redundant, technical, or merely trivial. They do not emphasize concepts and values like freedom, equality, rights, and responsibilities, the very values that patriotic assimilation encourages (Wucker 2006: 229–230).

Separating immigration management from homeland security matters would reduce mission complexity, a problem noted earlier. A major goal of the USCIS is to encourage the assimilation of permanent resident immigrants. In today's terminology, that is referred to as political incorporation. The political incorporation model holds that for a minority community to witness an effective response to its needs, minority leaders must come to occupy positions of government authority (Browning, Marshall, and Tabb 1984). Homeland security measures that target Muslim Americans and the implementation of a Muslim travel ban permanently color how many immigrants perceive the DHS and its current immigration functions. Separating immigration from homeland security would help, over time, to improve the reputation and perception of the immigration bureaucracy among legal immigrants. A conservative think tank noted the following:

> The Cato Institute calculated that even if the government's Terrorist Information Awareness program were 95 percent accurate, a search focused on the U.S. Muslim population would turn up 299,750 false positive IDs—with only 1.5 percent probability of finding a real terrorist. In other

words, the government was wasting time and money and alienating the groups whose help was needed—all for precious little benefit to American security. (Wucker 2006: 147–148)

Cyberattacks and Homeland Security

Another DHS problem involves its mission to secure the homeland against cyberattacks (Clarke and Knake 2010: 44). Cyber technology to protect against attacks has lagged behind what cyber warriors using it offensively have been able to do. And privacy and civil liberty concerns complicate the development and, more important, the utilization of that technology. In 1996, NSA (National Security Agency) wanted to use a clipper chip that would have allowed it to access every encryption program and would have enabled NSA to listen in without a court order. Privacy, civil liberty, and technology interest groups united in vehement opposition to NSA's proposal and effectively killed it (Clarke and Knake 2010: 107–108). Such opposition was increased by Patriot Act and Patriot Act II provisions.

Malware programs all too frequently seem to defeat, for a time at least, the systems designed to protect against them. It is clearly evident that defense against cyberattacks, such as what is called zero-day malware, needs technology development. The term refers to a specific type of malware or malicious software that has only recently been discovered. The zero-day phenomenon is one not previously known about or anticipated. Security teams respond to zero-day malware by tracking its ability in real time using deep-packet inspection system tied into Internet security to ferret out and stop a cyberattack (Clarke and Knake 2010: 163). Zero-day malware can affect specific operating systems in specific ways. It infiltrates a computer system or network usually attached to e-mail or otherwise disguised as harmless files. For example, zero-day malware affected the Microsoft Internet Explorer browser, which Microsoft has since addressed. Often zero-day malware instances are resolved with security upgrades or software patches (https://www.techopedia.com/definition/29741/zero-day-malware).

Defense against cyberattack is characterized by asymmetry. The National Institute for Public Policy defines "asymmetric threat" as the term used to describe forms of attack against the United States for which there are no defenses. It depicts tactics that Washington will not abide, because it is either morally reprehensible or restricted by legal agreement (http://www.nipp.org/wp-content/uploads/2014/11/Asymmetry-final-02.pdf; see also Bennett et al. 1999; Cordesman 2000).

A 2009 study by the National Academy of Sciences warned that cyber war policy was ill-formed, undeveloped, and highly uncertain (Clarke and Knake 2010: 261). Developing defensive cyber war policy and technology is problematic, in part, because of Congress and its policy-making processes. As Clarke and Knake note:

> Congress is a federation of fiefdoms, subject to the vicissitudes of constant fund raising and lobbying of those who have donated funds. That situation has two adverse consequences with regard to congressional involvement in cyber war oversight. First, everyone wants his or her own fiefdom. Congress has resisted any suggestion that there be one committee authorized to examine cyber security [there are now 28 committees and subcommittees that share some oversight responsibilities]. Second, Congress "eschews regulation" and spits it out. The influential donors of the information technology, electric power, pipeline, and telecommunications industries have made the idea of serious cyber security regulations as remote as public financing of congressional campaigns or meaningful limits on campaign contributions. (Clarke and Knake 2010: 264–266)

Quite a number of solutions have been proposed for the problem of the DHS being woefully behind in developing defenses against cyberattacks.

1. Negotiate an international Cyber War Limitation Treaty along the lines of the SALT Treaties.

2. Establish an internal Cyber Risk Reduction Center.

3. Establish within international law such concepts as the "obligation to assist" and "national cyber accountability."

4. Impose a ban on first-use cyberattacks against civilian infrastructure.

5. Prohibit the preparation of the battlefield in peacetime by the emplacement of trapdoors or logic bombs on such civilian infrastructures as electric power grids, railroads, and the like.

6. Prohibit altering data or damaging networks of financial institutions at any time, including especially the emplacement of logic bombs.

7. Create an International Cyber Threat Reduction Center.

8. Do significantly more research on more secure network designs, along the lines of the DoD's Defense Advanced Research Projects Agency (DARPA).

9. Establish a private network for the internal working of federal agencies that would deny access to those who could not prove who they were (a Govnet).

10. Increase presidential involvement in cyber defense policy making (Clarke and Knake 2010: 268–278).

Problems with Civil Liberties and Privacy versus Security

There is an inherent value conflict at issue in homeland security policy and civil rights and liberties policy. Striking a balance between those values in the ways in which homeland security is pursued while safeguarding traditional privacy and civil liberties protections is an ongoing problem and concern (LeMay 2006: 261–264). The fight against international terrorism focuses on granting the federal government powers that in their sweeping nature inevitably conflict with civil rights and civil liberties. Trying to achieve a balance has led to somewhat strange political bedfellows, to an unlikely coalition of liberal civil rights groups and conservative libertarians, and to gun-rights advocates and medical privacy advocates. Former conservative Republican congressman Bob Barr, who had voted for the USA Patriot Act, has since opposed Patriot Act II and has become a sharp critic. A new coalition, Patriots to Restore Checks and Balances, jointed conservative groups, like the American Conservative Union, the Center for Privacy and Technology Policy, and Free Congress, with such liberal groups as the American Civil Liberties Union (ACLU) and the American Librarians Association. A nationwide grassroots coalition claims that 383 communities and 7 states have enacted anti-Patriot Act laws, called "civil liberties safe zones," or sanctuary cities. The coalition lobbies Congress to scale back three provisions of Patriot Act II law: one that allows federal agents to conduct "sneak and peek" searches without notification, one that demands records from such institutions as libraries and medical offices, and one that uses a sweepingly broad definition of terrorism in pursuing suspects (LeMay 2006: 261).

DHS mandates that the FBI, CIA, state, and local governments share intelligence reports with DHS. Civil rights activists claim this endangers the rights and freedoms of law-abiding citizens by blurring the lines between foreign and domestic spying. The ACLU, for example, charges that the DHS will be 100 percent secret and 0 percent accountable. Although enacted to track down terrorists, information can be collected on any dissenter, citizen or not, violent or not. The classification within the DoD and FEMA documents of peace marches and protests as "terrorist events" in 2003 is but one example of the dangerous potential for civil liberties abuses by the DHS (https://www.projectcensored.org/2-homeland-security-threatens-civil-liberties).

Critics of the Patriot Act, which had been approved by a vote of 357–66 in the House of Representatives and 98–1 in the Senate, argue that it, and the DHS Act, allows government increased and nearly unprecedented access to the lives of citizens and results in an unrestrained imposition on civil liberties. Wiretaps, previously confined to one telephone, can now follow a person from place to place at the behest of government agents. People can be and have been detained on vague suspicion that they might be a terrorist. Detainees can be and have been denied the right to legal counsel (Wucker 2006: 141–142). Patriot Act II places the entire federal government under the jurisdiction of the Justice Department, DHS, and FEMA NORTHCOM. Critics note the lack of checks and balances to protect anyone who is tagged in error, even unintentionally. The ACLU charges that post-9/11, the federal government engaged in systematic policies of torture (e.g., walling and waterboarding at Gitmo), indefinite detention, mass surveillance, and religious discrimination through racial and religious profiling of Arab and Muslim Americans. It argues the Patriot Act, and the DHS in its manner of enforcing its policies and practices, has eroded many of America's most cherished values and in the process made us less free and less safe (https://www.aclu.org/issues/national-security).

Critics argue the approach of the Patriot Acts (I and II) and of the DHS in fighting the war on terrorism domestically involves a cure that is worse than the disease. David Cole articulates the concerns of those critics:

> Three principles in particular should guide our response to the threat of terrorism. First, we should not overreact in a time of fear, a mistake we made all too often in the past. Second, we should not sacrifice the bedrock foundations of our constitutional democracy—political freedom and equal treatment—absent a compelling showing of

need and adoption of narrowly tailored means. And third, balancing liberty and security, we should not succumb to the temptation to trade a vulnerable minority's liberties, namely the liberties of immigrants in general, or Arab and Muslim immigrants in particular, for the security for the rest of us. The USA Patriot Act violates all three of those principles. (cited in Etzioni and Marsh 2003: 35)

Proponents of the primacy of the value of public safety, by contrast, argue that foreign citizens in our midst have no entitlement to enter or to remain in the country and that prudence dictates measures that change the terms under which they are allowed to remain in the United States. Mark Krikorian, director of the Center for Immigration Studies, articulates that perspective:

It would be unfortunate, if, in our effort to prevent another 3,000 American deaths—or 30,000 or 300,000—we were inadvertently to deport some foreign citizens who pose no threat to us. But their presence here is a privilege we grant, not a right they have exercised, and we may withdraw that privilege for any reason. (cited in Etzioni and Marsh 2003: 33–34)

Sometimes groups inadvertently got caught up in the post-9/11 hysteria. An October 2004 raid by the FBI on the offices of a small charity known as the Islamic-American Relief Agency effectively shut down the charity. The Patriot Act expanded the International Emergency Economic Powers Act that allowed the government to seize assets of organizations while investigating it for links to terrorism. The FBI found no evidence of such links, and the raid was likely the result of confusing the Islamic-American Relief Agency with the Sudan-based charity called the Islamic-African Relief Agency, which the U.S. government claims does have links to terrorists (LeMay 2006: 263).

Critics of the DHS and Patriot Acts I and II charge the government with racial profiling. They look skeptically at programs like the Total Information Awareness of the DoD, which focuses on people who speak certain languages: Afghan languages, Arabic, Farsi, Korean, and Mandarin (Torr 2004: 61).

The Intelligence Authorization Act of 2004, which funds all intelligence activities of the U.S. government, changed the definition of "financial institution." Prior to 2004, that referred to banks. The new definition includes stockbrokers, car dealerships, casinos, credit card companies, insurance agencies, jewelers, airlines, and any other business "whose cash transactions have a high degree of usefulness in criminal, tax, regulatory" and now possible terrorist-related matters (Martin 2005: 1).

DHS greatly expanded its use of expedited removals, especially for persons ordered out of the country from countries known to harbor terrorists—although that threat may be small. A 2003 staff report of the September 11 Commission found that only 5,000 of the 400,000 were from countries known to have ties to Al Qaeda. Of some 1,100 persons from that group, moreover, none were ever charged with terrorism-related offenses (LeMay 2006: 264).

An intended solution to those myriad problems and concerns regarding matters of privacy and civil liberties versus security was the establishment, within DHS, of the Office for Civil Rights and Civil Liberties (CRCL). It was designed to integrate civil rights and civil liberties into all 22 of the agencies of the department by doing the following:

1. Promoting respect for civil rights and civil liberties in policy creation and implementation, and providing advice and support for incorporation of civil rights and civil liberties protections into the Department's immigration-related activities and policies;

2. Communicating with individuals and communities whose civil rights and civil liberties may be affected by Department activities and informing them of policies and avenues of redress;

3. Investigating and resolving civil rights and civil liberties complaints filed by the public regarding Department policies or activities;

4. Leading the Department's equal employment opportunity programs and promoting workforce diversity and the Department's efforts to implement proactive and effective programs for promoting diversity; and

5. Ensuring that the Department complies with constitutional, statutory, regulatory, and other requirements relating to civil rights and civil liberties. CRCL attempts to do so by assessing the impact of DHS policies and activities, training DHS personnel, and engaging with diverse communities. (https://www.dhs.gov/topic/civil-rights-and-civil-liberties)

The CRCL has trained privacy officials at 68 of the 78 fusion centers and provides technical assistance to those officials by training more than 1,000 fusion center staff since 2009. The CRCL has incorporated standards into the agency's cyber security programs and initiatives by providing specific training on the protection of privacy and civil liberties as they relate to computer network security activities provided to DHS personnel. To do so, it completed an overhaul of its civil rights investigations processes by creating a new complaint database system, by developing an easy-to-use online complaint submission form, by increasing access to comprehensive language services, by increasing transparency for complainants, and by improving coordination with components to track response to and implementation of recommendations (https://www.dhs.gov/topic/civil-rights-and-civil-liberties).

While supporting the creation of the CRCL within the DHS, the ACLU is less impressed with its accomplishments. The ACLU's solution to coping with problems of civil rights and civil liberties, and with privacy rights associated with the implementation of Patriot Act II and with the DHS itself, was to establish its own National Security Project. The project aims to educate the public about abuses and shape law so that courts,

Congress, and U.S. citizens can serve as an enduring check on abuse and seeks to have the federal government renounce policies and practices that disregard due process, enshrine discrimination, and turn everyone into a suspect (https://www.aclu.org/issues/national-security).

Comprehensive Immigration Reform

Without question, many problems of concern to homeland security arise from the flow of unauthorized immigration and the political issues it engenders. But illegal immigration is a problem exacerbated by the breakdown in legal immigration law and policy. Simply put, America's immigration system is broken. As Michael Bloomberg notes, "Reforming a broken immigration system is the single most important step the federal government could take to bolster the economy" (cited in Bush and Bolick 2013: 101). No realistic or lasting resolution of the illegal immigration problem can be achieved without a comprehensive reform of immigration law and policy. Enacting comprehensive immigration reform, however, is a public policy conundrum.

Congress has periodically attempted to reform immigration in a comprehensive way ever since the Immigration Act of November 29, 1990 (IMMACT, 104 Stat. 4981; summarized in LeMay and Barkan 1999: 288–295). Since 1990, however, and especially post-2001, it has become a toxic political issue.

The Republican Party, since 2007, has reached a near-schism on the issue between the more business-oriented, establishment wing of the party and the Tea Party Activist and Libertarian-leaning wing, as well as the grass roots of the party, and today what might best be called the Trump wing of the party. Senators John McCain (R-AZ) and Lindsey Graham (R-SC), who, in 2007, were among a Senate "Gang of Eight," cosponsored bills with Democrats to comprehensively reform immigration policy but have since backed off that position. The Tea Party/Libertarian/Trump base of the party has adamantly opposed what McCain and Graham had called "earned legalization" but that the Trump base of the party has labeled amnesty.

On the other hand, the progressive wing of the Democratic Party, including particularly the Hispanic Caucus, the Black Caucus, the Border States Caucus, and stalwarts of the liberal wing of the Democratic Party, exemplified by senators Bernie Sanders (I-VT) and Elizabeth Warren (D-MA), has an entrenched position, insisting that earned legalization and enactment of the Dream Act proposals be included in any reform measure before they will support it. The extreme partisan divide results in a stalemate on the issue.

What is politically most popular among Republicans today—a crackdown on illegal immigration through border control measures such as license laws and building a fence or a Southwestern border wall, as proposed by President Trump—makes for ineffective and inefficient policy, manifestly having cost billions of dollars with little or no impact on the rate of unauthorized immigration since 2001. Border control policy addresses "pull" factors influencing the unauthorized immigration flow. But the failed economies of Mexico and Central American countries like El Salvador, Honduras, and Guatemala and the drug cartel-instigated violence in those countries underpin "push" factors. The push factors are demonstrably more powerful influences on the migration flow than are any U.S. laws on the matter.

Events like the Arab Spring, the civil war in Syria, and the rise of ISIS in Iran and Iraq propel mass refugee movements, adding further pressure to the immigration issue. Foreign civil wars and domestic strife, often racially, ethnically, or religiously inspired, renew mass refugee movements compelling hundreds of thousands to millions to flee their nations of origin to migrate elsewhere. Such conditions affect both legal and unauthorized immigration flows, changing them in their overall size, composition, and origin (LeMay 2013: 70).

Other lobbying groups, like the No More Deaths organization, on humanitarian grounds, offer food, water, and medical aid to undocumented immigrants crossing the desert areas along the Southwestern border. They aim to reduce the number of deaths along the border that annually number in the several hundreds. The Irish Lobby for Immigration Reform pushes for provisions that would benefit Irish immigrants (both legal immigrants and visa overstayers). Hispanic groups, like LULAC and LaRaza, push for an amnesty provision (PEW Hispanic Center 2011).

The "immigration problem" is acute in several states. In Florida, for example, the 2010 census found that among Miami's 2.6 million residents, 51 percent were foreign born. That latest census found that among the total population, 39 million—just over 12 percent—were foreign-born residents (Bush and Bolick 2013: 139; LeMay 2013: 37; U.S. Bureau of the Census 2010). In June 2002, Florida was the first state to set up the 287 (g) Cross-Designation Program that allowed state and local law enforcement to act on behalf of the federal law enforcement officials (ICE) (Bush and Bolick 2013: Preface xi–xiii).

The attempt to pass comprehensive reform that came closest to passage was in 2007, when then president George W. Bush re-advocated a comprehensive immigration reform bill sponsored by senators John McCain and Ted Kennedy (D-MA). The legalization provision, however, aroused such opposition among Republicans that President Bush was forced to stop pushing the legislation, and Senator McCain, in an attempt to save his 2008 bid for the Republican presidential nomination, was likewise forced to withdraw his sponsorship. Although many business groups favored the plan, groups like the Minutemen opposed it, even forming vigilante groups along the Mexican border to stop illegal immigrants (*The Denver Post*, March 31, 2005). The National Council of State Legislatures and the National Governors Conference oppose any measure that does not include funding for state and local governments. They oppose what they charge are unfunded mandates on states and localities (LeMay 2013: 70–71).

Senate Democrats introduced the Comprehensive Immigration Reform Act of 2011 (S. 1251), but Senate Republicans insisted on a filibuster-proof vote of 60, killing the bill, as it did a Dream Act measure.

A Republican-favored approach to more piecemeal immigration reform, using a crackdown approach to illegal immigration instead of a comprehensive approach, is well exemplified by the Secure Communities program established by ICE in 2008. ICE prioritized the removal of public safety and homeland security threats, those who violated the nation's immigration laws, including those who failed to comply with a final order of removal, and those who engaged in fraud/willful misrepresentation with official government matters. The program uses a federal information-sharing partnership between the DHS, the FBI, and state and local law enforcement to help identify in-custody immigrants. Under the program, the FBI automatically sends to DHS the fingerprints of individuals arrested and/or booked into custody by any state or local law enforcement agency to see if they have outstanding warrants so that the DHS can check those against its immigration databases. If such checks reveal that an individual in custody is unlawfully present in the United States or is otherwise removable, ICE takes enforcement action against violent or serious criminals, as well as those who have violated the nation's immigration laws (https://www.dhs.gov/sites/default/files/publications/14_1120_memo_prosecutorial_discretion.pdf; https://www.dhs.gov/sites/default/files/publications/14_1120_memo_secure_communities.pdf).

ICE completed full implementation of Secure Communities to all 3,181 jurisdictions within the 50 states, the District of Columbia, and 5 U.S. territories on January 22, 2013. From its inception to its suspension, the Secure Communities Program led to the removal of 315,200 criminal immigrants. It was suspended during President Obama's second administration by order of secretary of DHS, Jeh Johnson, on November 20, 2014. The suspension lasted until January 25, 2017 (https://www.dhs.gov/sites/default/files/

publications/14_1120_memo_secure_communities.pdf). The Obama DHS suspended the program in reaction to general hostility to it among governors, mayors, and state and local law enforcement officials around the country who had refused to cooperate with the program, and due to a number of federal court decisions that rejected the authority of state and local law enforcement agencies to detain immigrants pursuant to federal detainment orders issued by the DHS. The suspension was also in response to recommendations of the Homeland Security Advisory Council Task Force. Secretary Johnson directed ICE to put in its place a program that will continue to rely on fingerprint-based biometrics, but ICE would only seek to transfer an immigrant in the custody of state and local law enforcement when the immigrant has been convicted of offenses listed under two priority lists or when, in the judgment of an ICE field office director, the immigrant posed a threat to national security. In other words, unless an immigrant posed a demonstrable homeland security risk, enforcement actions would only be taken against immigrants who are convicted of the enumerated crimes. In response to a number of federal court decisions that held that detainee-based detention by state and local law enforcement agencies violates the Fourth Amendment, Secretary Johnson ordered ICE to replace requests for detention with requests for notification.

Republican Donald Trump was elected president in November 2016. On taking office, he immediately reversed the Obama administration's executive orders on the matter. Using his executive order powers, President Trump ended the extension of Deferred Action for Childhood Arrivals and Deferred Action for Parental Accountability policies and ordered the Justice Department and DHS to crack down on illegal immigrants. Trump issued Executive Order 13768, Enhancing Public Safety in the Interior of the United States, on January 25, 2017. It ordered his secretary of Homeland Security, John Kelly, to reinstate the Secure Communities program. From that date until the second quarter of FY 2017, 10,290 criminal immigrants were removed via the Secure Communities program (https://www.ice.gov/secure-communities). Deportation hearings had backlogged during the Obama administration. They responded to the problem by suspending the Secure Communities program. With the renewal of the Secure Communities program, backlogs in deportation hearings again began to rise. President Trump's administration responded by shifting 100 immigration judges from elsewhere in the DHS to hold deportation hearings at the Mexican border.

A number of solutions have been suggested to better cope with the problems and concerns discussed earlier. As Jeb Bush and Clint Bolick (2013) note:

> Two thirds of Americans support a process by which illegal immigrants can obtain lawful status so long as they learn to speak English, pass background checks, and pay restitution. (9)

They propose a provision within a comprehensive immigration reform which they call "earned residency" (as opposed to the Democrats' "earned legalization"). Earned residency would provide a path to legal resident status as long as the unauthorized immigrants pay taxes, learn English, and have committed no substantial crimes. The legalizing immigrants would have legal resident status, but it would not be amnesty nor would it be a short-cut path to citizenship (40–47). Given Jeb Bush's lack of success in obtaining the Republican Party's nomination for president in 2016, losing out to Donald Trump, one can reasonably assume his earned residency solution was not favorably received by the party's base voters.

Another often-tried solution to the "control of the border" problem has been to increase the size of the Border Patrol and to assign more agents to the Southwest border with Mexico. The Border Patrol has been steadily increasing in its number of agents, dramatically so under the DHS. In 2006 there were 11,000 agents. By 2009 that rose to 17,000, and by 2016 the national total of Border Patrol agents stood at 19,828. Of those, 17,026 are assigned to the Southwest Border Sector, with only 2,059 to the Northern Border Sector (with Canada) and only 211 to the Coastal Border Sector (https://www.cbp.gov/sites/default/files/assets/documents/2017-Jan/USBP%20Stats%20FY2016%20sector%20profile.pdf).

Rather than building a wall, which they consider too costly and not very effective, Bush and Bolick recommend a combination of real and "virtual" fencing, aerial surveillance, and increased border security staffing, and extending DHS authority to take security actions in the 50 national parks located within 100 miles of U.S. borders. They favor biometric identification, including use of DNA, iris scans, facial recognition, and voice imprints (Bush and Bolick 2013: 52). They also argue that an enforcement-only, or secure-the-border-first, policy is self-defeating. They note that as the DHS has cracked down, more illegal immigrants in the country are staying rather than returning to Mexico (114).

Another piecemeal approach to better border control that has been tried, viewed as a stopgap measure until more border agents could be approved, funded, hired, and trained, was to assign National Guard units to the Southwest Border Sector to assist the Border Patrol/DHS. The first such program was called Operation Jump Start, in which 6,000 National Guard troops were ordered to the Southwest border by President Bush and served from 2006 to 2008. That approach was continued and expanded by President Obama in Operation Phalanx, which in July 2010 began a six-month mission assigning 1,210 Army National Guard troops along the 1,933-mile Southwest border to support the CBP. Their tasks included ground surveillance, criminal investigative analysis, command and control, mobile communications, transportation, logistics, and training support. Operation Phalanx used 12 National Guard helicopters and several fixed-wing aircraft to provide aerial operations to Operation River Watch II, which covered 200 miles of border from Laredo to the Gulf Coast. They were credited with assisting in the apprehension of 17,900 illegal immigrants from July 2010 to June 2011. The U.S. Government Accountability Office (GAO), however, warned that the use of National Guard troops at the border would hinder National Guard recruitment efforts and would fuel perception that the border is militarized, as well as hinder binational agreements between Mexico and the United States (https://www .army.mil/article/140752; https://www.army.mil/article/51819; https://www.cbp.gov/newsroom/national-media-release/ national-guard-supports-border-security-efforts).

Climate Change and the Frequency and Intensity of Natural Disasters

Another problem and concern for the DHS's FEMA is the impact of climate change that has contributed to the increasing frequency, intensity, and the costs of weather-related natural disasters. There is considerable political controversy and disagreement about climate change and the human role in contributing to it. Moreover, disagreement over the validity of climate change science and appropriate policy responses to the problem are deeply partisan. The anti-climate change policy position of the Trump administration exacerbates the concern about FEMA's reactions to natural disasters, which, as noted, will likely only increase in the number of such events and the intensity and destruction caused by them (such as the Category 5 hurricane that so devastated Puerto Rico in 2017).

"Climate change is defined as a change in global or regional climate patterns, in particular, a change apparent from the mid- to late twentieth century onwards and attributed largely to the increased levels of atmospheric carbon dioxide produced by the use of fossil fuels" (https://climate.nasa.gov/evidence/). A recent study found that 97 percent of climate scientists agree that climate warming trends over the past century are very likely due to human activities, and most of the leading scientific organizations worldwide have issued statements endorsing this position. They hold that there is a greater than 95 percent probability that the increased rate in global warming is due to human activity since the mid-20th century (https://www.climate.nasa.gov/evidence/).

The evidence of global climate change is indicated by the following:

1. Sea level rise of 8 inches in the last century and the rate of sea rise in the last two decades nearly doubled that of the last century.
2. Global temperature rise.
3. Warming oceans—a rise of 0.302°F since 1969.
4. Shrinking ice sheets.
5. Declining Arctic sea ice.
6. Glacial retreat.
7. Increase in extreme weather events.
8. Decreased snow cover.

The National Aeronautics and Space Administration (NASA) projects the following effects of climate change:

1. The continued rise in global temperature.
2. Frost-free seasons will lengthen.
3. Marked changes in precipitation patterns.
4. More draught and heat waves.
5. Hurricanes will become stronger and more intense.
6. The sea level will rise by 1–4 feet by 2100.
7. The Arctic will become ice free before 2050.

According to a recent PEW study, some 55 percent of the population accepts that climate change is real and influenced by human activity (https://www.pewinternet.org/2016/6/10/04/the-politics-of-climate-change/). They point to the increased frequency and intensity of recent hurricanes and the rising costs in lives and property damage from those storms.

Hurricane Katrina, for example, struck the Gulf Coast on August 29, 2005. It was a Category 3 hurricane on the Saffer-Simpson Hurricane Scale. It caused levee breeches in New Orleans that led to a catastrophic aftermath. Katrina had sustained winds of 100–140 mph. Hundreds of thousands of people had to be evacuated and were displaced in Louisiana, Mississippi, and Alabama. The storm killed nearly 2,000 people, caused more than $100 billion in damage, and affected 90,000 square miles. The U.S. Coast Guard rescued 34,000 people in New Orleans alone. The Superdome in New Orleans was the refuge center for 15,000 people who were not able to evacuate themselves or be evacuated by the local government. FEMA was notably unprepared to cope with the disaster (https://www.history.com/topics/hurricane-katrina/).

Shortly after Katrina, the Atlantic coast was again struck by Hurricane Rita, which hit Louisiana and Texas. It made landfall on September 23, 2005. It, too, was a Category 3 hurricane with 115-mph sustained winds. The storm and its storm surge caused 120 deaths. Its damage was estimated at $10.5 billion and was, up to that time, the ninth-costliest natural disaster storm in U.S. history. According to the National Climate Data Center of the NOAA, Rita caused the evacuation of more than 3 million residents from the Gulf Coast region (www.hurricanescience.org/history/storms/2000s/rita and www.nodc.noaa.gov/hurricane-rita).

Hurricane Gustav hit on August 25, 2008. It caused a coastal storm surge in Louisiana. It was a Category 2 hurricane, with sustained winds of 105 mph. It caused a total of $6.61 billion, and 77 lives were lost in the United States and 153 lives in Haiti. More than 10,250 homes were lost. The storm impacted the 2008 presidential election—forcing a delay in the Republican National Convention and causing the state of Louisiana to delay its congressional elections by three months.

Hurricane Irene hit on August 26–27, 2011. NOAA classified Irene as a Category 1 hurricane, with wind gusts of 115 mph. It spawned several tornadoes. Rainfall amounts exceeded 10 inches, and its storm surge was 10 feet. It caused five deaths in North Carolina, and it pounded the East Coast as far north as Canada (http://weather.gov/mhx/August272011EventReview/).

Hurricane Sandy struck New Jersey and New York on October 22, 2012. It was nicknamed "Superstorm Sandy." It caused 147 deaths as it ravaged the New York City and New Jersey shore. A Category 2 storm, it required 6,700 National Guard troops to assist coping with its destruction and threat to lives. It caused 110 homes to burn to the ground in Breezy Point, Queens, New York. Hurricane Sandy left 4.8 million customers without power in 15 states and the District of Columbia. More than 71,000 people applied for more than $385 million in housing assistance alone. New Jersey governor Chris Christie estimated the storm damage in his state at $36.8 billion, with another $29.4 billion in repairs and restoration and $7.5 billion in mitigation protection and prevention coverage. New York City mayor Michael Bloomberg estimated that Sandy caused $19 billion in damages to the city. Governor Andrew Cuomo placed its costs to the state of New York at $41.8 billion. According to the National Hurricane Center, Hurricane Sandy was the second costliest in U.S. history (https://edition.cnn.com/2013/07/13/world/americas/hurricane-sandy-fast-facts/index.html).

The 2016 Atlantic Hurricane season witnessed the highest amount in tropical cyclone activity since 2012. It saw 15 named storms and 7 hurricanes, among which 4 were major hurricanes (a Category 3 or greater storm). The first storm of the season struck in January 2016. Hurricane Alex was the first hurricane to strike the U.S. Atlantic coast in the month of January since 1938. The final storm of the season was Hurricane Otto, which hit on November 25. For the season, tropical cyclone storms caused 743 deaths and a total damage of $16.1 billion. Between 1981 and 2010, the average number of storms in a season was 10.8 but numbered 15 in 2016. If there were an average 5.6 hurricanes in a season from 1981 to

2010, there were 7 in 2016. From 1981 to 2010 a Category 3 or more major hurricanes occurred 2.5 times; in 2016, there were three such storms. The season's strongest storm was Hurricane Matthew, which struck the coast on October 12, 2016 (https://www.weather.com/storms/hurricane/news/hurricane-season-2016-atlantic-recap/).

The politics of climate change is characterized by strong lobbying opposition by climate change deniers. A 2015 study identified 4,556 individuals associated by network ties to 164 organizations. These organizations are the most responsible for efforts to downplay the threat of climate change in the United States. Notable lobbyist for climate deniers include Freedom Works, Americans for Prosperity, David and Charles Koch and the Koch Industries, Exxon-Mobil, the Heritage Foundation, the Marshall Institute, the Cato Institute, and the American Enterprise Institute (https://www.pewinternet .org/2016/6/10/04/the-politics-of-climate/).

Suggested solutions for problems and concerns linked to climate change are to increase solar and wind power usage and to decrease the use of fossil fuels/fracking/coal mining. Other solutions being tried are Data Gov, a climate data initiative; U.S. Climate Resilience Toolkit; the NOAA; the National Climate Assessment of 2014; the United States Department of Energy doing research in nonfossil and renewable energy sources and technology; the Environmental Protection Agency; the United Nations Framework on Climate Change; and the Paris Climate Accord of October 5, 2016, signed by President Obama, which was agreed to by every major country in the world. The United States, however, was alone in pulling out of the agreement by President Trump after the G-20 meeting in July 2017 (https://www.climate.nasa.gov/evidence/; http:// unfccc.int/paris_agreement/items/9485.php).

Besides pulling out of the Paris agreement, President Trump signaled his dramatic change regarding climate change from that of President Obama by continuing to cast doubts on the legitimacy of climate change science, by announcing budget cuts to FEMA and the Environmental Protection Agency, by increasing funds for the fossil fuel extractive industry, such as fracking, the Alaska oil pipeline, deregulation of the fossil fuel industry, by rescinding President Obama's executive orders canceling contracts to extract fossil fuels on national lands, and by opening up both Atlantic and Pacific coastal shelves to increased oil extraction despite opposition from the state governments along both coasts to such deep underwater drilling.

Secret Service Scandals and Reform Efforts

Founded in 1865, the U.S. Secret Service is one of the oldest federal investigative agencies. The service has 3,200 special agents and 1,300 uniformed officers who guard the White House, the Treasury building, and foreign diplomatic missions located in Washington, D.C. It is charged with protecting the president and First Family, the vice president, the president-elect, the vice president-elect, visiting heads of states, and representatives of the United States during special missions overseas. After the 9/11 attacks, it took on new responsibilities: providing security at nonpolitical events that could be the targets of terrorists, such as the Super Bowl (http://www.cnn.com/2016/04/18/us/secret-service-fast-facts/index.html).

Despite its expanded roles, the Secret Service suffered budget cuts, poor management, and poor morale that contributed to an exodus of agents: between 2011 and 2015, for example, the number of full-time workers at the agency fell from 7,024 to 6,315.

The Secret Service's field office in New York City was located in the World Trade Center and was destroyed in the 9/11 attacks, and its Special Officer Craig Miller was killed. The agency was moved from the Department of the Treasury to the DHS when that department was established in 2002.

The agency was rocked by several management problems, security breaches, and sex scandals and ethical failures in 2012–2016 (http://www.cnn.com/2012/04/19/us/secret-service/index.

html/; http://www.dailycaller.com/2015/12/03/cash-for-dem-hoes-check-and-more-disturbing-new-details-in-secret-service-scandals/).

The Secret Service came under critical examination due to an incident in which a Virginia couple crashed President Obama's first White House state visit and the agency's overspending in FY 2009. The director of the Secret Service at the time was Mark Sullivan, who became an agent with the service in 1983 and director of the Secret Service in May 2006. Questions of serious mismanagement arose in May 2012, when news broke about a sex scandal involving agents who were among 22 people from the DHS who contributed to the Interagency Working Group on U.S. Government-Sponsored International Exchanges and Training. A sizable group of Secret Service agents became embroiled in the scandal over use of prostitutes, bringing them to Cartagena, Colombia's Hotel El Caribe, during a visit a few days prior to President Obama's attendance at the Sixth Summit of the Pan-American Conference. Eleven agents/employees of the service were placed under investigation in the scandal. Two supervisors were forced to resign, and one was allowed to retire. Solicitation of prostitutes is legal for adults in Colombia, but the conduct was a breach of the Secret Service's conduct code (http://www.cnn.com/2012/04/19/us/secret-service/index.html). A number of Drug Enforcement Agency (DEA) agents attending the 2012 summit were also accused of using prostitutes. Then, in October 2014, the federal investigator probing allegations that Secret Service special agents had hired prostitutes in the Colombia probe had to resign when he was alleged to have hired a prostitute in Broward County, Florida (http://www.nydailynews.com/news/national/fed-probing-secret-service-prostitution-claims-resigns-report-article-1.1991034). The House Committee on Oversight and Government Reform (HOGR), then chaired by Jason Chaffetz (R-UT), sent a letter to the Secret Service requesting specifics about the incident. The committee brought in outsiders to examine whether or not the Colombia sex scandal incident was symptomatic of broader problems.

In 2013, the Secret Service was accused of repeated failures to follow procedures to protect the president, including allowing an armed intruder to jump the White House fence and storm into the East Room and, in September 2014, allowing President Obama to ride in an elevator with an armed security guard at the Center for Disease Control in Atlanta, Georgia. And in March 2015, another agent who was drinking heavily in the evening then crashed a government car into the White House barrier (http://www.dailycaller.com/2015/12/03/cash-for-dem-hoes-check-and-more-disturbing-new-details-in-secret-service-scandals).

Director Mark Sullivan retired in March 2013, and Julia Pierson was named the service's first female director. But scandals continued. In May, a senior agent from the presidential detail created a disturbance while trying to get back into a woman's hotel room after leaving a bullet from his gun. An internal review found the agent and another agent from the presidential detail had sent inappropriate e-mails to a female coworker. One agent was fired and the other reassigned. In December 2013, while President Obama was attending the memorial service for Nelson Mandela in South Africa, the detail allowed a man with forged security credentials to stand a few feet away from the president pretending to be a sign-language interpreter. In March 2014, a member of the service's elite counter assault team was found passed out in an Amsterdam hotel lobby after a night of alleged partying. He and two other members of the presidential detail were recalled home and placed on administrative leave. A review panel found a "leadership vacuum" within the agency, with a lack of focus and the need for more training. The panel recommended hiring 85 new agents and 200 uniformed officers to prevent future breaches. In October 2014, Director Julia Pierson resigned, and Joseph Clancy, a former special agent from the president's security detail, was appointed interim director (http://www.cnn.com/2016/04/18/us/secret-service-fast-facts/index.html).

In December 2015, the HOGR issued a scathing report on the service. It found that the agency had failed to implement many of the reforms recommended by the panel in 2014. The committee declared that "the agency's recent public failures are not a series of isolated events, but the product of an insular culture that has historically been resistant to change" (http://www.cnn.com/2016/04/18/us/secret-service-fast-facts/index.html).

In February 2017, Secret Service director Joseph Clancy retired, and on April 25, 2017, President Donald Trump appointed Randolph "Tex" Alles, a retired Marine two-star general, as director of the Secret Service.

Proposed solutions to these problems have been included in a Judiciary Committee–passed reform bill for the Secret Service, which passed the House and was sent on to the Senate on July 13, 2016. The reform measure was a bipartisan bill sponsored by House Judiciary chair Bob Goodlatte (R-VA); Ranking Member John Conyers (D-MI); Crime, Terrorism, Homeland Security, and Investigations Subcommittee chair Jim Sensenbrenner (R-WI); and the subcommittee's ranking member Sheila Jackson-Lee (D-TX). It was titled the Secret Service Improvement Act of 2015 (H.R. 1656) (https://judiciaryhouse.gov/press-release/goodlatte-conyers-sensenbrenner-jackson-lee-unvail-secret-service-reform-legislation; http://www.thebill.com/blogs/floor-actions/house/249365-house-passes-secret-service-reform-bill/).

The key components of the Secret Service Improvement Act of 2015 are as follows:

1. Strengthens security by clarifying that it is a federal crime to knowingly cause, with the intent to impede or disrupt the orderly conduct of government business or official functions, any object to enter restricted buildings or grounds, including the White House and the Vice-President's residence.

2. Requires the Secret Service to evaluate the use of additional weaponry, including non-lethal weapons.

3. Amends current law to permit the Secret Service to investigate threats against former Vice-Presidents.

4. Requires the Secret Service to devise and implement procedures for evaluating threats to the White House and protected by the Service, including threats from drones and explosives, and to report its findings to Congress.

5. Requires the Secret Service to evaluate technology at the White House, including ways that technology can be used to improve safety at the White House.

6. Requires the Secret Service to evaluate how it retains evidence and to report its findings to Congress.

7. Enhances agents' training and increases manpower by directing the Service to increase the number of hours spent training, and directs them to provide joint training between Uniformed Division officers and Special Agents; and authorizes the hiring of no fewer than 200 additional Uniformed Division officers and 80 additional special agents.

8. Improves transparency and accountability by requiring the Director of the U.S. Secret Service to be confirmed by the Senate. The measure contains a Sense of Congress that determinations by the DHS or the Secret Service regarding changes to the White House itself for protection reasons should be given significant deference with the many entities that have a role in approving such changes, including the National Capital Planning Commission and the Commission of Fine Arts.

The Travel Ban Controversy

As discussed in Chapter 1, President Trump issued two executive orders imposing a travel ban that, given his campaign rhetoric and continued messages on Twitter, were widely viewed as "Muslim bans." In late January 2017, he issued the first ban, which stipulated a 90-day ban on immigration from seven Muslim-majority countries, Iran, Iraq, Libya, Somalia, Sudan, Syria, and Yemen; blocked entry of Syrian refugees into the United States; and temporarily suspended (for 90 days) entry to other refugees from those seven countries. It included language that favored religious minorities. President Trump tweeted the provision would apply to persecuted Christians from the Middle East. The executive order was immediately challenged in several federal courts. On January 31, acting attorney general Sally Yates refused to defend the order, determining that it was unconstitutional. President Trump summarily fired her (as a cabinet-level department head, she served "at the pleasure of the president"). In mid-February, a judge of the Ninth Circuit Court of Appeals in Seattle, Washington, ruled that the ban was unconstitutional and halted its enforcement (www.seattletimes.com/seattle-news/politics/federal-judge-in-seattle-halts-trumps-immigration-order/; www.npr.org/sections/thetwo-way/2017/03/15/520171478/trump-travel-ban-blocked-nationwide-by-federal-judge-in-hawaii).

On March 6, 2017, President Trump issued a second version of the travel ban. The March executive order barred immigrants, including refugees, from six Muslim countries (dropping Iraq from the list). It suspended all refugees for 120 days—a period designed to give the new administration time to review and develop a set of new "extreme vetting" procedures for immigrant applications from the barred countries. It cut the number of refugees that the United States would accept in 2017 by more than half, from 110,000 to 50,000. The second version of the travel ban dropped the language that favored religious minorities. On March 15, U.S. district judge Derrick Watson, of Hawaii, put an emergency hold on the second ban, and a district judge of Maryland, Theodore Chuang, issued a nationwide preliminary injunction of the travel ban. The Trump administration's DOJ (Department of Justice) appealed the decision to the U.S. Supreme Court. DOJ lawyers argued that the executive order falls squarely within the president's lawful authority in seeking to protect national security. The Supreme Court, on June 21, 2017, just before closing its session for the summer, partially upheld the second executive order travel ban and announced it would hold full oral arguments on the ban in the fall session, 2017 (https://www.jdsupra.com/legalnews/muslim-country-travel-ban-upheld-in-part-70428/). The Supreme Court's ruling, however, exempted from the ban persons with previously approved visas and persons with a bona fide connection, such as individuals who were "close family members," to a U.S. citizen or permanent resident immigrant. Its exemptions included green card holders, those with approved visas for H-1B workers, F-1 students, J-1 exchange visitors, K-1 fiancés, L-1 intracompany executive managers, specialized transferees, O-1 extraordinary ability persons, P-1 performers, R-1 religious workers, and E-2 investors. Curiously, the Supreme Court did not mention that putting off its holding of full oral arguments to the fall session would make the stated rationale for the ban moot (i.e., beyond the 120 days supposedly necessary to develop a new set of extreme vetting procedures).

The DOJ complicated matters when it issued guidelines as to what constituted "close family ties," which excluded grandparents and other extended-family relatives. On July 15, Judge Derrick Watson issued a ruling interpreting the Supreme Court's June 21 decision, stating that common sense dictated that grandparents were the epitome of close family members. Attorneys for Hawaii offered the case of Ismail Elshikh, the imam of a Honolulu mosque, to demonstrate the "harm" the travel ban imposed on Hawaii citizens as the ban applied to his mother-in-law. Along with Hawaii, courts in Maryland and the state of Washington heard challenges to the new revised travel ban. Attorney General Jeff Sessions immediately stated that the Justice Department would appeal Judge Watson's ruling to the Supreme Court (www.npr.org/sections/thetwo-way/2017//03/15/520171478; https://www.washingtonpost.com/world/national-security/

judge-rejects-hawaii-bid-to-exempt-grandparents-from-
trumps-travel-ban/2017/07/06/8e3a3252-625d-11e7-
8adc-fea80e32bf47_story.html?utm_term=.c3101d02e8e3;
https://www.wsj.com/articles/trump-appeals-latest-travel-ban-
ruling-1500072777?med=cx_picks&cx_navSource-cx_picks/).

A partial solution to these travel ban concerns came with the
Supreme Court decision which upheld the travel ban executive
order as constitutional. The Court stipulated some exemptions,
however, and federal district court actions continue to limit the
application of the travel ban provisions.

Business Needs versus Security Concerns in Visa Application Processing

> Since 9/11 America has been turning its back on
> openness. . . . The result was that while the administration
> talked about balancing security and openness, almost all
> of its resources and effort went into time-consuming
> background checks on foreigners, new controls at the
> borders, and aggressive enforcement against anyone
> caught committing even the most minor infraction of the
> labyrinthine immigration regulations. (Alden 2008: 5, 9)

Business mogul and Microsoft founder Bill Gates noted that
before the 9/11 attacks the United States was remarkably open
to immigration, and the visa application process, particularly
for immigrants coming from our Western allied nations and
for business purposes, was streamlined to attract "the best and
the brightest" from abroad to infuse the nation's economy. He
characterized America as an IQ magnet. The success of the
United States in attracting the greatest talent helped the country to become a global innovation leader, enriching the culture
and creating economic opportunity for all Americans (cited in
Alden 2008: 49). As Alden so pointedly notes: "In an effort to
keep out anyone who might again inflict such grievous harm,

the United States is building a system of border controls that could rob it of much of what has made it such an impressive and successful country" (Alden 2008: 20). Amy Chua, in her book *Day of Empire,* argues that "to pull away from its rivals on a global scale, a society must pull into itself and motivate the world's best and the brightest, regardless of ethnicity, religion, or background" (cited in Alden 2008: 21).

Prior to September 11, 2001, each year more than 10 million visa applications were processed by 843 consular officers in 230 visa-granting U.S. embassies and consulates around the world, averaging more than 1,000 visa interviews per day. After the 9/11 attacks, that pace became impossible. Applicants had to undergo a personal interview and security clearance, and interviews doubled. Fareed Zakarian, editor of *Newsweek International,* noted that "every visa officer today lives in fear that he will let in the next Mohammad Atta. As a result, he is probably keeping out the next Bill Gates" (cited in Wucker 2006: 155).

From 1993 to 2001, nonimmigrant visa applications (many for business-related travel) adjudicated by consular officers rose from 7 million per year to more than 10 million. U.S. State Department's consular affairs used a "visa express" program for Saudi Arabia. By 2006, the United States, the European Union, and the United Kingdom had negotiated problems with visa processing. It foiled a nascent plot by homegrown U.K. terrorists to detonate bombs on several transatlantic flights (Alden 2008: 238).

After the 9/11 attacks, the State Department and DHS often clashed over the visa application program. The economic cost of strict immigration enforcement is still being measured. By 2006, 1 million people were waiting for the department to process their applications for permanent residency, and this delay created many problems for U.S. business, particularly technology companies. By 2007, 53 of the State Department's consulates reported long waits for visas to come to the United States (Alden 2008: 278–282). A new visa application program, dubbed "Visa Condor," slowed visa approval by months, and visa denials rose sharply, affecting short-term business travel. Visa Mantis, a technology alert list, increased the volume of required security checks from 1,000 per year in 2000 to 20,000 in 2003. Business applications for temporary visas fell from over 6 million in FY 2000 to 2.7 million in FY 2003 (Wucker 2006: 156–157).

In the 1990s, one-third of Silicon Valley's scientific and engineering workforce was foreign-born immigrants, as were 40 percent of physical and life scientists in the U.S. educational and health services and 25 percent of physical scientists in manufacturing (Alden 2008: 50). That changed after the 9/11 attacks and the security hysteria that followed.

The rush to get biometric requirements into use in an unrealistically short time created unnecessary friction when caution took precedence over common sense. This was a blow to entrepreneurial spirit in the United States and cost millions of dollars in lost business conferences, science meetings, and sporting competitions (Wucker 2006: 177–178). The demand for high-skilled workers soon outpaced the supply in the United States, as many of those "best and brightest" went, instead, to Australia, Canada, Ireland, New Zealand, and the United Kingdom. A host of U.S. businesses reported having trouble finding workers with the skills that they needed. This trend resulted in another related problem—the stagnation of the flow of ideas (Bush and Bolick 2013: 71; Wucker 2006: 206–209).

America's problem is not immigration itself, but how immigration occurs—that is, whether people come desperately across the border or give up in disgust at the failure of our bureaucracy and laws, or whether they can reasonably expect that the United States will make it feasible for the workers we need to comply with its immigration laws and to welcome them into our society as they work hard to participate in the civic life of their adopted communities. (Wucker 2006: 231)

Business-related immigration, spurred by an entrepreneurial spirit, has a major impact on business start-ups, creating jobs for native-born citizens. Between 1996 and 2011, start-ups by the native born *decreased* by 53 percent, but those by foreign born *increased* by 50 percent (Bush and Bolick 2013: 83). Business-related immigration is especially linked to high-tech industries located in what Enrico Moretti describes as the "brain hubs" phenomenon (Moretti 2012). And every high-tech job in a metropolitan area produces five service jobs in the local economy, compared to 1.6 jobs created by every job in the traditional manufacturing sector (Bush and Bolick 2013: 91–92).

Solutions to the business-related immigration problem and controversy are essentially policies that redress the balance between the need for security and the needs of business and the U.S. economy. A number of solutions have been suggested in the literature:

1. Create a National Border Administration to be comprised of the Coast Guard, Customs and Border Protection, Immigration and Citizenship Enforcement from the DHS, and the inspection arm of the Department of Agriculture (Alden 2008: 141; Bush and Bolick 2013: 15; Wucker 2006: 227).

2. Recognize that creating a "zero-defects visa system," currently a goal of the philosophy of the Department of State's visa and consular affairs bureaucracy, is unrealistic. The United States lacks the technology to do it. The sheer size of the applicant pool makes it unlikely if not impossible. There are inadequate resources to achieve it (Alden 2008: 218–219).

3. Expand the guest-worker program linked to market demand (Bush and Bolick 2013: 27–28; Wucker 2006: 225).

4. Recognize that the risk of terrorism can only be managed, not eliminated. Sometimes the consequences to eliminate

all risks are worse than learning how to live with them (Alden 2008: 291).

5. Establish a Western Hemisphere Travel Initiative (Alden 2008: 279). The United States has to get serious about once again encouraging good people to come to the United States (Alden 2008: 292).

6. Reverse the "brain drain" (Bush and Bolick 2013: 88–102).

7. Instead of focusing on what we are not, articulate what brings us together: a shared sense of faith and can-do optimism (Wucker 2006: 222).

8. Dream big again, stop blaming others for our problems, and instead rely on our strengths (Wucker 2006: 223).

9. Eliminate congressional micromanagement. Allow immigration agencies to revise regulations on their own rather than legislating such changes (Wucker 2006: 226).

10. Reduce family reunification preference visas, such as adult sibling allotment, and increase preference numbers allotted to business-related immigration tied to the changing needs of the U.S. economy/job market. Family reunification preferences now account for 63 percent of legal immigration (Wucker 2006: 227).

11. Enact major, comprehensive immigration reform that works for our country instead of acting as a drag on the economy (Wucker 2006: 232).

12. Encourage "brain circulation" and the creation of industries that will provide jobs in immigrant-sending countries and create markets for U.S.-produced goods (Wucker 2006: 237).

13. Business needs to legally bring in the workers they need, but policy needs to establish and enforce significant financial penalties on those employers who circumvent immigration and labor laws (Wucker 2006: 232–234).

14. "Staple green-cards to the back of every diploma our universities issue to a foreign-born student" (Wucker 2006: 237).

The Economic Impact of Tightening Visitors' Visas

Visas are legal documents issued by a consular or similar state department official allowing a person to travel to the United States for either permanent or temporary reasons, such as immigrant, student, tourist, government representative, business, or cultural exchange (LeMay 2015: 364). The fact that all of the terrorists involved in the 9/11 attacks had gotten non-immigrant visas and entered the United States legally (i.e., as documented nonimmigrants) led to calls to reform and revise the visa system. Ambassador Mary Ryan, the Department of State's (DOS) assistant secretary of state for consular affairs, which oversaw and implemented the visa application process, became a scapegoat for the failure to prevent the attacks (Alden 2008: 151–160).

A nonimmigrant who qualifies for the nonimmigrant status and visa seeks temporary entry into the United States for a specific purpose, which includes the following: foreign government officials, visitors for business, visitors for pleasure (tourist), immigrants in transit through the United States, treaty traders and investors, students, international representatives, temporary workers and trainees, representatives of foreign information media, exchange visitors, fiancé(e)s of U.S. citizens, intracompany transferees, NATO officials, and religious workers. Most nonimmigrants can be accompanied or joined by spouses and unmarried minor (or dependent) children (www.uscis.gov/tools/glossary/nonimmigrant).

Immigrant visas are issued to persons seeking permanent resident immigrant status, which may be subject to numerical limitations or not. Visas subject to numerical limitations are granted to persons qualifying for family-sponsored, employment-related, or diversity immigrant visas. Four categories of family-sponsored visa preferences include (1) unmarried sons and daughters and their children of citizens, (2) spouses and unmarried sons and daughters of legal permanent residents; (3) married sons and daughters of U.S.

citizens and their spouses and children; and (4) brothers and sisters of U.S. citizens aged 21 and over. There are five categories of employment-sponsored preferences: priority workers, professionals with advanced degrees or immigrants of exceptional ability; skilled workers; professionals (without advanced degrees), and needed unskilled workers; special immigrants (ministers, religious workers, employees of the U.S. government abroad); and employment creation immigrants or "investors" (http://immigration.findlaw.com/visas/immigrant-and-non-immigrant-visa-types).

These visas may be issued to persons living abroad from a consular office of the DOS and with the visa may enter the United States and become legal immigrants when they pass through the port of entry (airport or seaport). The other path is for immigrants already living in the country, including certain undocumented immigrants, temporary workers, foreign students, and refugees who file an application for adjustment of status—to legal permanent residence—with the Bureau of Citizenship and Immigration Service (USCIS). They can also, at that time, file for work permits. New legal immigrants are automatically granted work permits (immigrant registration cards/green cards) after becoming legal permanent residents (http://immigration.findlaw.com/visas/immigrant-and-non-immigrant-visa-types).

Problems and concerns developed with visa application and processing as a result of the 9/11 attacks and resulting legislation such as Patriot Acts I and II, the creation of DHS, the Border Protection, Anti-Terrorism, and Illegal Immigration Act of 2005 (also known as the REAL ID Act) (LeMay 2015: 348–349). A number of programs with visa-complicating features were used to implement these laws, three of which are highlighted here: NSEERS (National Security Entry-Exit Registration System), US-VISIT, and the Office of Biometric Identity Management—all of which resulted in some visa application and processing backlogs, especially for nonimmigrant visas, that had a negative impact on the U.S. economy.

The NSEERS was a port of entry registration and departure registration requirement. It was the first of these visa control programs established after the 9/11 attacks (Alden 2008: 222–223; Wucker 2006: 144). It was applied to certain nonimmigrant visitors from Iran, Iraq, Sudan, Syria, Pakistan, Saudi Arabia, and Yemen. It also required registration for nonimmigrants coming from any country if they are determined to meet criteria that were established by the secretary of the DHS if those individuals are referred to the DHS by State Department consular officers, or if the inspecting officer (at the port of entry) believes the immigrant should be registered in the interest of law enforcement or national security. NSEERS-registered immigrants were also required to register their departure at a designated port (http://www.immigration.com/visa/general-nonimmigrant-visa/national-security-entry-exit-registration-system). It was applied to temporary foreign visitors (nonimmigrants) from 25 countries listed by the attorney general as supporters and exporters of international terrorism and others who met a combination of intelligence-based criteria that identified them as potential security risks. By January 2005, individuals from 160 countries were registered on NSEERS (Alden 2008: 294; LeMay 2015: 27–28; Wucker 2006: 155–156).

US-VISIT essentially replaced NSEERS and applied the procedures, including collection of some biometric data such as fingerprinting, more generally to all nonimmigrants regardless of country of origin, beginning at the end of September 2004, when it expanded entry-exit procedures to include all visitors traveling to the United States under the Visa Waiver Program who arrive at airports and seaports (Alden 2008: 248–254, 294; https://epic.org/privacy/surveillance/spotlight/0705/editorial.html; Wucker 2006: 177).

US-VISIT was established in compliance with several laws requiring that the DHS create an integrated, automated entry-exit system that records the arrival and departure of immigrants (to get at the problem of visa overstayers), deploys equipment (e.g., 10-point fingerprint readers) at all ports of entry to verify identities and authenticate their travel documents through comparison with biometric identifiers, and utilizes an entry-exit system that records immigrant arrival and departure information from those biometrically authenticated documents. It is based on four acts of Congress: (1) the Illegal Immigration and Reform Act of 1996, (2) the Immigration and Naturalization Service Data Management Improvement Act of 2000, (3) the USA PATRIOT Act of 2001, and (4) the Enhanced Border Security and Visa Entry Reform Act of 2001 (https://epic.org/privacy/surveillance/spotlight/0705/editorial.html).

In March 2013, the DHS established the Office of Biometric Identity Management (OBIM) within its National Protection and Programs Directorate. OBIM supports the DHS's responsibility to protect the United States by providing biometric identification that helps federal, state, and local governments to accurately identify persons they encounter to determine whether or not such persons pose a risk to the United States. OBIM operates and maintains IDENT—a system to match, store, analyze, and share biometric data. It is used by USCIS, U.S. Coast Guard, USCBP, ICE, TSA, and the intelligence community, DOJ, DOS, DOD, state and local law enforcement, and international partners (https://www.federalregister.gov/documents/full_text/xml/2016/12/15/2016-30187.xml).

While developments with each of these programs and procedures between 2002 and 2013 have improved the biometric data used and the technology to catch, store, match, and analyze that data, as they were introduced and implemented, the programs each caused delays and backlogs in visa processing for both those seeking permanent residency status (legal immigrants) and, especially, nonimmigrants (temporary visas of various types). Those delays and an increased number of disapprovals resulted in millions of dollars lost to the U.S. economy. Wait times to get interviews for visa applications can take months for those coming from some countries, and security background checks for green cards and citizenship applications are measured in years rather than months (Alden 2008: 11–14; Bush and Bolick 2013: 91–101; Wucker 2006: 177–178).

There are no easy solutions to the problems and costs to the U.S. economy that are associated with the tightening of the visa process for homeland security purposes. The sheer volume of visa applications for permanent immigration and especially for nonimmigrant visas inevitably leads to increased backlogs resulting from increased concerns for security. The problem is being eased as biometric technology is improved and implemented. Three additional "solutions" that have been proposed are highlighted here: the Smart Border Partnership Action Plan, the Start Up Visa Act, and a guest-worker program geared to market demand wherein the guest workers would be prescreened in their country of origin.

The Smart Border Partnership Action Plan has been in negotiation with Mexico and Canada since 2002 and has entailed 22 to 30 points in an agreement between the country sending immigrants (Mexico or Canada) and the United States (Alden 2008: 132; https://2001-2009.state.gov/p/wha/ris/fs/18128 .htm). A number of points pertain to increased infrastructure security: (1) developing long-term planning to secure coordinated physical and technological infrastructure with growing cross-border traffic; (2) relief for bottlenecks; (3) infrastructure protection—conducting vulnerability assessment of transborder communication and transportation networks in need of protective measures; (4) harmonize port-of-entry traffic flow on both sides of the border; (5) demonstration proposals—establish "prototype" smart port-of-entry operations; (6) increased cross-border cooperation and mechanisms among local, state, and federal levels with a focus on operations at border-crossing points; and (7) financing projects at the border by exploring joint financing mechanisms to meet development and infrastructure needs.

Several points pertain to the secure flow of people: (1) preclearing travelers by expanding the Secure Electronic Network for Rapid Inspection (SENTRI) of dedicated commuter lanes at high-volume ports between borders; (2) establishing joint advanced passenger information on relevant flights; (3) NAFTA travel—exploring methods to facilitate the movement of NAFTA travelers, including dedicated lanes at high-volume airports; (4) safe borders and deterrence of immigrant smuggling—reaffirm mutual commitment to the Border Safety Initiative and develop cooperation to enhance authorities and specialized institutions to assist, save, and advise migrants as well as those specialized on curbing the smuggling of people by expanding the Alien Smuggling and Trafficking Taskforce; (5) visa policy consultations—increasing frequency of consultations on visa policies and visa screening procedures and share information from relevant consular databases; (6) joint training in the areas of investigation and document analysis to enhance ability to detect fraudulent documents and break up smuggling rings; (7) develop a system of compatible databases to share intelligence; and (8) enhancing efforts to detect, screen, and take appropriate measures to deal with potential dangerous third-country nationals and taking into consideration the threats they represent to security (https://openknowledge.worldbank.org/handle/10986/11140License: CCBy3.01GO18128; see also Alden 2008: 132).

The Start Up Visa Act of 2011 (S.565, 112th Congress) was a bill to establish an employment-based visa for immigrant entrepreneurs who have received significant capital from investors to establish a business in the United States. Then senator John Kerry (D-MA) sponsored the bill. Among its provisions, it has an amendment that directs the DHS to terminate the status of sponsored entrepreneurs (and their spouses, and children, if any) if, after three years, they fail to meet investment requirements or fail to meet job creation, capital investment, or revenue requirements (https://www.govtrack.us/congress/bills/112/s565; see also Bush and Bolick 2013: 27).

Finally, a guest-worker program that is geared to market demand and that would have the guest workers prescreened in the country of origin has been proposed (Bush and Bolick 2013: 27; Wucker 2006: 224–234).

Federalism's Impact—Relations with State and Local Governments

Homeland security policy making and implementation is complicated by the fact that the United States has a federal system of government. Homeland security policy making, like that of almost all areas of policy, illustrates the problems and concerns that emerge from the devolution of security policy implementation. Devolution is the transfer or delegation of powers to a lower level, for example, by a central government to local or regional administration (http://en.oxforddictionaries.com; see also Udani 2013: 151–172). The devolution of policy to state and local governments impacts the inclusion of immigrants and immigrant groups. Inclusion has been defined as an individual's or group's engagement with the processes or organizations that recognize the individual or group by conferring membership or by providing resources such as entitlements or protections. It provides a sense of security, stability, and predictability, understood primarily as an ability to plan for the future (Cook 2013).

With respect to homeland security policy, a considerable degree of devolution has taken place since the establishment of the DHS: 49 states have established state departments or offices of homeland security, as well as 4 territories and 6 tribal areas (https://www.hsdl.org/?collection&id=1176).

This section focuses on two concerns that illuminate the relationship between the national government (and particularly the DHS) and state and local governments: the Secure Communities program on the one hand and the sanctuary movement on the other hand (http://www.ojjpac.org/sanctuary.asp/; https://cis.org/map-sanctuary-cities-counties-and-states; http://www.apsanlaw.com/law-246.List-of-Sanctuary-cities.html; https://www.ice.gov/secure-communities/; https://www.whitehouse.gov/presidential-actions/executive-order-protecting-nation-foreign-terrorist-entry-united-states-2/).

State and local governments have varied considerably in their willingness to cooperate with federal law enforcement since some policing powers were devolved in 1996, with enactment of the Illegal Immigration Reform and Immigrant Responsibility Act signed into law by President Clinton on September 30 (http://www.visalaw.com/iirira-96-a-summary-of-the-new-immigration-bill/). Based on a provision in the 1996 law, the Secure Communities program was launched in 2008. It identified unauthorized immigrants for removal by checking the fingerprints of persons arrested or booked in custody by local authorities (Suro 2015: 117). Secure Communities (2008–2014; reactivated January 25, 2017) was a program to assist ICE's enforcement priorities for those immigrants detained in the custody of another law enforcement agency. It employs an information-sharing partnership between the DHS and the FBI that helps identify in-custody immigrants without imposing new or additional requirements on state and local enforcement. Under Secure Communities the FBI automatically sends the fingerprints to the DHS to be checked against its immigration database. If the checks reveal that an individual is unlawfully present or is otherwise removable, ICE takes enforcement action. It prioritizes the removal of individuals who are deemed the most significant threats to public safety, determined by the severity of their crime, their criminal history, and risk to public safety, and those who have violated immigration laws (http://www.ice.gov/secure-communities).

ICE completed full implementation of the Secure Communities program to all jurisdictions within the 50 states, the District of Columbia, and the 5 U.S. territories by January 2013. The program was suspended by the DHS through an executive order in November 2014, stating that the DHS should focus on deporting "felons, not families" (Suro 2015: 118). Secretary Jeh Johnson promulgated new priorities by memorandum to the acting director of the ICE, the director of the CRCL within the DHS, and the assistant secretary for intergovernmental affairs (http://www.ice.gov/secure-communities). Quite a number of state and local governments had already taken actions to neutralize federal regulations under the Secure Communities program. For example, in October 2014, the Catholic Legal Immigration Network had noted that 3 states, 26 cities (sanctuary cities), 233 counties, and the District of Columbia had restricted their cooperation (CLINIC 2014; Suro 2015: 118).

The suspension of Secure Communities under the Obama administration lasted until January 15, 2017, when President Trump, by Executive Order 13768, Enhancing Public Safety in the Interior of the United States, directed the secretary of Homeland Security, John Kelly, to renew the program. The DHS rescinded all of the Obama executive order procedures, and within six months the DHS had removed more than 10,000 convicted criminal immigrants under the newly reinstated Secure Communities program. Under all its years of operation (2008–2017), Secure Communities led to the removal of more than 315,000 criminal immigrants (http://www.ice.gov/secure-communities).

Sanctuary city is a name given to a city in the United States that follows certain procedures that shelter illegal immigrants. These procedures can be by law (de jure) or by action (de facto). The designation of sanctuary city has no legal meaning. The term is commonly used for cities that do not permit municipal funds or resources (e.g., police officers) to be applied in furtherance of enforcement of federal immigration laws. They do not allow police or municipal employees to inquire about one's immigration status (http://www.apsanlaw.com/law-246. List-of-Sanctuary-cities.html; http://www.ojjpac.org/sanctuary.asp).

Sanctuary cities are part of a broader sanctuary movement that goes back to the 1980s when churches sheltered unauthorized immigrants from Central America (El Salvador, Honduras, and Guatemala) who were seeking asylum in the United States (Couton 1993; Lippert 2005). The concept of sanctuary cities is deeply embedded in Western tradition, going back to biblical times. The 1980s' sanctuary movement put church and state in conflict over the fate of Central Americans fleeing civil wars and pleading for asylum in the United States. The Reagan administration, like the Trump administration, was reluctant to grant asylum to Central Americans (and today especially Mexicans), claiming they were economic refugees, not political refugees with legitimate "fear of persecution" in their homelands. Few were granted asylum. For example, in 1984, less than 3 percent of Central Americans were given asylum, as opposed to Poles fleeing communism, who were 10 times more likely to find asylum in the United States. Iranians fleeing the Ayatollah regime were 20 times more likely to be granted asylum. An estimated 2,000 refuge seekers were aided by churches in the sanctuary movement of the 1980s (https://www.nytimes.com/2017/07/26/us/politics/sessions-sanctuary-cities.html).

The movement has revived and spread since the inauguration of President Donald Trump and his appointment of Attorney General Jeff Sessions. Attorney General Sessions has led the department's campaign against sanctuary cities by threatening to cut off federal funding. Attorney General Sessions announced on July 26, 2017, that cities and states could lose millions of dollars in federal grants unless they began cooperating with immigration agents (https://www.nytimes.com/2017/07/26/us/politics/sessions-sanctuary-cities.html).

The threatened cities have fought back in U.S. courts. Judge William Orrick of the U.S. District Court in San Francisco temporarily blocked the Trump administration from withholding funding over sanctuary policies. The city attorney for San Francisco sued the Trump administration, arguing that the policy of withholding funding violated the Constitution. Attorney General Sessions ruled that to receive grants for local law enforcement, local governments had to agree to allow federal immigration agents access to their jails and to provide 48 hours' notice before releasing immigrants whom federal authorities wanted to be detained for immigration violations. Depending on how one defines a sanctuary city, there are hundreds of cities, counties, and states which are at least informally associated with the sanctuary movement (http://www.apsanlaw.com/law-246.List-of-Sanctuary-cities.html).

Local officials counter the attorney general's announced policy, arguing that separating local law enforcement from federal immigration authorities is good policy both from a legal standpoint and from a public safety standpoint. That separation of local law enforcement departments from federal agencies like the DOJ and DHS means that immigrants are more likely to come forward to report crimes and to serve as witnesses. New York's commissioner of immigration affairs holds that the concept of withholding federal funding that promotes public safety is counterproductive (https://www.nytimes.com/2017/07/26/us/politics/sessions-sanctuary-cities.html).

The solution to these problems may likewise be twofold. On the one hand, the federal government could induce more participation in the revived Secure Communities program by offering greater financial support and by offering more training to local governments that agree to participate. On the other hand, federal courts may resolve the sanctuary city issue by ruling at the appellate level, or even at the Supreme Court level—less likely, however, given its current make-up—on the constitutionality of the DOJ's policy to withhold funding to sanctuary cities. At the very least, the federal courts may clarify the legal definition of a sanctuary city.

The Brain-Drain Problem

"Brain drain" refers to a significant emigration of talented individuals from lesser-developed to developed countries. Emigration may be "pushed" by turmoil within a country or may be "pulled" by better professional opportunities in other countries drawing those seeking a better standard of living (http://www.investopedia.com/terms/b/brain_drain.asp).

Brain drain causes countries, industries, and organizations to lose valuable professionals: doctors, scientists, engineers, computer scientists, financial professionals. Such emigration affects the nation of origin in two ways: expertise is lost, diminishing the supply of professionals, and the country's economy is harmed as each professional represents surplus spending units. They earn larger salaries, so their departure removes significant consumer spending from the country of origin. According to a World Bank study, in the past decade, the largest numbers of highly educated migrants are from Europe, Southern and Eastern Asia, and Central America. In terms of a proportion of the potential educated labor force, the highest brain-drain rates are in the Caribbean, Central America, and Western and Eastern Africa (documents.worldbank.org/curated/en/4268888146812).

The United States has a long tradition of benefiting from the brain-drain phenomenon. Foreign students studying in the United States grew from 50,000 in 1980 to 600,000 by the year 2000, when nearly 40 percent of the doctorates in science and engineering and 30 percent of master's degree students were foreign born. In mathematics, computer science, and physical and life sciences, 60 percent of postdoctoral students doing research were foreign born. One-third of American Nobel Prize winners were foreign born, and between 1990 and 2001, 50 percent of the Nobel Prize winners in the United States were foreign born (Alden 2008: 50, 188–189).

The nation's openness to immigrants, and the benefits received from the brain-drain flow, changed after the 9/11 attacks and the enactment of the USA PATRIOT Act. The DHS initiated the Student and Exchange Visitor Information System (SEVIS). SEVIS had been approved in 1996 but not implemented until after the attacks (for a summary of the 1996 law, see LeMay and Barkan 1999: 304–310). SEVIS required regular reporting by educational institutions on the enrollment status of their international students (Alden 2008: 200–202; LeMay 2013: 84; Middelstadt et al. 2011). The electronic monitoring system was rushed to implementation, and bugs in the system led to backlogs and protracted delays in correcting the data for months at a time. SEVIS produced 1,000 alerts each week, and between 2003 and 2005, 81,000 students were tagged as potential violators of the SEVIS program (Wucker 2006: 160–161). The

Institute of International Education reported foreign student enrollment in the United States declined by 46 percent from 2002 to 2003 and increased by 23 percent in the United Kingdom, by 15 percent in Canada, and by 10 percent in Australia. By 2004, Chinese students attending U.S. graduate schools dropped by 45 percent; those coming from the Middle East dropped by 50 percent. America's loss was other countries' gain: Australia, Canada, Ireland, New Zealand, and the United Kingdom all gained students (Alden 2008: 212–213). A National Science Foundation study noted that foreign doctoral students from China, India, and Taiwan dropped dramatically (Wucker 2006: 161–164). The United States is experiencing much greater competition for the highly talented immigrants from Canada, China, the European Union, Japan, and South Korea. As of 2017 Europe and Asia now produce more science and engineering PhDs than does the United States (www.weforum. org/agenda/2017/02/countries-with-most-doctoral-graduates/ STEM/.) By 2020, the United Kingdom is expected to triple its international student enrollment. India, Singapore, and Hong Kong are now "knowledge centers" in information technology (IT). In 1975, the United States held 75 percent of all global science and engineering degrees. By 2010, that fell to 15 percent (Wucker 2006: 189–191).

Visa Mantis, a technology alert list, increased dramatically the volume of required security checks from a 1,000 per year in 2000 to 20,000 such checks in 2003 (Wucker 2006: 156). The United States now must seriously compete with other countries for highly talented immigrants and the needed skills they bring (Bush and Bolick 2013: 71; Wucker 2006: 195). For the first time in its modern history, the United States began to experience a negative brain-drain flow.

The negative brain-drain flow accelerated after the election of President Trump, whose nationalist-populist animosity toward immigration created unintended consequences. Tech workers who would have otherwise sought opportunities in

Silicon Valley are starting to seek such opportunities in Mexico, China, and other countries overseas. President Trump signed an executive order for a government review of H-1B visas for foreign workers, which is making it harder for U.S. companies to get tech talent. Even workers already in the United States are being wooed by countries, such as Canada, hoping to capitalize on the H-1B mess in the United States. Canada launched a new visa program called Global Skills Strategy, which makes it easier to recruit highly skilled foreign workers. Where in the United States approval waits are for months, in Canada, they are in just two weeks. Canada launched another tech recruitment program, Go North, in 2016. It is aimed at Canadian expats who had settled in Seattle and San Francisco's Bay Area. Canada has 71,000 tech companies that comprise 5.6 percent of its total employment. President Trump complained that three-quarters of engineers in Silicon Valley aren't Americans. Canada and China have jumped to attract them. After President Trump announced withdrawal of the United States from the Paris climate accord in June 2017, French president Emmanuel Macron called on U.S. climate scientists, engineers, and other innovates to seek refuge in France, and Macron launched a website "Make Our Planet Great Again," encouraging them to emigrate. Indian IT companies plan to double their operations in Mexico as the United States makes it more difficult for Indians to get H-1B visas (https://www.vanityfair.com/news/2017/07/silicon-valleys-trump-brain-drain-continues).

Solutions to this growing negative brain drain from the U.S. economy have been proposed. The Start Up Visa Act cited earlier is one such response. Another action would be making student visas plentiful and readily accessible again, as would a guest-worker program for highly skilled workers geared to market demand. In STEM fields (science, technology, engineering, and mathematics), foreign students should be entitled to work visas for jobs in those fields (Bush and Bolick 2013: 26–28).

Another suggested solution is to develop and enact a carefully designed guest-worker program that balanced promoting integration into the U.S. economy and society with a degree of brain circulation of those skilled workers back to their homelands, providing jobs in migrant-sending countries, and increasing markets for U.S.-produced goods. Michele Wucker suggests that the United States "staple green cards to the back of every diploma our universities issue to a foreign-born student" (2006: 237).

The Impact of Immigration on Social Security

There has been ongoing controversy as to the costs versus the benefits of immigration, particularly illegal immigration and especially as one projects those costs versus benefits into the future. What the analyst finds depends very much on the assumptions used in the study or for the projections. There is less such controversy, however, in measuring the impact on immigration on Social Security. Analysis by the Social Security Administration, the Labor Department, the Congressional Budget Office, the Center on Budget and Policy Priorities, and the Rand Corporation has found the impact of both legal and illegal immigration on the Social Security system and its Trust Fund to be positive in its net impact, even projecting the effect out to 75 years (https://economix.blogs.nytimes.com/2013/07/02/immigration-and-social-security/; https://www.cbpp.org/research/immigration-and-social-security/; https://www.thedailybeast.com/how-immigrants-will-save-social-security/; see also National Research Council 1997).

Opponents of immigration reform argue pervasively that illegal immigrants don't contribute their fair share in taxes and drain government benefits. Government economists with the Congressional Budget Office and Social Security actuaries, as well as think tank analysis, like the Center on Budget and Policy Priorities, however, find that undocumented workers are helping to keep the Social Security Trust Fund in the black because they are paying into the system, typically with false Social Security numbers, which means they will never collect benefits. Their contributions, collected over many years, help keep the system solvent and benefits flowing for aging baby boomers (https:// www.cbpp.org/research/immigration-and-social-security; www.thedailybeast.com/how-immigrants-will-save-social-security). When the U.S. Senate passed a comprehensive immigration bill in 2013, the Social Security Administration studied the likely effect of its legalization program and concluded that if passed and implemented, it would have added $276 billion in revenue over 10 years, while adding only $33 billion in costs. Its chief actuary projected that even 75 years out, there would be a net gain from immigrants because their withdrawals will be offset by their children's contributions. High-skilled workers pay in to the system more than they get out, and in recent years, high-skilled workers have comprised a larger percentage of immigrants. Economists specializing in labor market economics agree that more immigration is better in terms of its effect on Social Security. In projecting immigrant impact into the future, two pools must be considered: those who are already here as unauthorized immigrants, about a third of whom pay Social Security taxes, and the additional legal immigrants who will come. The Center for American Progress, a supporter of immigration reform, estimates that if 70 percent of illegal immigrants are legalized, they will contribute $500 billion on net in 36 years, the period that baby boomers will put a strain on the Social Security system (https://economix.blogs.nytimes. com/2013/07/02/immigration-and-social-security/).

Labor Department economists who studied the effect of comprehensive immigration reform projected that the benefits are even greater when looked at on a longer horizon. The Social Security Administration estimated that in 2010 illegal immigrants paid a net contribution of $12 billion. If such immigrants gained legal status, they would contribute on balance even more, according to the director of the National Immigration Law Center. In general, researchers conclude that increases in immigration will improve the financial status of Social Security and that decreases in immigration will worsen it (https://www.cbpp.org/research/immigration-and-social-security).

To the extent that these economists' estimates are accurate, the current crackdown on immigration, both legal and unauthorized, as advocated by the Trump administration for reasons of homeland security concerns, will have an adverse effect on the Social Security Trust Fund. That adverse impact on the U.S. economy and on the Social Security system will be greater if, as happened over the past decade, a greater number of high-skilled workers who are already here opt to leave or if such immigrants not yet here decide to immigrate elsewhere, as noted in the brain-drain section.

Another aspect of the impact of immigration on the system that must be noted is the fact that immigrants have a higher percentage of participation in the labor market than do native-born citizens. This reflects the demographic aspects of the immigrant population. They come during their prime working ages. They tend to have more children than do the native born. Increased birth rates and higher labor market participation have a net positive effect on the financial status of Social Security resulting from an increase in payroll tax collections and more years of contributing to the fund before withdrawing benefits (https://www.cbpp/research/immigration-and-social-security).

The obvious solution to the problem or concern with the negative impact on the Social Security system because of decreased immigration associated with the security aspects of the crackdown approach to border control is to enact comprehensive immigration reform. Although an obvious solution, as discussed earlier, it is not a politically likely solution, particularly given the policy priorities of the Trump administration on both immigration and homeland security matters.

Conclusion

The problems, controversies, and possible solutions discussed here may enable planning for better homeland security policy making and implementation in the future. Groupthink aspects in the rush to establish the DHS under a decidedly crisis atmosphere led to a number of unanticipated consequences. The very behemoth size of the DHS entailed management problems that plagued the new department for more than a decade. The mission complexity associated with merging 22 agencies continues to make effective and efficient implementation of homeland security policy a difficult-to-achieve goal. Cyber offense has to date outstripped the nation's cyber defense capabilities. There is ongoing tension between the perceived needs for security with traditional values of civil liberties and privacy rights. Comprehensive immigration reform presents a policy conundrum that exacerbates problems with a broken immigration system. Climate change trends portend increasingly frequent and severe weather-related natural disasters that strain the financial and administrative capacity of FEMA and the DHS to cope with them. The Secret Service has been rocked by scandals and poses an ongoing management problem that may be beyond the capability of the DHS to resolve.

The travel ban controversy of the Trump administration embroils the government in ongoing conflict between the administration and the federal court system. Analysts suggest, moreover, that the ban will not really do anything to increase homeland security. Security concerns have resulted in visa processing that has negatively affected business needs and adversely impacted the nation's economy, as has the tightening of visitors' visa. The United States is a federal system of government. That structural arrangement intentionally limits the power of government, especially of the federal government. It complicates the relationship between the national government and its bureaucracies with those of the state and local levels of government, as illustrated by the Secure Communities program and by the conflicts and controversies associated with the sanctuary movement. Until the 9/11 attacks, the United States greatly benefited from a brain-drain flow. That flow has shifted markedly since 2001. Homeland security policy concerns and how the national government administers policy to ensure greater security have contributed to a growing competition from other advanced-nation economies for the highly talented migrants. Finally, the chapter examined the impact of immigration on the Social Security system and how homeland security concerns have led to a change in the immigration flow that portends a long-term negative impact on the financial stability of the Social Security system.

References

Alden, Edward. 2008. *The Closing of the American Border.* New York: HarperCollins.

Browning, Rufus P., Dale Rogers Marshall, and David H. Tabb. 1984. *Protest Is Not Enough.* Berkeley: University of California Press.

Bush, Jeb, and Clint Bolick. 2013. *Immigration Wars: Forging an American Solution.* New York: Simon and Schuster.

Clarke, Richard, and Robert K. Knake. 2010. *Cyber War: The Next Threat to National Security and What to Do About It.* New York: Ecco/HarperCollins.

CLINIC. 2014. "State and Localities That Limit Compliance with ICE Detainee Requests," *State and Local Immigration Project.* Washington, DC: Catholic Legal Immigration Network, Inc.

Cook, Maria Lorena. 2013. "Incorporation of Unauthorized Immigrants Possible? Inclusion and Contingency for Nonstatus Migrants and Legal Immigrants," in Jennifer Hochschild, Jacqueline Chattopadhyay, Claudine Gay, and Michael Jones-Correa, eds. *Outsiders No More? Models of Immigrant Political Incorporation.* Oxford: Oxford University Press. http://dx.doi.org/10.1093/acprof:oso/9780199211113.003.0003.

Cordesman Anthony H. 2000. "Homeland Defense: Asymmetric, Indirect, Covert, Terrorist and Extremist Attacks with Weapons of Mass Destruction: Defending America: Redefining the Conceptual Borders of Homeland Defense Project." http://www.csis.org/homeland/analysis/islam-and-patterns-in-terrorism-and-violent-extremism.pdf. Accessed July 18, 2017.

Couton, Susan Bibler. 1993. *The Culture of Protest: Religious Activism and the U.S. Sanctuary Movement.* Boulder, CO: Westview Press.

Econ.worldbank.org/WEBSITE/EXTERNAL/EXTDEC/EXT. Accessed 7/29/2017.

https://openknowledge.worldbank.org/handle/10986/1140 License:CCBy3.oIGO

Etzioni, Amitai, and Jason H. Marsh, eds. 2003. *Rights vs. Public Safety after 9/11: America in the Age of Terrorism.* Lanham, MD: Rowman and Littlefield.

General Accounting Office. 2002. *Alien Smuggling: Management and Operational Improvements Needed to Address Growing Problem.* Washington, DC: U.S. Government Printing Office.

Haynes, Wendy. 2004. "Seeing around Corners: Crafting the New Department of Homeland Security," *The Review of Policy Research,* May, 21 (3): 369–396.

http://en.oxforddictionaries.com. Accessed July 28, 2017.

http://immigration.findlaw.com/visas/immigrant-and-non-immigrant-visa-types. Accessed July 27, 2017.

http://unfccc.int/paris_agreement/items/9485.php. Accessed 7/24/2017.

http://weather.gov/mhx/August272011EventReview/. Accessed July 24, 2017.

http://www.apsanlaw.com/law-246.List-of-Sanctuary-cities.html. Accessed July 28, 2017.

http://www.cnn.com/2012/04/19/us/secret-service/index.
html/. Accessed July 25, 2017.

http:// www.cnn.com/2016/04/18/us/secret-service-fast-facts/
index.html/. Accessed July 25, 2017.

http://www.decision-making-solutions.com/group-decision-
making-problems-group-think-theory. Accessed July 17,
2017.

http://www.hurricanescience.org/history/storms/2000s/rita/.
Accessed 7/24/2017.

http://www.immigration.com/visa/general-nonimmigrant-
visa/national-security-entry-exit-registration-system.
Accessed July 27, 2017.

http://www.investopedia.com/terms/b/brain_drain.asp.
Accessed July 29, 2017.

http://www.nipp.org/wp-content/uploads/2014/11/
Asymmetry-final-02.pdf. Accessed February 18, 2017.

http://www.nydailynews.com/news/national/fed-probing-
secret-service-prostitution-claims-resigns-report-
article-1.1991034. Accessed July 17, 2017.

http://www.ojjpac.org/sanctuary.asp. Accessed July 28, 2017.

http://www.thebill.com/blogs/floor-actions/house/249365-
house-passes-secret-service-reform-bill. Accessed July 25,
2017.

http://www.visalaw.com/iirira-96-a-summary-of-the-new-
immigration-bill/. Accessed 7/28/2017.

https://cis.org/map-sanctuary-cities-counties-and-states.
Accessed July 28, 2017.

https://climate.nasa.gov/evidence/. Accessed July 24, 2017.

https://economix.blogs.nytimes.com/2013/07/02/
immigration-and-social-security/. Accessed 7/27/2017.

https://edition.cnn.com/2013/07/13/world/americas/
hurricane-sandy-fast-facts/index.html. Accessed 7/24/2017.

https://epic.org/privacy/surveillance/spotlight/0705/editorial.
html. Accessed July 27, 2017.

https://judiciaryhouse.gov/press-release/goodlatte-conyers-
sensenbrenner-jackson-lee-unvail-secret-service-reform-
legislation/. Accessed July 25, 2017.

https://www.gao.gov/products/GAO-16-7071.

https://2002-2009.state.gov/p/wha/ris/fs/18128.htm.
Accessed July 28, 2017.

https://www.aclu.org/issues/national-security. Accessed
July 20, 2017.

https://www.army.mil/article/51819. Accessed July 24, 2017.

https://www.army.mil/article/140752. Accessed July 24,
2017.

https://www.cbp.gov/newsroom/national-media-release/
national-guard-supports-border-security-efforts.
7/19/2017.

https://www.cbp.gov/sites/default/files/assets/
documents/2017-Jan/USBP%20Stats%20FY2016%20
sector%20profile.pdf. Accessed 7/24/2017.

https://www.cbpp.org/research/immigration-and-social-
security/. Accessed July 19, 2017.

https://www.climate.nasa.gov/evidence/. Accessed July 24,
2017.

https://www.dhs.gov/science-and-technology/first-responders.
Accessed July 18, 2017.

https://www.dhs.gov/sites/default/files/publications/14_1120_
memo_prosecutorial_discretion.pdf. Accessed 7/20/2017.

https://www.dhs.gov/sites/default/files/publications/14_1120_
memo_secure_communities.pdf. Accessed 7/20/2017.

https://www.dhs.gov/topic/civil-rights-and-civil-liberties.
Accessed July 20, 2017.

https://www.federalregister.gov/documents/full_text/
xml/2016/12/15/2016-30187.xml. Accessed July 28, 2017.

https://www.govtrack.us/congress/bills/112/s565. Accessed July 28, 2017.

https://www.history.com/topics/hurricane-katrina/. Accessed July 24, 2017.

https://www.hsdl.org/?collection&id=1176. Accessed July 28, 2017.

https://www.ice.gov/secure-communities. Accessed July 20, 2017.

https://www.jdsupra.com/legalnews/muslim-country-travel-ban-upheld-in-part-70428/.

Accessed 7/15/2017.

https://www.nodc.noaa.gov/special-reports/rita.html. Accessed 7/24/2017.

https://www.nytimes.com/2017/07/26/us/politics/sessions-sanctuary-cities.html. Accessed 7/28/2017.

https://www.pewinternet.org/2016/6/10/04/the-politics-of-climate/. Accessed July 24, 2017.

https://www.projectcensored.org/2-homeland-security-threatens-civil-liberties. Accessed February 20, 2017.

https://www.techopedia.com/definition/29741/zero-day-malware

https://www.thedailybeast.com/how-immigrants-will-save-social-security. Accessed July 29, 2017.

https://www.vanityfair.com/news/2017/07/silicon-valleys-trump-brain-drain-continues. Accessed 7/28/2017.

https://www.washingtonpost.com/world/national-security/judge-rejects-hawaii-bid-to-exempt-grandparents-from-trumps-travel-ban/2017/07/06/8e3a3252-625d-11e7-8adc-fea80e32bf47_story.html?utm_term=.c3101d02e8e3. Accessed 7/15/2017.

https://www.weather.com/storms/hurricane/news/hurricane-season-2016-atlantic-recap/. Accessed July 24, 2017.

https://www.whitehouse.gov/presidential-actions/executive-order-protecting-nation-foreign-terrorist-entry-united-states-2/. Accessed 7/28/2017.

https://www.wsj.com/articles/trump-appeals-latest-travel-ban-ruling-1500072777?med=cx_picks&cx_navSource-cx_picks. Accessed July 15, 2017.

Immigration Act of November 29, 1990, 104 Stat. 4981.

Janis, Irving. 1972. *Victims of Groupthink.* Boston: Houghton-Mifflin.

Janis, Irving. 1982. *Groupthink: Psychological Studies of Policy Decisions and Fiascoes,* 2nd ed. Boston: Houghton-Mifflin.

Kayyem, Juliette N. 2003. "The Homeland Security Muddle," *The American Prospect,* November, 14 (10): 46–49.

Kemp, Roger L. 2003. "Homeland Security: Trends in America," *National Civic Review,* Winter, 92 (4): 45–53.

Kowert, Paul. 2002. *Groupthink or Deadlock: When Do Leaders Learn from Their Advisors?* Albany, NY: SUNY Press.

Krause, Elisha. 2003. "Building a Bigger Bureaucracy: What the Department of Homeland Security Won't Do," *The Public Manager,* Spring, 32 (1): 57–59.

Lehrer, Eli. 2004. "The Homeland Security Bureaucracy," *Public Interest,* Summer, 1156: 71–86.

LeMay, Michael. 2006. *Guarding the Gates: Immigration and National Security.* Westport, CT; and London: Praeger Security International.

LeMay, Michael. 2013. *Transforming America: Perspectives on U.S. Immigration. Vol. 3: Immigration and Superpower Status, 1845 to the Present.* Santa Barbara, CA: Praeger.

LeMay, Michael. 2015. *Illegal Immigration: A Reference Handbook,* 2nd ed. Santa Barbara, CA: ABC-CLIO.

LeMay, Michael, and Elliott Barkan, eds. 1999. *U.S. Immigration and Naturalization and Naturalization Laws and Issues.* Westport, CT: Greenwood Press.

Light, Paul C. 2002. *Homeland Security Will Be Hard to Manage*. Washington, DC: Brookings Institution's Center for Public Service.

Lippert, Randy K. 2005. *Sanctuary, Sovereignty, Sacrifice: Canadian Sanctuary Incidents, Power, and Law*. Vancouver, BC: University of British Columbia Press.

Martin, David. 2005. "With a Whisper, Not a Bang: Bush Signs Parts of Patriot Act II into Law—Stealthily," *San Antonio Current*. http://www.cacurrent.com/site/news/cfm? Accessed August 23, 2005.

Middelstadt, Michelle, Bureke Speaker, Doris Meissner, and Muzaffer A. Chishti. 2011. *Through the Prism of National Security: Major Immigration Policy and Program Changes in the Decade since 9/11*. Washington, DC: Migration Policy Institute.

Moretti, Enrico. 2012. *The New Geography of Jobs*. Boston: Houghton-Mifflin Harcourt.

National Research Council. 1997. *The New Americans: Economic, Demographic, and Fiscal Effects*. Washington, DC: NRC/National Academy Press.

PEW Hispanic Center. 2011. "Unauthorized Immigration." www.pewresearch.org/topics/Unauthorized-Immigration. Accessed August 20, 2011.

Riley, Michael. 2005. "1,000 Activists to Patrol Border for Migrants." *The Denver Post*, March 31: A-06.

Roots, Roger. 2003. "Terrorized into Absurdity: The Creation of the Transportation Security Administration," *Independent Review*, Spring, 7 (4): 503–518.

Suro, Roberto. 2015. "Mitigating Federal Immigration Law: Inclusion at the Local Level," in Michael LeMay, ed. *Illegal Immigration*, 2nd ed., 116–121. Santa Barbara, CA: ABC-CLIO.

Torr, James D., ed. 2004. *Homeland Security*. San Diego, CA: Greenhaven Press.

Udani, Adriano. 2013. "Thwarting Federal Immigration Reform: The Politics of Welfare Devolution in the United States," in Michael LeMay, ed. *Transforming America: Perspectives on U.S. Immigration, Vol. 3,* 151–172. Santa Barbara, CA; and Denver, CO: Praeger Press.

U.S. Bureau of the Census. 2010. "2010 Census Quick Facts." www/xmarks.com/site/quickfacts.census.gov/gfd/states/48000.html. Accessed August 20, 2011.

Wucker, Michele. 2006. *Lockout*. New York: Public Affairs/Perseus Books.

www.dhs.gov/sites/default/files/publications/TSA. Accessed September 1, 2017.

www.hurricanescience.org/history/storms/2000s/rita; and www.nodc.noaa.gov/hurricane-rita

www.npr.org/sections/thetwo-way/2017/03/15/520171478.html. Accessed July 15, 2017.

www.oig.dhs.gov/assets/Mgmt/OIG_08_67_June08.pdf. Accessed September 1, 2017.

www.seattletimes.com/seattle-news/politics/federal-judge-in-seattle-halts-trumps-immigration-order/. Accessed September 1, 2017.

www.uscis.gov/tools/glossary/nonimmigrant. Accessed July 27, 2017.

Yehiv, Steve A. 2003. "Groupthink and the Gulf Crisis," *British Journal of Political Science,* July, 33 (3): 419–443.

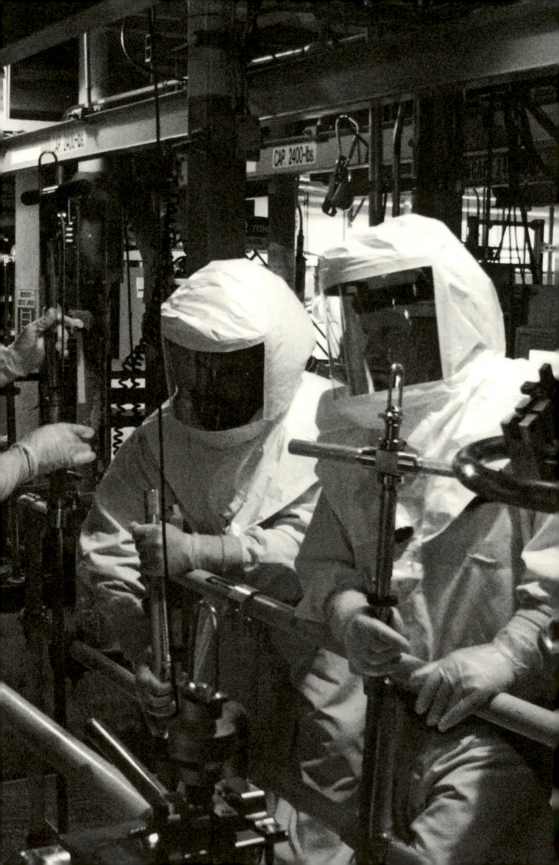

3 Perspectives

Introduction

This chapter presents eight original essays on the topic of homeland security policy making in the United States. It includes essays written by established scholars of the topic, by scholars just beginning their professional careers, and by activist stakeholders who make up those working on the frontline of the politics and policy making of homeland security. The essays collectively provide insights and a perspective beyond and different from the expertise of the author.

Within These Walls: The Sanctuary Movement
Dianne Aid

Introduction

It was an early spring morning in 2007 when I received a phone call from my friend Maria stating: "La Migra tiene" Rene (her husband). I thought she was joking, 60 seconds later I knew she was not. Employees who had gotten away from a work place raid at a horse racing track were hiding out in a nearby field notifying families of loved ones who had been

---

Hanford workers transfer highly radioactive material out of underwater storage in a reactor basin located about 400 yards away from the Columbia River on June 1, 2012. Hanford, in Washington State, is the largest nuclear cleanup site in the United States. Nearly a million gallons of radioactive material is expected to reach the Columbia River sometime in the next fifty years if cleanup efforts are not effective. (Department of Energy)

detained. Rene's brother-in-law was one of the eye witnesses. Rene, Maria, and their two U.S.-born citizen children (ages seven and five) were members of St. Matthew/San Mateo Episcopal Church in Auburn, Washington.

Rene was a "Show Case Story." He entered the United States each year on a valid work visa and, until he was detained, had no idea he had fallen out of status through no fault of his own. The attorney who took care of the worker visas for foreign workers missed a filing date on Rene's paperwork knocking him out of status. In the immigration system, there was no forgiveness for "attorney error." All responsibility is placed on the immigrant. Rene was a model citizen: no traffic tickets, no criminal activities or even minor infractions. He was squeaky clean. He volunteered at his children's school and community activities. He was a member of the Vestry of St. Matthew/San Mateo.

St. Matthew/San Mateo declared sanctuary for Rene and accompanied him for the following nine years it took his case to work through the broken immigration system. His case was finally closed by prosecutorial discretion in 2016.

The Sanctuary movement, offering places of safety and protection, has deep roots in the ancient faiths of Judaism, Christianity, and Islam, as well as other faith traditions.

> But the stranger that dwells with you shall be to you as one born among you, and you shall love him as yourself; for you were strangers in the land of Egypt: I am the LORD your God. (Lev. 19:34)

The flight into Egypt is a biblical event described in the Gospel of Matthew (Matthew 2:13–23). Soon after the visit by the Magi, who had learned that King Herod intended to kill the infants of that area, an angel appeared to Joseph in a dream to tell him to flee to Egypt with Mary and Jesus. Since biblical times, faith communities have continued to offer safety and protection. Quakers are well known for safe houses they offered on the Freedom Trail traveled by escaped slaves. Hymns such as "Swing Low Sweet Chariot" and "Go Down Moses" were code songs for escape imbedded in the faith message. The *Assisi Underground* is a 1985 American *film* that tells the story of a Franciscan friary offering assistance to Jews escaping Nazi regimes.

The past 35 years have moved humanity into a fluid, global world. Increased technology and corporatization have assailed indigenous, mostly farming communities, and pushed groups out of traditional lands and occupations. This has been a driving factor of immigration. We most certainly have seen this in the United States as asylum seekers from Central America fled political wars in their home countries. The Sanctuary movement was founded in the 1980s, and churches opened their doors to house-fleeing immigrants from Central America. Tensions broke out between federal agencies responsible for immigration law enforcement and religious communities. The religious communities used their moral position as the rationale for taking the risk of sanctuary work. In 1986, under President Ronald Regan, a general amnesty was offered for undocumented immigrants then living in the United States. The General Amnesty ended in 1989, followed by the 1996 Immigration Reform Act, which placed extensive limitations on immigration. There has not been any significant reform since then.

The New Sanctuary Movement

In 2005, immigration enforcement became very active. The Immigration and Citizenship Services ceased as a government agency to be replaced by the current Department of Homeland Security (DHS), which had been established in response to the September 11 terrorist attacks. Immigration bills pending before Congress were put aside. Immigration has been a political football since, based in racism, religious discrimination, and a false sense of "why don't they just apply for citizenship." It has made it very difficult for immigrant families. The political times led churches and other religious communities to step up to the plate and offer sanctuary.

On May 7, 2009, the New Sanctuary movement was launched in several cities across the United States. The launch in Seattle took place at St. Mark's Episcopal Cathedral. St. Matthew/San Mateo Episcopal Church in Seattle announced at that time that Rene Martinez and his family would become a Sanctuary family. Rene never needed to take shelter in the church. Our form of Sanctuary took on the work of accompaniment. The Washington New Sanctuary movement and the several communities of faith that comprised it partnered with Saint Matthew/San Mateo to raise the funds to pay the four attorneys who worked on Rene's case. Rene, since he was not confined to residency in the church, was free to go about giving public testimony of his story. Rene defied the negative images of undocumented immigrants as law breakers, drug dealers, and persons living high off public assistance. He really did change minds and hearts. Accompaniment involves emotional and temporal support and advocacy. Advocacy is an extremely important aspect of sanctuary support, especially when it comes to immigration court hearings and accompanying an individual to mandatory check-ins with DHS. They are un-nerving. Rene would leave home in the morning for his check-in, saying goodbye to his family, all the while not being sure whether he would be detained or be allowed to continue living at home with his family as his case was being adjudicated. That process took nine years, four attorneys, and many thousands of dollars. The presence of people from the New Sanctuary movement, including lay and clergy, had a profound impact. Security officers at the DHS headquarters would comment on how impressive it was to see the large group gathered in support of Rene. Immigration judges at the beginning of each hearing would ask who the people in the gallery were. We identified ourselves as members of the New Sanctuary movement and named our various faith communities. This assured the immigration court that Rene was not a flight risk. Rene was fortunate that he never needed to take shelter in the church. But that did not mean he had an easy time of it, nor did his family. Rene's children were aged five and seven when he was detained and put into immigration proceedings. They were 14 and 16 when his case was finally closed. This simply is not fair to his children, U.S. native-born citizens, who spent nine years of their critical development as children wondering on any given day whether their father would come home that day.

Along with the accompaniment of Rene and the family, Saint Matthew/San Mateo became the center in our area of King County for the immigrant community and their allies to meet and to organize. We drew the attention of the press as immigration was becoming the political football of the time. One reporter interviewing immigrants and members of the New Sanctuary movement asked, "Why here, why this church?" Antonio, a community leader/organizer and undocumented migrant himself, replied, "Because it is safe here."

Work of the New Sanctuary Movement—Creating Public Awareness and Education

There are many misconceptions about who are the undocumented immigrants, about their motives for coming to the United States, and a lack of knowledge about how broken the U.S. immigration system is. A common question is, "Why don't they just apply for citizenship and get legal?" We also cannot ignore the element of racism and popular nationalism that is involved, especially in the political climate during and since the 2016 U.S. elections. There are several educational resources available through such organizations as Catholic Legal Immigration Network (CLINIC at Cliniclegal.org) and Church World Services.

When we talk about a broken immigration system we can point to the time it takes for a case to get through the immigration system (e.g., Rene) because there is such a backlog of cases and not enough immigration judges, so hearings are often scheduled a year apart and even a simple case requires three hearings, if the immigrant is fighting deportation. A U.S. citizen may apply for the legal immigration of certain family members: spouses, children, and siblings. But the waiting time for a visa for a child over 21 or a sibling is currently around 25 years.

Actions and vigils are important. The Washington New Sanctuary movement and our sister organization in Oregon hold an annual Mother's Day Weekend vigil at the Northwest Detention Center to highlight the painful separation of families. I suggest the thoughtful reader might try researching the for-profit immigration detention centers. Hosting "Las Posadas" has been another action. This involves the reenactment of Mary and Joseph seeking room in the inn for the impending birth of Jesus and being turned away over and over again. Such reenactments project a powerful image for immigrants seeking hospitality in the United States.

Advocacy, the accompaniment of an individual, is critically important. The other form of advocacy is advocating for public policy and for compassionate, humane immigration reform. Now and then we are questioned as to the appropriateness of churches being involved in political issues. For us, these are not necessarily political issues, but are moral and ethical actions and, as mentioned at the beginning of this essay, are rooted in our faith traditions.

Sanctuary Now

Although deportations were at record high during the Obama administration, the workplace raids had stopped, and many deportations were happening through warrants for expired visas, detention in county jails and local court systems. The focus was on immigrants who had committed violent crimes. This has changed under the Trump administration. Now people are being profiled and picked up in sweeps. It is very unsettling.

School teachers report the fear their students feel that mom or dad may be taken from them. Sanctuary is resurging. In December 2016, in Seattle, we called the members of the New Sanctuary movement to re-gather. We were expecting about 20 people, but more than 100 showed up.

The strategy now is forming rapid response teams in communities. Through our network we receive text messages if ICE (Immigration and Customs Enforcement) is observed. Members of response teams show up as witnesses. This has actually resulted in some cases of ICE leaving.

Hub Churches

Saint Matthew/San Mateo is a hub church for our area. Should there be a major ICE action, for example in the case of a workplace raid, the community will know to gather at the hub, and attorneys and mental health professionals will be available to families. We are also preparing ourselves to offer physical sanctuary as the need for this type of sanctuary arises.

How safe is a church? A Memorandum of Sensitive Places was released by the DHS in 2011. It basically declares churches, schools, and medical facilities as places where ICE will not conduct enforcement activities. Although this is not a law, to date that policy has been respected.

Conclusion

In closing I want to recognize the "Spirit of Sanctuary" that exists at Saint Matthew/San Mateo. We knew our own story, which included elders, Japanese American farmers of the White River Valley who were faithful members of our congregation and were taken from their homes to be placed in the camps for Japanese Americans during World War II. In 2005, they saw the persecution happening to the Mexican immigrant community in Auburn, many of them were members of our congregation. They were the encouragement for Sanctuary. They are no longer with us, but their story and our stories today are within the walls of the Sanctuary of St. Matthew/San Mateo.

Dianne Aid, TSSF (Third Order Society of St. Francis), has been an immigration reform advocate for 28 years, working with Episcopal Church and interfaith communities. She studied anthropology in college and specialized in Latin American ethnography and cognitive anthropology. She currently serves as the president of the Episcopal Network for Economic Justice.

Evolution of Emergency Management in the United States: Innovation, Collaboration, and Focusing Events
DeeDee M. Bennett

Several changes have shaped emergency management in the United States and the way it is perceived. Since the World Trade Center Terrorist Attacks on September 11, 2001 (often referred to as 9/11), the Federal Emergency Management Agency (FEMA) has undergone various paradigm shifts in terms of its hierarchical structure, mission priorities, and public interests. In 2002, the Homeland Security Act established the Department of Homeland Security (DHS) with the primary mission to "prevent terrorist attacks within the United States" (S. 2794, 107th Congress 2002, 116 Stat. 2142). The head of DHS was also established to be a cabinet-level secretary, appointed by the president of the United States. The newly appointed secretary of the DHS would displace the FEMA administrator as a cabinet-level appointment. Furthermore, FEMA, along with Customs and Immigration, Travel Security Agency, Secret Service, and other agencies, was consolidated within DHS.

Many scholars have criticized this change (Birkland 2006; Harrald 2012; Sylves and Cumming 2004). Researchers saw the creation of the DHS as a reactive policy measure in response to the 9/11 attacks, remodeled from earlier proposals. As a low-probability, high-consequence event, terrorist attacks are not as frequent or as damaging (in terms of lives lost or property damaged) as are flooding, hurricanes, or tornadoes in the United States over time. Therefore, scholars saw the shift in perceived mission priority adjustments due to the changes in hierarchical structure as potentially problematic in the face of frequent natural hazards (Birkland 2006; Harrald 2012). The response and recovery efforts in the gulf coast following Hurricane Katrina in 2005 immediately highlighted scholarly concerns. However, beyond the obvious changes in organization structure, the evolution of emergency management in the United States since 2002 has been punctuated by three other challenges: the influence of technological innovation, a renewed emphasis on collaboration, and continued reactionary legislation predicted by focusing events.

Influences in Innovation

Innovation has shaped the perception of FEMA. Prior to the 9/11 attacks, many Americans did not have access to 24-hour cable news channels. Similarly, mobile phones, tablets, and laptop computers were not as ubiquitous as they are now. The introduction of user-friendly "plug-and-play" cable systems in 2002 led to approximately one-third of U.S. households having access to cable television and mobile wireless devices (CCTA n.d.). In 2007, the prime-time cable viewership of 24-hour cable news channels reached approximately 2.7 million. In 2016, that viewership neared 5 million (Matsa 2017). A new theory in political science and media studies, the CNN-Effect, questions whether 24-hour cable news can drive policy and/or military intervention (Gilboa 2005). While some question the real impact of these cable channels with regard to policy and military intervention, some propose that the power of real-time images of active incidents shapes the perception and social construct of disasters (Sylves 2012). Following the destruction left in wake by Hurricane Katrina, the 24-hour cable news channels were accessible in millions of homes and raised public concerns regarding emergency management in the United States (Gall and Cutter 2012). Disaster scholars have noted that disaster coverage within the news media also led to a perpetuation of disaster myths of mass looting, panic, and other antisocial behavior (Tierney, Bevc, and Kuligowski 2006). Birkland (2006) also noted that media attention may promote political learning during disasters.

The increase in viewership of cable television is not the only advancement in technology that has impacted emergency management in the United States. The progression and evolution of communications technology and devices has introduced a method to warn the public and a new, prevalent form of journalism from citizens. Advancements in mobile wireless devices and social media platforms impact the way in which we (as citizens) learn about disaster and process information and allow us to refine disaster media coverage. FEMA's Partnership with the Federal Communications Commission and Wireless Carriers has introduced the Wireless Emergency Alerts (WEA) allowing government authorities to geographically target emergency messaging to WEA-enabled mobile devices using cell broadcast technology (www.fcc.gov/consumers/guides/wireless-emergency-alerts-wea). Since 2012, emergency alerts have been sent to mobile devices using WEA, reaching individuals and not just households. The reach of WEA is potentially huge; as of 2015, nearly 91 percent of Americans own a cell phone (Raine 2013). Furthermore, this new system has had a significant impact on reaching previously underserved populations; research regarding people with disabilities shows that messages via WEA are especially important (Bennett, Baker, and Mitchell 2017; Bennett, Phillips, and Davis 2017).

Social media platforms, such as Facebook and Twitter, have also had an impact on emergency management. Facebook, founded in 2004, has infiltrated our homes and lives, serving more than 1 billion active users worldwide (https://www.facebook.com/pg/facebook/about/?ref=page_internal). As of

2016, approximately 68 percent of American adults use Facebook at all age groups, including 62 percent of individuals aged 65 and older and 88 percent of individuals aged 18–29. Scholars have noticed a rise in the level of citizen journalism given the increased use of social media platforms and mobile wireless devices (Crowe 2012). Emergency messaging can no longer be maintained and controlled solely by government authorities when the public is allowed to contribute, process, and refine the news in real time. Vieweg and colleagues (2008) noticed the use of social media platforms following the Virginia Tech shootings in 2007 and since then have researched public contributions on social media platforms following various disasters (Bennett 2017; Bennett, Baker, and Mitchell 2017). As of 2017, majority of emergency management agencies at federal and state levels have an online presence on at least one social media platform (Bennett 2017).

Emphasis on Collaboration

The emphasis on collaboration has evolved over time. Over 450 organizations were involved, during the response efforts to the 9/11 terrorist attacks, with 35 percent being privately owned and nearly 15 percent nonprofit organizations (Comfort and Kapucu 2006). Evidence of this type of cross-sector collaboration during disasters has increased with the scale of the incident (Waugh and Streib 2006). After Hurricane Katrina, criticisms of the response and recovery efforts centered around communication and collaborative failures (Simo and Bies 2007). A study by Kapucu, Arslan, and Collins (2010) identified 580 organizations involved in response to Hurricane Katrina, and 71 percent of the organizations were from the public sector.

In 2011, then FEMA administrator, Craig Fugate introduced the "Whole Community Approach," giving a name to the collaborative trend in disaster management. In a statement to Congress, Fugate is quoted as saying that while government will serve following disasters, "a government-centric approach to disaster management will not be enough to meet the challenges posed by a catastrophic incident" (FEMA 2011: 2). The changes in the federal guidelines over time mimic the same trend. The Federal Response Plan in 1992 described means for a federal response to augment state and local efforts. The National Response Plan in 2004 renewed a focus on all-hazards approaches and described a means by which all levels of government would work together. The National Response Framework in 2008 included a broader audience of nonprofit organizations and private sector entities. It also changed the name from "plan" to "framework" to emphasize the nature as a guide to encourage partnership and the provision of a unified response for all disasters. Following Hurricane Sandy in 2012, the National Response Framework in 2013 emphasized a holistic approach to response and fostering the need for whole community involvement (FEMA 2013). Scholars have also highlighted the importance of collaboration and the whole community approach for reaching often-underserved populations (Bennett, Phillips, and Davis 2017). Ironically, wording in the Robert T. Stafford Act has been amended to include broader collaborative efforts beyond American Red Cross to include faith-based organizations: the Mennonite Disaster Service and the Salvation Army.

Legislation: Focusing Events and Politics

The renewed emphasis on collaboration has been led in part due to legislative changes. Legislation has influenced the implementation of emergency management functions, often predicated by focusing events as defined by Birkland (1997). Beyond the significant changes following 9/11 due to the creation of DHS, FEMA has had several changes since 2002. Following Hurricane Katrina, the Post Katrina Emergency Management Reform Act of 2006 reorganized FEMA and established new positions to assist with guidelines during response and recovery that considered the needs of individuals with access and functional needs (S. 3791, 109th Congress, 2006). Following

Hurricane Sandy, Congress introduced and passed legislation related to supplemental appropriations and the subsequent delivery of federal disaster assistance to survivors (H.R. 219, 113th Congress, 2013). According to FEMA, the Sandy Recovery Improvement Act of 2013 may be one of the "most significant legislative change to FEMA authorities since the Stafford Act" (as worded on the FEMA website: https://www.fema.gov/sandy-recovery-improvement-act-2013).

Foreseeing the Future

If the past is any indication, we can anticipate changes in the implementation of emergency management based on the progression of innovation, the enhanced need for collaboration, and from reactive policy measures following larger, increasingly frequent focusing events. The impact of innovation on the field will reinforce a need for scientific literacy among emergency management professionals. The next-generation emergency management core competencies document highlights this future necessity. Additionally, professionals will need to understand how to incorporate evolving technologies (Next Generation Core Competency Focus Group 2016). The enhanced need for collaboration will also encourage an understanding of how to build capacity within communities, as well as the increasingly interconnected and interdependent world in which we live. Ideally, this will bring forth a renewed respect for mitigation measures to limit future vulnerabilities to potential hazards. Finally, perhaps research and lessons learned in the hazards and disasters field can incite more proactive legislative measures without waiting for the next focusing event.

References

Bennett, DeeDee. 2017. "Providing Critical Emergency Communications via Social Media Platforms: Cross-Case Analysis," in Yu-Che Chen and Michael Ahn, eds. *Routledge Handbook on Information Technology in Government*. New York: Routledge.

Bennett, DeeDee, Paul Baker, and Helena Mitchell. 2017. "New Media and Accessible Emergency Communications," in Katie Ellis and Mike Kent, eds. *Disability* and *Social Media*. New York: Routledge.

Bennett, DeeDee, Brenda Phillips, and Elizabeth Davis. 2017. "The Future of Accessibility in Disaster Conditions: How Wireless Technologies Will Transform the Life Cycle of Emergency Management," *Futures Journal*, 87: 122–132.

Birkland, T. A. 1997. *After Disaster: Agenda Setting, Public Policy, and Focusing Events*. Washington, DC: Georgetown University Press.

Birkland, T. A. 2006. *Lessons of Disaster: Policy Change after Catastrophic Events*. Washington, DC: Georgetown University Press.

California Cable & Telecommunications Association (CCTA). n.d. History of Cable. CCTA. https://www.calcable.org/learn/history-of-cable/. Accessed October 25, 2017.

Comfort, L. K., and N. Kapucu. 2006. "Inter-Organizational Coordination in Extreme Events: The World Trade Center Attacks, September 11, 2001," *Natural Hazards*, 39(2), 309–327.

Crowe, A. 2012. *Disasters 2.0: The Application of Social Media Systems for Modern Emergency Management*. Boca Raton, FL: CRC Press.

Federal Emergency Management Agency (FEMA). 2011. *A Whole Community Approach to Emergency Management: Principles, Themes, and Pathways for Action*. Washington, DC: Department of Homeland Security, Federal Emergency Management Agency.

Federal Emergency Management Agency (FEMA). 2013. *National Response Framework*, 2nd ed. Washington, DC:

Department of Homeland Security, Federal Emergency Management Agency.

Gall, M., and S. Cutter. 2012. "2005 Events and Outcomes: Hurricane Katrina and Beyond," in Claire Rubin, ed. *Emergency Management: The American Experience*, 1900–2010, 2nd ed., 191–213. Boca Raton, FL: CRC Press.

Gilboa, E. 2005. "Global Television News and Foreign Policy: Debating the CNN Effect." *International Studies Perspectives*, 6(3): 325–341.

Harrald, J. R. 2012. "Emergency Management Restructured: Intended and Unintended Outcomes of Actions Taken since 9/11," in Claire Rubin, ed. *Emergency Management: The American Experience*, 1900–2010, 2nd ed., 167–189. Boca Raton, FL: CRC Press.

Homeland Security Act of 2002, S. 2794, 107th Congress, 2002.

https://www.facebook/pg/facebook/about/?ref=page_internal. Accessed October 25, 2017.

https://www.fema.gov/sandy-recovery-improvement-act-of-2013. Accessed October 25, 2017.

Kapucu, N., T. Arslan, and M. L. Collins. 2010. "Examining Intergovernmental and Interorganizational Response to Catastrophic Disasters: Toward a Network-Centered Approach." *Administration & Society*, 42(2): 222–247.

Matsa, K. E. 2017. "Cable News Fact Sheet. Pew Research Center: Journalism & Media." http://www.journalism.org/fact-sheet/cable-news/. Accessed October 25, 2017.

Next Generation Core Competency Focus Group. April, 2016. "The Next Generation Emergency Management Core Competencies." Report for the FEMA Higher Education Program. Emmitsburg, MD. https://training.fema.gov/hiedu/docs/emcompetencies/ngcc%20final%20competencies%204-28-2016.pdf

Post-Katrina Emergency Management Reform Act of 2006, S. 3791, 109th Congress. 2006.

Raine, L. 2013. "Cell Phone Ownership Hits 91% of Adults." Pew Research Center. http://www.pewresearch.org/fact-tank/2013/06/06/cell-phone-ownership-hits-91-of-adults/. Accessed October 25, 2017.

Sandy Recovery Improvement Act of 2013, H.R. 219, 113th Congress. 2013.

Simo, G., and A. L. Bies. 2007. "The Role of Nonprofits in Disaster Response: An Expanded Model of Cross-Sector Collaboration." *Public Administration Review*, 67(s1): 125–142.

Sylves, R. T. 2012. "Federal Emergency Management Comes of Age: 1979–2001," in Claire Rubin, ed. *Emergency Management: The American Experience*, 1900–2010, 2nd ed., 115–166. Boca Raton, FL: CRC Press.

Sylves, Richard T., and William R. Cumming. 2004. "FEMA's Path to Homeland Security: 1979–2003." *Journal of Homeland Security and Emergency Management*, 1(2): 53–75.

Tierney, K., C. Bevc, and E. Kuligowski. 2006. "Metaphors Matter: Disaster Myths, Media Frames, and Their Consequences in Hurricane Katrina," *The Annals of the American Academy of Political and Social Science*, 604(1): 57–81.

Vieweg, S., L. Palen, S. B. Liu, A. L. Hughes, and J. N. Sutton. 2008. *Collective Intelligence in Disaster: Examination of the Phenomenon in the Aftermath of the 2007 Virginia Tech Shooting*. Boulder: University of Colorado.

Waugh, W. L., and G. Streib. 2006. "Collaboration and Leadership for Effective Emergency Management," *Public Administration Review*, 66(s1): 131–140.

www.fcc.gov/consumers/guides/wireless-emergency-alerts-wea. Accessed March 2, 2018.

DeeDee M. Bennett is an assistant professor in the Emergency Services Program in the School of Public Administration, University of Oklahoma at Nebraska. She has her Ph.D. from Oklahoma State University's Political Science Department in Fire and Emergency Management.

Congressional Staffing and Homeland Security Policy Making
Sara Hagedorn

September 11, 2001, dawned bright and sunny in Washington, D.C., and New York City, without a cloud in the sky (the author was working in the U.S. Senate on September 11 and vividly remembers the day). It would end very dark. That day was the catalyst for the creation of the Department of Homeland Security (DHS).

In 2002, it appeared members of Congress were working hard to draft legislation that would form the DHS, the newest cabinet-level department to be created in nearly 15 years (the Veterans Administration was the last in 1989), but what was occurring behind the scenes is equally interesting. Congressional staff and members of Congress were playing key roles in drafting and negotiating much of this legislation and setting the policy agenda.

One morning in the fall of that year, the Senate office I was working in got the call, and three of us (policy staffers) grabbed our suit jackets and rushed to the basement where we caught the subway to the Capitol building. It was our office's turn. We briskly made our way to the Republican cloak room just off the Senate floor, where on a small round table sat the Republican's copy of a bill that was easily five inches thick. We divvied up the respective titles which fell into our policy areas and began reading. That is how Republican Senate staff, and their bosses, got to read the Homeland Security Act of 2002, the bill that would establish the DHS (the author worked in the U.S. Senate from 2000 to 2007, for two different senators. At the time of the authorization of the DHS, she worked for Senator Conrad Burns [R-MT]).

So, who are these congressional staffers, and what do they do? We learned in our high school civics class, and many college classrooms, the members of Congress themselves do all the work and make all the decisions regarding policy. However, that is not necessarily always the case. Congressional staff first appeared on Capitol Hill in the mid-19th century (Malbin 1980), and their numbers grew as a result of the passage of a number of bills (namely the Legislative Reorganization Act of 1946, the Legislative Reorganization Act of 1970, and the Congressional Budget Act of 1974 [Peterson 2008]). A majority of them are male, but women make up 40 percent of all congressional staff (Hagedorn 2015). They are young, with over 60 percent of them under the age of 35. They serve on the personal staffs of members of Congress, work for committees, and work for those in leadership. They research and draft legislation and amendments, negotiate policies, help oversee executive departments, and meet with constituents. These individuals are coming up with policy ideas for the country and often setting the policy agenda in Congress.

The creation of the DHS was no exception to this phenomenon. Congressional staffers played key roles in its creation, and continue to play key roles in providing oversight, and outlining the budget, of the DHS.

This bill had been drafted by staffers and was being vetted by staffers. Yes, members of Congress are the key player in the process, negotiating the high-level items and making the big decisions, but the role of staff was clear.

But wait you are asking, that was over 15 years ago; what about now? A similar story emerges. A recent survey of over 500 current and former congressional staff members showed us that congressional staff are large drivers of policy (Hagedorn 2015). They are proposing policy ideas, in all areas of policy, and their bosses are acting upon them. They have a great deal of discretion in policy negotiation and approval.

Out of the 530 staffers to complete the survey, 64 handled some aspect of homeland security (including immigration, security, emergency management and FEMA, domestic terrorism preparedness, and counterterrorism, as well as communications) for their bosses or committees.

Are these homeland security staffers different from their colleagues? Yes and no. They are older (48 percent are over the age of 35), and more males cover these issues (75 percent are male) than congressional staff overall. Of our 64 homeland security staffers, 56 percent of them work in the House and 44 percent in the Senate. Forty percent work for Democrats, and 60 percent for Republicans. Only 4 of them are former staffers, with 60 currently working in Congress. Sixty-four percent of them work in a personal office, 33 percent on a committee, and the remaining 3 percent in a leadership office.

When asked how important they are to the overall agenda-setting process in Congress, 77 percent of our homeland staffers reported being somewhat, very, or extremely important. (Seventy-eight percent of non-homeland staffers reported these same levels of important; thus these staffers look exactly like the larger congressional staff population.) What does this mean exactly; what are they doing? They are drafting bills and amendment language. In fact, almost 90 percent of our homeland staffers reported having been involved with drafting such language for their bosses.

You may be thinking that individual congressional staffers might be exaggerating their own importance, especially with the importance question. This is definitely a possibility, which is why so many different factors are used for this analysis. Further, it should be noted that congressional staff do their jobs in the shadows, often as completely unseen actors (Kingdon 2003). These individuals are writing the speeches, the legislation, and press releases, yet their name goes on none of it. They do everything on behalf of their bosses. Thus, we can safely make the assumption a majority of our survey respondents are not embellishing their own importance; it is not in their nature.

These staffers were asked how often they negotiate bill language or policies on their boss's behalf, without running everything by their boss. This might seem excessive to some who believe members of Congress are in absolute control, but 93 percent of these staffers reported doing this at least once, with a full 34 percent reporting they do it most of the time. This is more important than you might think; this means staffers are enabled by their bosses to make decisions on their behalf, without prior approval. Even though the members are the ones who are constitutionally obligated to pass legislation (and they are still the only ones who cast all votes on the floor of the House and Senate), they have empowered staff to do a great deal of the daily work required to draft and pass legislation.

Finally, these staffers were asked how often their boss takes their advice on new policy ideas and vote recommendations. Not a single one of our homeland security staffers reported that their boss never took their policy ideas and acted upon them. This shows us homeland security staffers, as least in this survey, appear to have a bit more power in their offices than the average staffer. They also are providing important input into the overall shape of homeland security policy of our country.

One of the biggest and most important responsibilities of a member of Congress is casting votes both in committee and on the House or Senate floor. In an average day, the issues span the full gamut from clean air to worker visas, and forest policy to Indian health care. Members are intelligent individuals, but they cannot be expected to know every detail of every policy issue, which comes before Congress. Thus, members rely on their staffers to research each vote in depth and provide them recommendations and justifications on how to vote. These recommendations are based on the member's stated opinions on issues, his or her past voting behavior, voters' preferences, and campaign promises. When asked if their boss takes their vote recommendations, 98 percent of our staffers reported having this happen, with 30 percent saying their bosses *always* take their vote recommendations, which was higher than staffers who do not handle homeland security issues (22 percent).

A number of interviews were also conducted with this research; when a Senate staffer was asked if his boss followed his vote recommendations, he said, "Yes, he listens to my vote recommendations. If he went against it, he will come back and explain why. He has never gone against an important one." A staffer from a different Senate office, when asked this same question, said, "He generally trusts what we tell him. If he disagrees it's because he talked to another member and has other information."

It cannot be denied high-level government officials such as members of Congress, presidents, and cabinet secretaries are making the big policy decisions dealing with homeland security and the DHS. However, it should not be assumed they are the only players in setting the policy agenda. Congressional staff, as evidenced by the survey data presented here, are playing a very important role in policy development.

References

Hagedorn, Sara L. 2015. "Taking the Lead: Congressional Staffers and Their Role in the Policy Process." Dissertation. University of Colorado-Boulder.

Kingdon, John. W. 2003. *Agendas, Alternatives, and Public Policies*. Boston: Little, Brown.

Malbin, Michael J. 1980. *Unelected Representatives: Congressional Staff and the Future of Representative Government*. New York: Basic Books Inc.

Petersen, R. Eric. 2008. "Legislative Branch Staffing, 1954–2007." *Congressional Research Service*. Report R40056. October 15, 2008.

Sara Hagedorn is an assistant professor at the University of Colorado-Colorado Springs and teaches in the Department of Political

Science. She teaches courses in American government and politics and, in her research, specializes in the U.S. Congress. She earned her Ph.D. from the University of Colorado-Boulder in 2015. Hagedorn worked on the staff of Senator Conrad Burns (R-MT), and Senator John Thune (R-SD).

Our Legacy Waste: Chemical and Nuclear
Irene Kornelly

The traditional definition of "legacy wastes" applied exclusively to wastes remaining from nuclear weapons facilities. Since the late 1980s and the beginning of military base closures in 1988, this term has evolved to include all wastes left behind after the closure of defense or energy facilities.

While wastes from chemical weapons destruction and nuclear waste containment are a large part of the legacy wastes, there are many other wastes that have remained stored, buried, or remediated at military and energy sites: active, closed, and formerly used defense sites (FUDs). Thousands of acres of soils and water throughout the United States have been contaminated by military industrial processes and training. While many sites can be easily remediated by the removal of contaminated soils, others require complicated and long-term cleanup methodologies. The total costs for the cleanup for all sites have not been calculated, but will no doubt be extremely high. While sites await cleanup, changes to environmental laws at the state and federal levels often add to these costs and require changes in remediation technologies (www.energy.gov/about-us).

Even after remediation has been completed, new laws and the discovery of additional toxins can force the Department of Defense to return to a site for additional cleanup. Recent examples of new chemicals determined to be harmful to human health are perfluorooctanoicacids (PFOAs), perfluorinated compounds (PFCs), and perfluorooctanes (PFOs) that have been found in water sources throughout the United States. Various types of cancer have been attributed to these chemicals that were in widespread use in firefighting foam employed at both civilian and military airports. Local water districts and military installations are now scrambling to find the dollars to clean up local water sources in order to protect their customers. While local agencies may eventually be reimbursed for the cost of the cleanups, with over 600 sites throughout the United States and cleanup costs estimated to be in the billions of dollars, the local cleanup costs will be paid by ratepayers at this time (https://www.peoacwa.army.mil/).

Remediation of a site does not mean that a site is now in "pristine" condition and suitable for all development activities. Land use restrictions (LUCs) can remain with the property that dictates the types of usage for a parcel of land, for example, industrial only, open space only, no residential use, no digging. Keeping track of LUCs can be difficult as property is sold and resold over time (https://www.hanford.gov).

In addition to the more common legacy wastes, the remains from nuclear and chemical weapons, both stored and buried, will continue to plague the United States for years (www.opcw.org/about-opcw).

The Chemical Weapons Convention (CWC), ratified by the U.S. Congress in April 1997, required all participants to destroy their chemical weapons and production facilities by 2007. To date, 192 countries have signed this treaty, encompassing 98 percent of the world's population. Four countries have not signed the treaty: Egypt, Israel, North Korea, and South Sudan; and it is unknown as to when or if these countries will become a part of the treaty. While the 2007 destruction deadline was not met, significant progress has been made, specifically by the United States and Russia in meeting their treaty obligations. To date about 96 percent of the world's known stockpile has been destroyed. It is now projected that all known stockpiles of chemical weapons will be destroyed by December 31, 2023. Two sites in the United States, Pueblo, Colorado, and Blue Grass, Kentucky, have yet to be fully destroyed. All sites in Russia have been destroyed, but many hazardous wastes remain from their destruction process. Without question additional stockpiles will be found and buried munitions will be recovered. It is estimated that in the United States at least half of the states potentially have buried chemical munitions within their borders. The cost to destroy these weapons and facilities and ensure the safety of workers in the destruction facilities and the surrounding environment is enormous (https://www.peoacwa.army.mil/).

The challenge to the CWC is the continuous use of chemical weapons by "rogue" nations and nonstate actors (terrorists). The use of sarin, sarin-like substances, chlorine, and mustard agent in Syria, Iran, and Iraq is well documented, as is the use in Malaysia for assassination and as a weapon of terror in a subway in Japan. Success in eliminating the use of chemical weapons can be achieved only through global, multinational efforts. Future challenges include the convergence of chemistry and biology that has led to huge advances in technology for the good of humanity and the potential for a new class of weapons that will employ both chemicals and biologics in one weapon.

While the United States, Russia, and virtually every other nation on the planet have signed on to the CWC, no such universal agreement exists for nuclear weapons. The Nuclear Test Ban Treaty has been signed by 166 countries, although not all of the countries have ratified the treaty. The moratorium on nuclear weapons testing has been adhered to by almost all countries with one notable exception, North Korea. The treaty, however, does not ban the development of nuclear weapons nor ban the upgrading of current stockpiles. The United States and Russia have entered into numerous unilateral agreements to reduce the number of nuclear weapons they each possess, but at the same time continue to upgrade and improve the effectiveness of their nuclear stockpiles. In fact, the proliferation of nuclear arms is a major topic of discussion in world affairs and diplomacy (North Korea, Iran, Israel, Pakistan, India, China, Russia, and the United States).

The safe storage of nuclear wastes is technically difficult, and destruction virtually is unknown at this time. Most nuclear wastes are sealed and stored at highly secure sites. The Department of Energy manages the cleanup of 107 nuclear sites in the United States, ranging from relatively small laboratories to thousands of acres.

The Waste Isolation Pilot Plant (WIPP) is located in Carlsbad, New Mexico, and began accepting wastes in 1999. It was designed to accept transuranic wastes generated from defense operations in the United States. The salts from the caverns in the Carlsbad area encapsulate the properly packaged wastes. In February 2014 WIPP was closed as a result of a minor radioactive leak. Cleanup at the site took almost three years and cost $500 million to remediate. The site was reopened in January 2017. As of mid-November 2017, over 12,000 shipments had been received at the WIPP facility. Hanford, Washington, is the site of one of the largest and most challenging cleanup sites for nuclear weapons in the world. The Hanford facility is located on 580 square miles of property near the Columbia River and operated for 44 years of plutonium production. During that time millions of tons of solid wastes and contaminated soils and billions of gallons of liquid wastes were created. The site has been under remediation for over five decades. The Savannah River Site in South Carolina is just now breaking ground for its second Saltstone Disposal Unit for the storage of liquid wastes. The new facility, when completed in December 2018, will store approximately 32.8 million gallons. The first facility has been completed. The Rocky Flats site near Denver, Colorado, was finally closed after years of remediation. Much of the industrial/plant area remains under the control of the Department of Energy and off limits to the public where monitoring of groundwater plumes will continue indefinitely. The former security buffer zone is scheduled to open as a wildlife refuge in 2018. The Yucca Mountain site near Las Vegas, Nevada, was intended as another place to store nuclear wastes on a long-term basis. This site is no longer under consideration due to environmental concerns and its proximity to Las Vegas (https:// www.hanford.gov; https://www/energy.gov/em/waste-isolation-pilot-plant).

The cleanup and management of sites contaminated by nuclear and chemical wastes will remain a major concern in the United States and around the world. Yet to be determined is the full extent of contamination in the oceans as a result of the dumping of weapons following World Wars I and II. Who will pay, who will do the cleanup, and where to begin are just a few of the questions to be answered. The destruction of chemical weapons and the safe storage of nuclear wastes will be the subject of continuous discussions in a rapidly changing technical and political climate.

References

Department of Energy. https://www.hanford.gov (Hanford site). Accessed November 9, 2017.

Department of Energy. www.energy.gov/about-us. Accessed November 9, 2017.

https://www.energy.gov/em/waste-isolation-pilot-plant. Accessed November 9, 2017.

Organization for the Prohibition of Chemical Weapons. www.opcw.org/about-opcw. Accessed November 9, 2017.

Program Executive Office, Assembled Chemical Weapons Alternatives. https://www.peoacwa.army.mil/. Accessed November 9, 2017.

Irene Kornelly is the president of Kornelly & Associates, a consulting firm specializing in military facility cleanup, redevelopment, and privatization of assets on military facilities. Her clients include government agencies as well as private companies. Prior to starting her own business, Irene was the director of the Colorado Office of Statewide Defense Initiatives for Governor Roy Romer. Irene also worked for Senators Gary Hart and Tim Wirth focusing on defense and aerospace issues.

Homeland Insecurity, Personal Security, and Constitutional Safeguards
Alemayehu G. Mariam

Benjamin Franklin's aphorism inscribed on a plaque in the stairwell of the Statue of Liberty warns, "They that can give up essential Liberty, to purchase a little temporary Safety, deserve neither Liberty nor Safety." Could he have foreseen enactment of the Patriot Act to purchase "a little temporary safety" in a world menaced by terrorism? Samuel Johnson condemned false "patriotism" as "the last refuge of scoundrels" (Boswell and Hibbert, 1986). Should we believe demagogic politicians-cum-patriots who pledge to save us from ourselves and protect us from terrorists seen and unseen?

In a democracy, there is often a need to balance public safety with the individual's right to privacy, with the right to be left alone from unreasonable government intrusion, surveillance, and control. Given the recurrence of indiscriminate and deadly terrorist violence, how can the government balance the liberty interests of citizens with the equally vital necessity of ensuring public safety?

Congress passed the Patriot Act of 2001 to "enhance domestic security against terrorism" (https://www.gpo.gov/fdsys/pkg/PLAW-107publ56/pdf/PLAW-107publ56.pdf). It granted law enforcement broad investigative powers to conduct searches of homes, businesses, and other premises without the consent or knowledge of owners or occupants, and use of National Security Letters (NSLs; see, e.g., Twitter, https://g.twimg.com/blog/blog/attachments/Redacted-NSL-16-422732-Twitter.pdf), which allows without warrant searches of telephone, e-mail, financial, or other records, including library privileges and roving wiretaps (www.cato.org/blog/patriot-powers-roving-wire-taps) to surveil "lone wolf" terrorists.

The American Civil Liberties Union (ACLU) has decried the Patriot Act and claimed that, contrary to what most Americans believe, it has "made it easier for the government to spy on ordinary Americans by expanding the authority to monitor phone and email communications, collect bank and credit reporting records, and track the activity of innocent Americans on the Internet" and has "turn[ed] regular citizens into suspects" (https://www.aclu.org/issues/national-security/privacy-and-surveillance/surveillance-under-patriot-act?redirect=infographic/surveillance-under-patriot-act). The Heritage Foundation applauds the Patriot Act and particularly its roving wiretap provision, which it claims is a "gigantic step forward in terms of helping law enforcement fight terrorism in a modern, technological world" (www.heritage.org/terrorism/report/after-bin-laden-support-the-patriot-act).

Should law enforcement be able to access the records, communications, and physical premises of individuals suspected of actual or potential involvement in terrorism playing loosey-goosey with the Fourth Amendment? Does a terrorist suspect have a Fourth Amendment protected right against unreasonable government searches and seizures?

In 2008, the Department of Justice's Office of Inspector General (OIG) documented systematic and widespread abuse of NSLs by the FBI and Section 215 orders for business records (https://oig.justice.gov/reports/2014/s1408.pdf). A 2015 OIG report on Section 1001 compliance for civil rights and civil liberties violations was inconclusive on the issue of abuse due to jurisdictional issues in investigating the complaints (https://.oig/justice.gov/reports/2015/s1503.pdf).

Representative Jim Sensenbrenner, the principal author of the Patriot Act, argued the Obama administration abused the act by engaging in "unrestrained surveillance" and "sift[ing] through details of our private lives" (https://www.theguardian.com/commentisfree/2013/jun/09/abuse-patriot-act-must-end). He claims that Congress, leery of potential abuses, placed certain "sunsetting provisions" for automatic expiration.

In 2007, a New York federal court struck down the amended provision of the Patriot Act's NSL for persons in the United States, and to gag those who receive NSLs from discussing them (https://www.aclu.org/files/pdfs/safefree/nsldecision.pdf;

see also https://www.washingtonpost.com/world/national-security/
appeals-court-rules-nsa-record-collection-violates-patriot-
act/2015/05/07/c4fabfb8-f4bf-11e4-bcc4-e8141e5eb0c9_story.
html?utm_term=.f08eb3b9c5b5). In 2015, the Second Court of
Appeals ruled that the Patriot Act does not allow the government
to collect domestic phone records. The DOJ has credited the
Patriot Act for tearing down the "wall separating the intelligence
officers from law enforcement agents" and facilitating "robust
information sharing between intelligence and law enforcement
personnel" (www.global/security.org/security/library/report-to-
congress-on-implementation-of-section-1001-of-the-USA-
PATRIOT-ACT). Yet, a 2015 DOJ report admits that mass surveillance capabilities authorized by Section 215 of the Patriot Act
have not helped solve any big terrorism cases (https://www./oig.
just.gov/reports/2015/01505.pdf#page-1).

A 2013 leaked document (http://www.washingtonpost.com/
wp-srv/special/politics/prism-collection-documents/) revealed
that the National Security Agency (NSA) and the FBI, using a
secret program called Prism, have been harvesting audio, video,
photographs, e-mails, and documents from the internal servers
of nine major technology companies. Are citizens more secure
today as a result of the Patriot Act? Have the rights of innocent
citizens been violated by abuses of the act?

The balancing between liberty and security was made when
the framers commanded in the Fourth Amendment that there
shall be no unreasonable searches and seizures by government.
They required judicial review of probable cause before autho-
rizing searches and seizures. In the Third Amendment, the
framers sought to ensure the individual's right to domestic privacy by forbidding the quartering of soldiers in private homes.
Could the government secretly "quarter" electronic eavesdrop-
ping devices in private homes to aid its soldiers fighting terrorist forces?

Unquestionably, the Patriot Act has broadened the government's power to encroach on the privacy of individuals protected by the Fourth Amendment. There have been anecdotal

evidence of gross abuses, misuses, and mismanagement of executive authority under the act. Because of the secrecy and lack of transparency of law enforcement agencies, the only credible evidence of widespread abuse comes from reports of the OIG of DOJ and court challenges by the ACLU and similar organizations.

In terms of mitigation of terrorism, between September 11, 2001, and December 31, 2014, there were 580 international terrorism-related convictions in the United States. A Senate subcommittee determined that at least 380 (66 percent) of those individuals were foreign-born (www.politifact.com/ truth-o-meter/statements/2017/mar/02/donald-trump/ trump-misleads-claim-about-terrorism-convictions-9/). The number of convictions for terrorist attacks planned or executed in the United States was only 40 of the 580 (www. politifact.com/truth-o-meter/statements/2017/mar/02/ donald-trump/trump-misleads-claim-about-terrorism-convictions-9/). It is noteworthy that clear acts of terrorism committed by white supremacists, including Dylann Roof who massacred nine black parishioners in Charlestown, South Carolina, are not counted as "terrorism" (https:// www.huffingtonpost.com/entry/domestic-terrorism-white-supremacists-islamist-extremists_us_594c46e4b0da2c731a84pdf; www.nytimes.com/2017/01/10/us/dylann-roof-trial-charleston.html).

Intelligence agencies have the technical capacity to snoop on digital communications. These agencies have classified capabilities in addition to the Patriot Act, as Edward Snowden has revealed (www.govtrack.us/congress/bills/110/hr6304/text; https://www. pbs.org/wgbh/frontline/article/how-edward-snowden-leaked-thousands-of-nsa-documents/). How much abuse occurs in the use of these capabilities remains to be determined.

The problem of domestic and international terrorism is ongoing. Most Americans are acutely aware of the devastating consequences of terrorist acts. Should we dispense with our constitutional protections to meet the increasing challenges of domestic and international terrorism?

Supreme Court justice Arthur Goldberg reflected, "This Court has gone far toward accepting the doctrine that civil liberty means the removal of all restraints from those crowds and that all local attempts to maintain order are impairments of the liberty of citizens. The choice is not between order and liberty. It is between liberty with order and anarchy without either. There is danger that, if the Court does not temper its doctrinaire logic with a little practical wisdom, it will convert the constitutional Bill of Rights into a suicide pact" (*Terminello v. City of Chicago*, 1949; https://supreme.justia.com/cases/federal/us/337/1/case.html). Our liberties are secure only so long as we are prepared to defend them. "Eternal vigilance is the price of liberty," as the maxim says. Liberty dies on the branch if each generation does not diligently water, cultivate, and fertilize the tree of liberty.

Congress must monitor and rectify abuses of the Patriot Act to ensure the constitutional rights of citizens are protected. The true guardians of liberty must always be citizens who remain vigilant and engaged to prevent government abuses committed in the name of public safety. Congress should subordinate the Patriot Act to the following language: "The right of the people to be secure in their persons, houses, papers, and effects, against unreasonable searches and seizures, shall not be violate, and no warrants shall issue, but upon probable cause, supported by oath or affirmation, and particularly describing the place to be searched, and the persons of things to be seized."

My deepest concerns and fears are best expressed in the metaphor (https://www.youtube.com/watch?v=sypsLSDgFK4) of the boiling frog. "If you plunge a frog into boiling water, it will immediately jump out. But if you place the frog into cool water and slowly heat it to boiling, the frog won't notice and will slowly cook to death." Will American citizens notice if encroachments on their privacy occur in incremental steps over a period of decades? Will they sacrifice the Bill of Rights on the altar of promised homeland security?

References

American Civil Liberties Union. https://www.aclu.org/files/pdfs/safefree/nsldecision.pdf.

American Civil Liberties Union. www.aclu.org/issues/national-security/privacy-and-surveillance/surveillance-under-patriot-act?/redirect=infographics/surveillance-under-patriot-act. Accessed March 2, 2018.

Boswell, James, and Christopher Hibbert, eds. 1986. *The Life of Samuel Johnson*. New York: Penguin Classics, p. 186.

Caselaw. https://supreme.justia.com/cases/federal/us/337/1/case.html. Accessed March 2, 2018.

Cato Institute. www.cato.org/blog/patriot-powers-roving-wiretaps. Accessed March 2, 2018.

Department of Justice, Office of Inspector General. https://oig.justice.gov/reports/2014/s1408.pdf. Accessed March 2, 2018; https://oig.justice.gov/reports/2015/s1503.pdf. Accessed March 2, 2018.

The Guardian. https://www.theguardian.com/commentisfree/2013/jun/09/abuse-of-patriot-act-must-end. Accessed March 2, 2018.

Heritage Foundation. www.heritage.org/terrorism/report/after-bin-laden-support-the-patriot-act. Accessed March 2, 2018.

http://www.washingtonpost.com/wp-srv/special/politics/prism-collection-documents/.
Accessed March 2, 2018.

https://archive.org/web/201609906022314/. Accessed March 2, 2018.

Huffington Post. https:// www.huffingtonpost.com/entry/domestic-terrorism-white-supremacist-islamist-extremist_us_594c46e4boda2c731a84.pdf. Accessed March 2, 2018.

Internet Archive: Wayback Machine. Web.archive.org/
web/20160906022314. Accessed March 2, 2018.

National Public Radio. https:// www.npr.org/
documents/2004/071304_doj_patriot.pdf. Accessed
March 2, 2018.

National Security Letters. https://g.twing.com/blog/blob/
attachments/Redacted-NSL-16-422732-Twitter.pdf.
Accessed March 2, 2018.

New York Times. www.nytimes.com/2017/01/10/us/dylann-
roof-trial-charleston.html?mcubz=3. Accessed March 2,
2018.

Politifact. www.politifact.com/truth-o-meter/
statements/2017/mar/02/donald-trump/trump-misleads-
claim-about-terrorism-convictions-9. Accessed March 2,
2018.

Public Broadcasting System. https://www.pbs.org/wgbh/
frontline/article/how-edward-snowden-leaked-thousands-
of-nsa-documents/. Accessed March 2, 2018.

United States Government Printing Office. https://www.gpo.
gov/fdsys/pkg/PLAW-107publ56/pdf/PLAW-107publ56.
pdf. Accessed March 2, 2018.

Washington Post. https://www.washingtonpost.com/world/
national-security/appeals-court-rules-nsa-record-collection-
violates-patriot-act/2015/05/07/c4fabfb8-f4bf-11e4-bcc4-
e8141e5eb0c9_story.html?utm_term=.f08eb3b9c5b5.
Accessed March 2, 2018.

www.oig/justice.gov/reports/2015/01505.pdf#page-1.
Accessed March 2, 2018.

YouTube. www.youtube.com/watch?v=sypsLSDgFk4.
Accessed March 2, 2018.

*Alemayehu G. Mariam is professor of political science, at Cali-
fornia State University-San Bernardino. He teaches constitutional
law, American government, and civil rights. He authored two*

constitutional law books. He practices law and has argued a case before the California Supreme Court. He earned his Ph.D. from the University of Minnesota and a J.D. from the University of Maryland.

All Souls Unitarian/Universalist Church: Why We Became a Sanctuary Church
Rev. Nori Rost

In some regard, the decision to ask my congregation to become a host Sanctuary congregation was a no-brainer. As Unitarian Universalists, we don't follow a common creed, nor do we all share a common belief. In my congregation there are humanists, atheists, Buddhists, pagans, theists, and more. What binds us together as a faith community is our attempts to embody seven guiding principles. These are:

> Belief in the inherent worth and dignity of every human;
>
> Justice, equity, and compassion in human relations;
>
> Acceptance of one another and encouragement to spiritual growth;
>
> A free and responsible search for truth and meaning;
>
> The right of conscience and the use of the democratic process in our Congregations and society at large;
>
> The goal of world community with peace, liberty, and justice for all; and
>
> Respect for the interdependent web of all existence, of which we are a part.

Unitarian Universalist churches don't seek to give you a road map for how to navigate this life (or make it to any future destinations, afterlife!); rather we use these seven principles to provide a compass by which folks can steer by their own north star. As such, we also draw on the wisdom of many sources of inspiration to guide us: sacred texts of all religions, humanist understandings of how we evolve as a species, the prophetic voices of leaders in the cause for justice and more.

So again, a no-brainer to ask my congregation to become a Sanctuary congregation. In fact, it was an idea that I had been toying with for the past few years, ever since hearing that our sister congregation, First Unitarian Society in Denver, Colorado, had made that leap.

Several years ago, they had joined a coalition of faith communities in the metro Denver area and had offered Sanctuary to two guests in the ensuing years; both of their guests were able to work out a deal with Immigration Control and Enforcement (ICE) to stay in the United States longer, as their cases were being reviewed.

So, I had been thinking of taking such a leap, myself, but hadn't made it a priority to do so until after the 2016 presidential election which put into power a man who was very vocal about not only further intimidating and attacking immigrants, but who also used racist metaphors to fan the flames of bigotry and ignorance of the immigrant communities in our midst.

The justification for our Unitarian Universalist church taking on this challenge was easily found. In fact, it's not really surprising that to learn that virtually every religion exhorts believers to show hospitality to strangers.

Judaism teaches: "When a stranger lives with you in your land, do not mistreat him. The stranger living with you must be treated as one of your native-born. Love him as yourself, for you were strangers in Egypt. I am the LORD your God" (Leviticus 19:34).

In Islam, the Quran states, "Do good unto your parents, and near of kin, and unto orphans, and the needy, and the neighbor from among your own people, and the neighbor who is a stranger, and the friend by your side, and the wayfarer, and those whom you rightfully possess. Verily, God does not love any of those who, full of self-conceit, act in a boastful manner" (Surah 4:36).

According to the Christian scriptures, Jesus tells his followers, in the Gospel of Matthew 25:25:31–46, that those who will inherit the realm of God are those who have clothed and fed, and cared for him. "Then the righteous will answer him, 'Lord, when did we see you hungry and feed you, or thirsty and give you something to drink? When did we see you a stranger and invite you in, or needing clothes and clothe you? When did we see you sick or in prison and go to visit you?' 'The King will reply, "Truly I tell you, whatever you did for one of the least of these brothers and sisters of mine, you did for me." ' "

Other faith traditions hold equally strong teachings: Hinduism, Ba'hai, Sikhism, Native American teachings. This makes sense to me. In every age, people of every stripe have experienced the brutality of famine, wars, disease, and other conditions that have made of them refugees and social outcasts, struggling to find a new home and a new hope for survival. Each learned from this to feel compassion, empathy for others who might find themselves in similar straits. It is sacred work that aligns us with the holy: the ability to put ourselves in the shoes of another who is suffering is at the core of the great religions.

And so, in May 2017, All Souls Unitarian Universalist Church voted overwhelmingly to become a host Sanctuary congregation. Over 90 percent of the members present said a resounding *yes* to being the first (and so far, only) such congregation in Colorado Springs, Colorado. We, too, are lucky, in that as we were considering making this move as a congregation, a Sanctuary Coalition was being formed in our city. From the moment we said yes, we were a part of a larger community of folks from different faith traditions, including the members of the First United Church of Christ and the Colorado Springs Quakers, both congregations who wholeheartedly came aboard the Sanctuary movement, even though they did not have the space to house an immigrant guest family, as well as a sprinkling of individuals from other faith traditions whose churches had not or would not make the decision to join the coalition.

We were not alone. Still this wasn't a decision made rashly by members of All Souls. There were many valid concerns raised during the forums held in advance of the vote. What about safety issues? What if the church were vandalized? What if an immigrant guest had an accident and was injured? Would I, as the minister, be open to arrest? What about the board of trustees?

I answered these questions the best I could, trying to assuage any fears, but the reality is, I told them, we don't know what will happen; we can't prepare for every contingency. We must step out in faith that, regardless of what may happen, this is the right decision to make.

And of course, nothing went in the linear fashion we had hoped. In July 2017, our church basement flooded after a series of torrential rains. This meant our children's religious education department had to be moved temporarily; that was also the space we were preparing for an immigrant guest. In August, well before any repairs could even be started, we had a request for Sanctuary referred to us by the Metro Denver Sanctuary Coalition. I have to be honest: I was very resistant. Not only was our basement flooded, we hadn't even begun construction on a shower project that would provide a place for any guests to get clean! It was clear that All Souls wasn't ready, and I expected the rest of the Coalition to see that. Instead, an immigrant woman said, "I would live in a closet with no running water if it meant I was able to stay with my family."

With that perspective, I changed course. At the end of August we welcomed our first guest, Elmer, and his three-year-old son, David. Elmer's wife and two other children remained in the Denver suburb where they owned a house, but David, a U.S. citizen himself, came with his father, because they couldn't afford childcare. They moved into my office—the only space available and I moved into the Small Hall, a fellowship area where we serve coffee and treats on Sunday following our worship services.

Currently, it has been over two months since Elmer and David have taken up residence at All Souls. David has become a great "coworker" bringing his race tracks and cars out into the Small Hall to play. Elmer is a cheerful, easygoing man who waits to hear from his lawyer what his next best move will be.

I don't know what will happen; I don't know if Elmer's case is compelling enough to be granted a stay of deportation with an opportunity to present why he should be allowed to stay. As for me, it's a clear choice: Elmer and his wife both work full-time, pay taxes, own a home, and are active members of their communities. They present no threat to any individuals or to the well-being of our nation. They are, in fact, assets to our nation, with so many gifts to share. It saddens me to think their family may fall prey to racist, xenophobic policies.

"Who is my neighbor?" asked the expert in legalities in the parable of the Good Samaritan, found in Luke 10:26–37. Jesus had just told him to love his neighbor as much as he loved himself, but he was looking for permission to continue to be exclusive—to name some people, *neighbors* and other people, *strangers*—the other, dangerous, to be avoided. Of course, most Christians know how this story ends: the neighbor is the one in need. The one in need is the one we are to love as much as we love ourselves.

And that's why it's alarming to see so many who profess to be people of faith rejecting the pleas of the immigrants and refugees in great need. With greater threats to family stability and well-being due to ICE deportation raids and the newly minted, controversial revised travel ban executive order signed by the president, we see a marked departure from the major tenets of our faiths.

I guess that's not surprising either. In tumultuous times such as these, it can be easy—comforting, even—to want to define our "enemies" by race, ethnicity, religious identity. If "they" are dangerous, then the solution is clear: keep "them" out. If they're already here, living among us, drive "them" out.

But, of course, humankind is so much more complex than the good guy/bad guy name tags we want to put on people at the door of our heart. Still, I believe, at the end of the day, that we Americans line up with the words of the poem by Emma Lazarus, inscribed on the Statue of Liberty that welcomes new arrivals to our shores.

"Give me your tired, your poor,
Your huddled masses yearning to breathe free,
The wretched refuse of your teeming shore.
Send these, the homeless, tempest-tossed, to me:
I lift my lamp beside the golden door."

That's at the heart of what we hold dear, what our faith traditions call us to, what our humanity demands: to see our humanity in strangers and call them kin. To echo the words of another spiritual leader, Ram Dass, at the end of the day, "we're all just walking each other home."

I don't yet know what will happen with Elmer's case. I do know I am honored to call him kin, to companion him on this journey that will hopefully lead to the home he has made for himself and his family. If not, at the very least, we have provided an opportunity for him to have more time with his family. I think Jesus, and Gandhi, and the Buddha, and Dr. King, and all the other spiritual luminaries we aspire to emulate, would agree.

The Rev. Nori Rost is the settled minister of All Souls Unitarian Universalist Church in Colorado Springs, Colorado. She has an MDiv from Iliff School of Theology, Denver, and a DMin from Episcopal Divinity School in Cambridge, Massachusetts.

Cyber Security and the Department of Homeland Security
Adilene Sandoval

The Department of Homeland Security (DHS) was created in response to the September 11 attacks. The mission of the DHS is to ensure a homeland that is safe, secure, and resilient against terrorism and other hazards (ODNI Home 2015). Within the mission of the DHS there are five main concepts that are emphasized in order to protect the United States from any outside harm such as that happened on September 11, 2001. The five core concepts are to prevent terrorism and enhancing security, secure and manage our borders, enforce and administer our immigration laws, safeguard and secure cyberspace, and ensure resilience to disaster (Review of the DHS Implementation 2015). Each concept provides an understanding that encompasses the responsibility of the DHS to the nation. Safeguarding and securing U.S. cyberspace is a core concept of the federal government due to the interconnectedness the Internet is able to provide around the world that places critical infrastructure at risk of cyberattacks. In securing cyberspace, the DHS works to analyze and reduce cyber threats and vulnerabilities, distribute threat warnings, and coordinate the response to cyber incidents to ensure that our computers, networks, and cyber systems remain safe (https://www.oig.dhs.gov/assets/Mgmt/2016/OIG-16-142-Sep16.pdf). The DHS, like many other federal agencies, depends on information technology (IT) systems and computer networks for essential day-to-day operation.

Securing cyberspace is a main goal of DHS. There are essential components of the DHS that help ensure the security of cyberspace. In January 2016, the U.S. Government Accountability Office (GAO) reported to the Congressional Committees that the DHS needs to enhance capabilities, improve planning, and support greater adoption of its National Cybersecurity Protection System ("Our Mission" 2016). During the inspection in January 2016, the GAO discovered that the DHS's National Cybersecurity Protection System (NCPS) had partially met its stated system objectives. There are four objectives that the NCPS focuses on; they are intrusion detection, intrusion prevention, analytics, and information sharing ("Our Mission" 2016). For intrusion detection the NCPS did not fully meet its objective because there was limited ability to detect possible malicious activity entering or leaving computer networks in federal agencies. In order for intrusion detection to fully work, the NCPS needs to scan network traffic for potential malicious activity by detecting abnormalities in the network. Having limited ability to detect intrusions within observed network traffic places the DHS with a massive obstacle that needs to be overcome to prevent cyberattacks. Intrusion prevention then becomes a proactive strategy in securing cyberspace from malicious e-mails. Its limitation lies in the fact that malicious content within web traffic is not detected. The analytics of the NCPS are tools that help analyze the characteristics of malicious code ("Securing Federal Networks" 2017). Lastly, information sharing is one of the most valuable objectives within the NCPS of the DHS. Information sharing between federal agencies and the private sector is crucial in securing U.S. cyberspace.

The mission of the DHS's Network Security Development (NSD) division is to "improve cybersecurity to federal departments, agencies, and partners by developing the technologies and establishing the services needed to fulfill CS&C's cybersecurity mission." On December 8, 2015, President Barack Obama signed into law the Cybersecurity Act of 2015. The law establishes information sharing between the federal government and the private sector for cybersecurity purposes. Within the Cybersecurity Act of 2015, provision Title IV, Section 406, states that "Covered Agencies" (in this case DHS) operate "Covered Systems." Covered systems refer to national security systems that use telecommunications or information systems operating in federal agencies (covered agencies). Under the aforementioned provision of the Cybersecurity Act of 2015, there was a list by which the DHS had to abide by no later than 240 days after the enactment of the act. By September 26, 2016, the Office of Inspector General reviewed the DHS in regards of the implementation of Title IV, Section 406 of the Cybersecurity Act of 2015 ("DHS Needs to Enhance . . ." 2016). In this review, the DHS was finally able to implement procedures and policies that are able to ensure the protect the information sharing between the DHS, other federal agencies, and the private sector that together will protect the critical infrastructure of the United States.

Even after all the technological advances achieved over the past decade, federal agencies are still having trouble protecting their computer networks and systems. Whether it is a lack of resources or a lack of personnel, the DHS's Network Security Development has not been able to fully meet its objectives to ensure that no vulnerability exists in the cyber realm. Protecting U.S. cyberspace is crucial for the safety of the nation and its citizens because any form of intrusion to federal computer networks and critical infrastructure could be catastrophic to the day-to-day functions of the U.S. government. Any form of intrusion into the computer networks and systems by a foreign or domestic enemy can lead the United States into chaos, thereby threatening the well-being of its citizens. It is the DHS's responsibility to ensure that all other federal and state agencies computer networks are functioning at its highest standard. Thus, it is crucial that the DHS is equipped with all the necessary instruments, resources, and labor to prevent cyberattacks from any adversary.

References

"DHS Needs to Enhance Capabilities, Improve Planning, and Support Greater Adoption of Its National Cybersecurity Protection System." United States Government Accountability Office. January 2016. http://www.gao.gov/assets/680/674829.pdf.

"ODNI Home." Home. December 18, 2015. https://www.dni.gov/index.php/ic-legal-reference-book/cybersecurity-act-of-2015.

"Our Mission." Department of Homeland Security. May 11, 2016. https://www.dhs.gov/our-mission.

"Review of the Department of Homeland Security's Implementation of the Cybersecurity Act of 2015." United States Government Publishing Office. September 26, 2016.

https://www.oig.dhs.gov/assets/Mgmt/2016/OIG-16-142-Sep16.pdf.

"Securing Federal Networks." Department of Homeland Security. March 16, 2017. https://www.dhs.gov/topic/securing-federal-networks.

Adilene Sandoval is a candidate for a master's degree in National Security Studies at California State University-San Bernardino.

Congressional Oversight of the Department of Homeland Security Undermines Security and Accountability
Christina Villegas

In the wake of the September 11 terrorist attacks, the Bush administration and Congress worked together to pass the Homeland Security Act of 2002. The objective was to streamline federal efforts to combat national security threats by consolidating 22 executive branch agencies, ranging in scope from the U.S. Customs Service to the Coast Guard and Secret Service, into the newly created Department of Homeland Security (DHS). Congress, however, failed to consolidate its own oversight of the fused agencies and instead retained its pre-DHS jurisdictional structure. Consequently, since its inception, DHS has reported to between 80 and 120 largely unrelated congressional committees and subcommittees. This fragmented system of oversight effectively cripples the agency's mission and undermines its accountability to the American people.

Over the past half century, the country has experienced a dramatic expansion of executive power as Congress has continued to delegate widespread authority to executive departments to implement often vaguely defined congressional objectives. Congressional oversight, which occurs at the committee level and involves a variety of activities from authorization and appropriation of funds to investigative and confirmation hearings, is meant to ensure that agency action complies with the intentions of the people's elected representatives in Congress. As Oleszek et al. (2016) explain in a manual on congressional procedure, "A fundamental objective of legislative oversight is to hold executive officials accountable for the implementation of delegated authority" (376). In other words, since members of Congress are ultimately accountable to voters, they have a duty both to ensure that the bureaucrats staffing agencies are not misusing or abusing their delegated authority and to make legislative adjustments to agency mandates to promote efficient, effective, and accountable policy making.

The DHS, which is endowed with the task of preventing terrorism and enhancing the nation's security, has a budget ranging from $40–65 billion and interacts with more people on a daily basis than any other federal agency. Congressional oversight is, thus, critical for ensuring that resources are properly allocated and that the department is working to achieve its mission without violating important civil liberties. Unfortunately, the disjointed and incoherent system of congressional oversight of DHS inhibits the effective exercise of delegated authority and diminishes accountability.

The Center for Strategic and International Studies (2004) reports that, in comparison with the Department of Defense, in which 80 percent of oversight is conducted by those with defense-related expertise in the House and Senate Armed Services Committees and the Defense and Military Construction Subcommittees, all 100 senators and over 90 percent of representatives oversee some aspect of DHS. Thus, there is little incentive for anyone in Congress to acquire expertise or a comprehensive view of homeland security beyond the particular jurisdiction of their committee. Shortly after DHS's inception over 15 years ago, the National Commission on Terrorist Attacks upon the United States (2004) recognized in the *9/11 Commission Report* that this system of oversight is dysfunctional. Listing several recommendations for improving homeland security efforts, commissioners specifically warned Congress to "create a single principal point of oversight and review for homeland security" (421). Yet, in spite of the *Commission Report* and multiple other bipartisan calls for reform over the years, Congress has made no effort to streamline its oversight structure and has failed to pass even a single reauthorization bill clarifying which goals it wants DHS to prioritize. Instead, members of Congress have fought to preserve their jurisdictional slice of DHS oversight, which gives them the ability to engage in valuable re-election activities such as holding public hearings, political grandstanding, and influencing agency actions on behalf of interest groups and constituents.

While maintaining the status quo helps serve the election goals of incumbent members of Congress, congressional inaction hinders U.S. national security. Under the current level of oversight, DHS officials are forced to respond to thousands of requests for information and testimony from various congressional committees every year. In many instances, the committees requesting information have priorities only loosely related to homeland security and often require duplicative information or emphasize unrelated and even incongruous goals. This state of affairs not only prevents DHS from acting as a coordinated unit, but it also leads to a huge diversion of critical financial and personnel resources that would be better utilized identifying, preventing, and responding to security threats. In a letter to the chair of the House Homeland Security Committee, former secretary of DHS Janet Napolitano complained that members of her staff "spend more time responding to congressional requests and requirements than executing their mandated homeland security responsibilities" (Caldwell 2011).

Another problem for national security arises when committees do not act when they need to because they are focused on other priorities that fall more directly under their jurisdiction. For example, Congress largely blamed DHS for its failure to identify the Christmas "Underwear" bomber, Umar Farouk Abdulmutallab, as a threat before he boarded a plane headed for Detroit in December 2009. But little attention was given to the fact that the Senate Finance Committee, which retained jurisdiction over DHS's newly organized Customs and Border Patrol (CBP) unit, was so consumed by debate over the Patient Protection and Affordable Care Act that they failed to hold confirmation hearings on Obama's nominee for CBP commissioner, Alan Berson. Thus, the Finance Committee left CBP, the agency in charge of preventing dangerous individuals from boarding aircraft headed to the United States, without a leadership team for months before and after Abdulmutallab's attempted attack (Kaniewski 2010).

The dispersed nature of congressional oversight also creates problems for responsibility and accountability. When the directives coming from the various committees are disjointed, ambiguous, and even contradictory, DHS lacks the incentive and ability to comply with congressional mandates. Authority is, thus, ceded to DHS to act and implement policies as it wishes. Furthermore, parochial interests and single issue lobbies have an easier time influencing policy in their favor even if their demands fall outside the scope of DHS's mission. In such a situation, congressional lawmakers are better able to serve special interests behind the scenes and are also shielded from the blame when something goes wrong. Whenever there is a failure in policy, the party responsible is usually elusive to the press and the public. Lawmakers can therefore hide their own failure to provide clear direction by engaging in high-profile critiques and investigations of agency actions. This deprives voters of the ability to hold responsible individuals accountable for waste, fraud, and abuse.

Without major reform of the current oversight regime, the DHS will continue to operate in an inefficient and unaccountable way. Until members of Congress are electorally rewarded for prioritizing security and accountability above power and influence, however, they are unlikely to adopt positive changes on their own. Voters and members of the media, who are concerned about restoring accountability and improving security, should demand that Congress implement the 9/11 Commission's recommendation to consolidate oversight of DHS and that Congress pass an authorization bill providing clear statutory direction for agency action.

References

Caldwell, Alicia. 2011. "DHS Most Overseen Department." *The Associated Press.* https://homeland.house.gov/press/associated-press-inside-washington-dhs-most-overseen-department/

Center for Strategic and International Studies. 2004. *Untangling the Web: Congressional Oversight and the Department of Homeland Security.* https://csis-prod.s3.amazonaws.com/s3fs-public/legacy_files/files/attachments/041210_dhs_whitepaper.pdf

Kaniewski, Daniel. 2010. "Congress Should Consider Its Own Failures in Attempted Bombing." *Roll Call.* http://www.rollcall.com/news/43351-1.html

National Commission on Terrorist Attacks upon the United States. 2004. *The 9/11 Commission Report.* http://govinfo.library.unt.edu/911/report/911Report.pdf

Oleszek, Walter J., Mark J. Oleszek, Elizabeth Rybicki, and Bill Heniff Jr. 2016. *Congressional Procedures & the Policy Process,* 10th ed. Los Angeles, CA: Sage.

Christina Villegas is an assistant professor of political science at California State University, San Bernardino. She has a Ph.D. from the Institute of Philosophical Studies, University of Dallas.

4 Profiles

Introduction

This chapter profiles the organizations and people involved in the homeland security issue. It begins with brief descriptions of the key stakeholder organizations that are active in providing for homeland security policy or its implementation or lobby for or against proposals to cope with homeland security problems.

After describing and discussing the organizational actors in the arena of homeland security policy making, the chapter profiles individual actors involved. These stakeholders include government officials, leaders of nongovernmental groups active in the politics of the issue, and leading scholars/analysts from the major "think tank" organizations active on the issue. These organizational and individual profiles are presented in alphabetical order.

Organizations

Al Qaeda

The international radical Islamic terrorist organization has roots going back to 1979–1989 and the Soviet War in Afghanistan. When the Soviets invaded the country, young Muslims

---

A New Orleans resident in the Upper Ninth Ward talks with a Federal Emergency Management Agency (FEMA) officer as he clears debris from his home following Hurricane Katrina in 2005. Some failures by FEMA led to harsh criticisms of the Department of Homeland Security, FEMA's departmental home in the federal executive branch. (FEMA)

from around the world volunteered to fight a jihad, or holy war, against them. Osama bin Laden, the son of a wealthy Saudi Arabian construction magnate, volunteered, funding the movement generously and fighting actual battles.

When the Soviets departed, the leadership established a base (Al Qaeda), and bin Laden became its emir and led the movement to prepare to fight anywhere in the world. He had been exiled from Saudi Arabia and leaving Afghanistan moved to a sanctuary in Sudan, from where he laid the groundwork for his jihad against the West. Beginning a fatwa against the United States, Al Qaeda fought the U.S. deployment in Somalia, downing two Black Hawk helicopters in 1993. It took credit for bombing the World Trade Center in 1993. Responding to mounting international pressure, Sudan forced bin Laden and Al Qaeda to leave, and they returned to Afghanistan. He issued a new fatwa against the United States in 1998 and merged with the Egyptian Islamist Jihad headed by Ayman al Zawahiri, who became the number two leader in Al Qaeda. In 2000, Al Qaeda operatives attacked the USS *Cole* in Yemen, killing 17 sailors. On September 11, 2001, Al Qaeda terrorists hijacked four U.S. passenger jet airliners and executed their devastating attack against the United States, killing nearly 3,000 civilians. The Taliban government in Afghanistan protected bin Laden and Al Qaeda, and the United States launched its war to topple the Taliban government. It has since become the longest war in U.S. history. Osama bin Laden fled, decentralizing Al Qaeda. Despite the United States' killing of Osama bin Laden and many of the leadership of Al Qaeda, recent National Intelligence estimates show Al Qaeda is once again gaining strength and has rebuilt itself despite U.S. efforts against it. Today, Al Qaeda and the Islamic State of Iraq and Syria (ISIS, also known as Daesh) are the leading international terrorist groups supporting and inspiring attacks on the West and on the United States, in particular, and thus are the leading threat to homeland security.

American Civil Liberties Union

Founded in 1920, the American Civil Liberties Union (ACLU) works nationally and through local chapters to protect the civil rights of citizens as guaranteed by the U.S. Constitution. It annually publishes many policy statements, pamphlets, studies, and reports on civil rights issues. It has frequently criticized the DHS and its implementation of Patriot Acts I and II. It publishes semiannually a newsletter, *Civil Liberties Alert*. It has been a leading partner in efforts to reform or amend the USA Patriot Act and to rectify what it determines are civil rights abuses in procedural matters designed to cope with homeland security issues, in particular, with the efforts of the DHS to remove unauthorized immigrants in an expedited manner. The ACLU has promoted a guest-worker program and legalization programs, more generally, and advocates for enactment of the Dream Act and for comprehensive immigration reform. It has sections for LGBT rights, civil liberties, and immigration. It opposes the Trump-ordered travel ban.

American Conservative Union

The American Conservative Union (ACU) is the oldest and largest of the numerous conservative lobbying organizations. Its purpose is to communicate effectively and advance the goals and principles of conservatism through one multi-issue, umbrella organization. ACU supports capitalism, belief in the doctrine of original intent of the framers of the Constitution, traditional moral values, and commitment to a strong national defense. Since 1994 it has sponsored "town meetings" to spearhead the conservative response to support such issues as military protection and defending the homeland against international terrorists. It lobbies against liberalization of immigration policy reforms. One device it uses effectively is to rate the members of Congress according to their votes on issues of concern to conservatives. Those ratings are used by a host of almanac and reference guides across the political spectrum. ACU's rating system has been copied by many other organizations. It publishes many print, audio, and video materials and television documentaries to promote public opinion on its issues of concern. Since 1974 it has hosted the annual Conservative Political Action Conference attended by thousands of conservative activists and leaders from across the country to discuss issues and controversies and has become an important factor in the Republican Party's presidential nomination process.

American Enterprise Institute

Founded in 1938, and headquartered in Washington, D.C., American Enterprise Institute (AEI) is a public policy think tank, a nonpartisan, nonprofit, 501 (c) (3) educational institute defending human dignity, expanding human potential, and building a freer and safer world whose scholars advance ideas rooted in a belief in democracy, free enterprise, American strength and global leadership, and those at the periphery of society, and a pluralistic, entrepreneurial culture. It is unaffiliated with any academic institution. AEI studies pursue data-driven research about a broad range of topics, focusing on current critical challenges and pursuing ideas not yet to be widely recognized. Its studies are multidisciplinary from the perspectives of economics, education, health care, poverty, foreign and defense studies, public opinion, politics, society, and culture. It engages with those who hold different points of view, believing a competition of ideas is essential to a free society. This approach gives it access and credibility with decision makers and government leaders across the country, fostering cooperation at a time when the United States is rent by deep divisions. It promotes reform in many policy areas, including privacy rights, civil liberty rights, and national and homeland security concerns.

American Immigration Control Foundation

Founded in 1983, the American Immigration Control Foundation (AICF) is a nonprofit research and educational organization (a think tank) whose primary goal is to inform Americans about the need for a reasonable immigration policy based on the nation's interests and needs. It has published reports on what it labels America's immigration crisis. It is a prominent national voice for immigration control and for educating Americans on what it views as the disastrous effects of uncontrolled immigration, and most particularly advocates for amendments of immigration law to better control the border, homeland security issues, and lone-wolf terrorism. AICF conducts public education campaigns to influence public opinion on the issue, campaigning through direct mail, paid advertisements, opinion surveys, and public appearances by its organization's leadership on radio and television.

American Immigration Law Foundation

Founded in 1987 as a tax-exempt, nonprofit educational, and service organization, the American Immigration Law Foundation (AILF) promotes understanding among the general public of immigration law and policy through education, policy analysis, and support of litigation. It has three core program areas: the Legal Action Center, the Public Education Program, and the Exchange Visitor Program. It has often been a critic of the USA Patriot Act and of the DHS's expedited removal program. It considers the current reaction to international terrorism influencing immigration policy to be a threat to civil liberties that is as great as is international terrorism itself. It opposed enactment of Patriot Act II. It is headquartered in Washington, D.C.

American Immigration Lawyers Association

The American Immigration Lawyers Association (AILA) is the national association of immigration lawyers created to promote justice and to advocate for fair and reasonable immigration law and policy. It seeks to advance the quality of immigration and nationality law and practice, and to enhance the professional development of its members who defend individuals charged with being in the United States illegally and in deportation hearings. It lobbies against what it considers to be unfair or anti-civil liberty provisions in immigration law, particularly the USA Patriot Act and the Department of Homeland Security Act. It has been an outspoken critic of and has supported litigation against the Muslim travel ban, and generally of the Trump administration's approach to homeland security by cracking down on immigration control. It supports comprehensive immigration reform legislation. It is headquartered in Washington, D.C.

American Library Association

Based in Chicago, Illinois, the American Library Association (ALA) is the oldest and largest library association in the world, with more than 64,000 members. Its stated mission is to promote the highest-quality library and information service and public access to information. ALA offers professional services and publications to its members and to nonmembers. It entered the homeland security political fray by joining in a coalition with other organizations attempting to amend the USA Patriot Act and the alleged privacy and civil liberties concerns by the manner in which the DHS implements its policies.

Americans for Prosperity

This organization is a 501 (c) (4) PAC, founded in 2004, as one of the first of this type of "Superpac" organizations. It is a very conservative political advocacy group lobbying on conservative issues, including a hard-line crackdown at the border immigration policy approach for the DHS and ICE. It was founded by David Koch and Karl Rove and raises huge amounts of "dark money" for funding negative TV ads, lower taxes, and government deregulation. It is headquartered in Arlington, Virginia.

Association of Patriotic Arab-Americans in the Military

Created shortly after September 11, 2001, the Association of Patriotic Arab-Americans in the Military (APAAM) is an organization of current and former Arab-Americans in the military, of whom there are about 3,500 serving in the U.S. armed forces. It is the first organization to organize them, building a contact list of all military members, past and present. APAAM seeks to represent them with one voice. It promotes education of Americans and American Arab communities of a dual patriotism to their ancestral heritage and dedication of the United States by emphasizing service and sacrifice as military men and women. It attempts to close the gap between bigotry, ignorance, and prejudice, on the one hand, and tolerance, on the other. APAAM was founded by U.S. Marine Corps gunnery sergeant Jamal S. Baadani, whose father was a refugee from Yemen who immigrated to the United States from Egypt. Jamal joined the corps at age 17. He founded APAAM as a nonpolitical association to represent Arab Americans in the military, to highlight their service and sacrifice and the sacrifice of Arab Americans post-9/11. Arab Americans experienced a backlash after the attacks, including Jamal's family. As U.S. military members, APAAM members have sworn an oath to protect and defend the Constitution of the United States against all enemies, foreign and domestic, and are prepared to sacrifice their lives for the protection of freedom for all Americans. They are headquartered in Ontario, California.

Border Policy Research Institute

Border Policy Research Institute (BPRI) is a multidisciplinary research institute (think tank) housed at Western Washington University (WWU). It conducts research to inform policy makers on matters relating to the Canada-U.S. border that focus especially on trade and transportation, economics, immigration, and border security. WWU established BPRI to promote research, academic programs, and public forums and programs on critical policy issues affecting the Pacific Northwest region. BPRI works closely with cognate programs and departments at WWU and collaborates with many public and private entities in the Pacific Northwest region. It is directed by Professor Laurie Trautman who leads a staff of six WWU faculty researchers and six visiting fellows.

Bureau of Immigration and Customs Enforcement

The Bureau of Immigration and Customs Enforcement (ICE) is within the Department of Homeland Security (DHS). It enforces all federal laws governing border control, customs, trade, and immigration to promote homeland security and public safety. It was established in 2003 with the creation of the DHS and through the merger of the investigative and enforcement elements of the former Immigration and Naturalization Service (INS). Currently, ICE has more than 20,000 employees located in more than 400 offices in the United States and in 46 foreign countries, and has an annual budget of $6 billion. ICE has three operational directorates: Homeland Security Investigations, Enforcement and Removal Operations, and the Office of the Principal Legal Advisor (OPLA). OPLA provides legal representation in all exclusion, deportation, and removal proceedings, against criminal immigrants, terrorists, and human rights abusers in immigration courts across the country. OPLA provides critical legal support to ICE components focusing on customs, cyber security, worksite enforcement, ethics, employment law, tort claims, and administrative law issues. These directorates of ICE are supported by the DHS's Directorate of Management and Administration. It is headquartered in Washington, D.C.

Business Roundtable

The Business Roundtable is an association of chief executive officers of leading corporations, who have a combined workforce of more than 10 million employees in the United States. It advocates public policies that foster vigorous economic growth, a dynamic global economy, and a well-trained and productive workforce essential for future competitiveness. It is selective in the issues it studies. A major criterion it uses is the impact the problem will have on the economic well-being of the nation. Working in task forces on specific issues, it directs research, supervises the preparation of position papers, recommends policy options and lobbies Congress and the administration on selected issues. It supports establishing an expanded guest-worker program, earned legalization, and comprehensive immigration reform. It opposes the travel ban and the impact of the homeland security law for causing backlogs in visa applications for foreign workers (e.g., H-1B, L-Visas). It is headquartered in Washington, D.C.

Catholic Legal Immigration Network

Catholic Legal Immigration Network promotes the dignity and protects the rights of immigrants in partnership with a dedicated network of Catholic and community legal immigration programs, including sanctuary churches. It is headquartered in Silver Spring, Maryland. It provides research and analysis of the significant changes in immigration policy announced by the Trump administration and proposed legislation backed by the administration. It provides summary and analysis of federal court cases, such as those concerning the travel ban. It provides a three-part guide to counter hateful anti-immigrant narratives through legislative testimony, local media work, and social media outlets. It provides a webinar series for advocates in removal orders and proceedings, and "practice tips" for counsels involved in enhanced enforcement of border security rules and procedures. It studies and publishes a state-by-state overview of legal mechanisms to combat the unauthorized practice of immigration law to assist noncitizen victims of that practice.

The Cato Institute

The Cato Institute was founded in 1977 as a public policy research foundation headquartered in Washington, D.C. Named for the *Cato Letters,* a series of libertarian pamphlets that helped lay the philosophical foundation of the American

Revolution, the institute describes its mission as seeking to broaden the parameters of public policy debate to allow consideration of the traditional American principles of limited government, individual liberty, free markets, and peace. To pursue those goals, the Cato Institute strives to achieve greater involvement of the intelligent, concerned lay public in questions of policy and the proper role of government. It is a nonprofit, tax-exempt educational foundation or "think tank."

Center for American Progress

The Center for American Progress (CAP) was founded in 2003 by John Podesta as a progressive policy research and advocacy think tank organization. It is based in Washington, D.C. It advocates for comprehensive immigration reform, the Dream Act, and President Obama's DACA (Deferred Action for Childhood Arrivals) and DAPA (Deferred Action for Parental Accountability) programs, and opposes the immigration "crackdown" approach of conservative organizations, the Muslim travel ban, and the civil liberties and privacy concerns arising from the USA Patriots Acts I and II, and the DHS law.

Center for Democracy and Technology

The Center for Democracy and Technology (CDT) promotes democratic values and constitutional liberties in the digital age. By bringing together experts in law, technology, and policy, CDT seeks practical solutions to enhance free expression and privacy in global communications technologies and cyber war issues. It states that it is dedicated to building a consensus among all parties interested in the future of the Internet and other communications media. It has become a lobbying organization on the issue and has joined in coalition with other organizations concerned with civil liberty issues around the establishment of the DHS and USA Patriot Acts I and II. It is headquartered in Washington, D.C.

Center for Immigration Studies

The Center for Immigration Studies (CIS) is an independent, nonpartisan, nonprofit research organization founded in 1985. It is a think tank devoted exclusively to research and policy analysis of economic, social, demographic, fiscal, and other impacts of immigration on the United States. It seeks to expand knowledge and understanding of the need for an immigration policy that gives first concern to broad national interests. It describes itself as pro-immigrant but favors low immigration that seeks fewer immigrants but a warmer welcome for those admitted. Led by Mark Krikorian, it publishes *Immigration Review*. It is notably anti-illegal immigration. It is located in Washington, D.C.

Center for Migration Studies

The Center for Migration Studies (CMS) of New York was founded in 1964. It is one of the premier institutes for migration studies in the United States. It strives to facilitate the study of sociodemographic, historical, economic, political, legislative, and pastoral aspects of human migration and refugee movements. In 1969 it incorporated as an educational, nonprofit institute. It brings an independent perspective to the interdisciplinary study of international migration and refugees without the institutional constraints of government analysis and special interest groups, or the profit considerations of private research firms. It claims to be the only institute in the United States devoted exclusively to understanding and educating the public on the causes and consequences of human mobility at both origin and destination countries. It generates and facilitates the dissemination of new knowledge and the fostering of effective policies. It publishes a leading scholarly journal in the field, the *International Migration Review*. For many years it held an annual conference in immigration policy in Washington, D.C., that brought together government officials, academic scholars of the issue, lawyers involved in immigration matters, and activists in immigration-related advocacy organizations, such as church-affiliated groups.

Center for Privacy and Technology Policy

The Center for Privacy and Technology at Georgetown Law Center is a think tank 501 (c) (3) nonprofit focused on privacy and surveillance law and policy. It studies the impact of government surveillance and commercial data practices on vulnerable communities, such as racial and ethnic minorities, immigrants, LGBT persons, and the poor. It provides intellectual and legal foundations for reform of U.S. consumer privacy law, especially on new technologies such as biometrics, wearables, and the Internet of things, and cyber software and hardware. It offers technology-intensive courses for students to become leaders in privacy practice, policy making, and advocacy. It supports fellows doing research in the field. Its six faculty directors work under the founding executive director of Georgetown Law Center on Privacy and Technology, Alvaro Bedoya. It has several research fellows and deputy technologists. Its experts work with companies and legislators to craft innovative policy and technical solutions to cyber and IT-related problems.

Center for Strategic and International Studies

The Center for Strategic and International Studies (CSIS) was founded in 1962 in Washington, D.C., by David Abshire and Admiral Arleigh Burke as a bipartisan, nonprofit, policy research think tank to provide strategic insights and policy resolutions to help decision makers chart a course toward a better world. Its CEO and president is John Hamre. It is an international policy institution focused on defense and security, regional study, and transnational challenges ranging from energy to global development and economic integration, ranked number one for international security. It has 220 full-time staff and a large network of affiliated scholars conducting research and analysis and developing policy initiatives. CSIS conducts research for Congress, the executive branch, and the media to explain current events and to make bipartisan policy recommendations to improve U.S. strategy.

Center for the Study of Hate Crimes and Extremism

A nonpartisan, domestic research and policy center, it examines bigotry on both the regional and national levels, on methods used to advocate extremism, and on the use of terrorism to deny civil or human rights to people on the basis of race, ethnicity, religion, gender, sexual orientation, disability, or other relevant status characteristics. The center sponsors public conferences, collaborates with international and national news media outlets, and maintains an Internet site with information about and in cooperation with government organizations, human relations organizations, nonprofit organizations, and law enforcement. It is housed within the Department of Criminal Justice at California State University-San Bernardino. Its director, Professor Brian Levin, was prominently interviewed by the national media after the lone-wolf terrorist attack in San Bernardino in 2015.

Center on Budget and Policy Priorities

The Center on Budget and Policy Priorities (CBPP) is a nonpartisan research and policy institute that studies federal and state policies to reduce poverty and inequality and to restore fiscal responsibility in equitable and effective ways. It was founded in 1981 to analyze federal budget priorities with a focus on how budget choices affect lower-income Americans. Currently, it responds to new developments and has entered into new areas of research. In the states, CBPP collaborates with nonprofits, including more than 40 members of the State Priorities Partnership, to build their capacity for budget and policy analysis and to participate effectively in policy debates, including, most recently, climate change. It is headquartered in Washington, D.C.

Congressional Research Service

Begun in 1914 at the insistence of Senator Robert La Follette, Sr. (R-WI), and Representative John Nelson (R-WI), the Congressional Research Service is sometimes known as the think tank of the U.S. Congress. It publishes an annual *Congressional Research Services Review*. It works exclusively for Congress, providing policy and legal analysis to committees and to members of both the U.S. House of Representatives and the Senate, regardless of political party affiliation. It is a legislative branch agency within the Library of Congress. It has been a valued and respected resource for more than a century. Its analyses are authoritative, confidential, objective, and nonpartisan. It has recently issued research reports on national security topics, on secrecy and information policy, on intelligence, on homeland security, and on terrorism. It has a staff of 600 employees located in Washington, D.C.

Council of Graduate Schools

The Council of Graduate Schools conducts research and coordinates programs and activities to advance graduate education and to promote U.S. competitiveness in the global economy. It has been a sharp critic of the negative impact on graduate education and graduate enrollments of the USA Patriot Acts, the SEVIS program of the DHS, and the State Department's tightening of the student visa applications programs generally. Its Best Practices Initiatives addresses common challenges to graduate education by supporting innovations and sharing effective practices with the graduate community, providing millions of dollars to support innovative projects at member institutions. It is a leading source of information and data analysis for benchmarking trends in graduate education, documenting the "brain-drain" outflow since 2001. It is a national advocate lobbying for graduate education and a resource for policy makers on issues concerning graduate education, research, and scholarship. It is an authority on global trends in graduate education. Its headquarters is located in Washington, D.C.

Council on Foreign Relations

The Council on Foreign Relations (CFR) is an independent, nonpartisan member organization, think tank, and publisher of research reports, and publishes *Foreign Affairs,* the leading magazine on U.S. foreign policy and international issues. It began in 1921 and is now a 4,900-member organization that is headquartered in New York City at the prestigious Harold Pratt House. It also has offices and conference/meeting rooms in Washington, D.C. It is a valued resource for its members of government officials, business executives, journalists, educators and students, civic and religious leaders, and other interested citizens. CFR takes no institutional position on matters of public policy.

Department of Homeland Security

Created as a cabinet-level department in 2002 with the merger of 22 agencies, the Department of Homeland Security (DHS) now has a staff of more than 240,000 employees. Its tasks include aviation security, border security, emergency response, cyber security, chemical facility inspection, customs inspection, immigration control and services, guarding the nation's coasts, and protecting the president, vice president, the White House, and visiting heads of states. It combined agencies drawn from the following departments: Agriculture, Defense, Energy, Health and Human Services, Justice, Treasury, and Transportation. It merged into the DHS such notable previous agencies as the Federal Protective Service, Federal Emergency Management Agency, the Federal Computer Incident Center, the U.S. Coast Guard, and the U.S. Secret Service. It is located in Washington, D.C.

Department of Justice

The Department of Justice was founded in 1870 (16 Stat. 162) to defend the interests of the United States according to the law, to ensure public safety against foreign and domestic threats, to provide leadership in preventing and controlling crime, to punish those guilty of unlawful behavior, and to ensure fair and impartial administration of justice. It is headed by the attorney general of the United States, created by the Judiciary Act of 1789. The 1870 Act established the Office of Solicitor General, which presents U.S. cases before the Supreme Court. Its 2017 budget is $48.5 billion. Among its more notable components and programs are the Bureau of Alcohol, Tobacco and Firearms, the Civil Rights Division, Criminal Division, Drug Enforcement Agency, Office for U.S. Attorneys, the Federal Bureau of Investigation, the Federal Bureau of Prisons, INTERPOL Washington, Tax Division, U.S. Marshals Service, and U.S. Victims of Terrorism Abroad Task Force. As are all cabinet-level departments, its headquarters is in Washington, D.C.

Federation for American Immigration Reform

Founded in 1979 by John Tanton, the Federation for American Immigration Reform is a national, nonpartisan, nonprofit, public-interest membership organization of conservative citizens sharing a common belief that the mass immigration that has occurred since 1980 should be strictly curtailed. It advocates a moratorium on all immigration except for the spouses and minor children of U.S. citizens. It advocates for a strict limitation on the number of refugees and supports President Trump's travel ban. It argues that the United States needs a strict and reduced immigration policy to allow time to regain control of the borders, secure the nation against terrorism, and reduce overall levels of immigration to about 300,000 a year. It advocates for a U.S. immigration policy that is nondiscriminatory while designed to serve the social, economic, and environmental needs of the United States. It is located in Washington, D.C.

Free Congress Foundation (Now American Opportunity Foundation)

Free Congress Foundation is a politically conservative, culturally conservative think tank that is more of an advocacy organization that promotes the "culture war" and advocates returning the nation and its policies to the "traditional, Judeo-Christian, Western" cultural heritage by stopping what it labels the long slide into the moral and cultural decay of "political correctness." It was founded in 1945. It strenuously opposes illegal immigration and any program of amnesty or earned legalization or earned residency programs; favors strict enforcement of immigration laws, of an English-only policy; and rejects all forms of multiculturalism. On homeland security issues, it favored the creation of the DHS and the USA Patriot Acts I and II. It is headquartered in Arlington, Virginia.

Freedom Works

Founded in 1984, Freedom Works has full-time staffed offices in 10 states and claims to be a coalition of about 700,000 volunteers nationwide. It was chaired by former U.S. House of Representatives majority leader Dick Armey. It advocates lower taxes, less government, and more freedom. It strongly backs a private business-based approach to a guest-worker program developed by the Krieble Foundation. It has grown into a serious force within the Republican Party and, in particular, in its presidential nomination process, tilting to the extreme right of the political spectrum. It advocates for strict border control and favored enactment of the USA Patriot Acts and the DHS act. It supports enhanced interrogation and expedited deportation policies. It is a libertarian advocacy group headquartered in Washington, D.C.

Government Accountability Office

The Government Accountability Office (GAO) is an independent, nonpartisan agency that works for Congress. Often referred to as the "congressional watchdog," the GAO investigates how the federal government spends taxpayer dollars. The GAO is headed by the comptroller general of the United States, who is appointed to a 15-year term by the president from a slate of candidates proposed by the Congress through a bipartisan, bicameral commission. The current comptroller general is Gene Dodaro, who became the eighth comptroller general on December 22, 2010, when he was nominated by President Obama and confirmed by the U.S. Senate. The GAO seeks to improve the performance and accountability of the federal government by providing Congress with timely information based on objective, fact-based, nonpartisan, nonideological, fair, and balanced studies. Its core values are accountability, integrity, and reliability.

GAO's studies and analyses are done at the behest of congressional committees or subcommittees or are mandated by public laws or committee reports. The GAO supports congressional oversight by auditing agencies and operations, investigating allegations of illegal or improper activities, reporting on the effectiveness and efficiency of policies in meeting their objectives, performing policy analyses and outlining options for congressional consideration, and issuing legal decisions and opinions. The GAO advises Congress and heads of executive agencies about ways to make government more efficient, effective, ethical, equitable, and responsive. It is consistently ranked as one of the best places to work in the federal government in the annual list of the Partnership for Public Service.

Heritage Foundation

Founded in 1973 by Joseph Coors, Paul Weyrich, and Edwin Feulner, the Heritage Foundation is a conservative think tank and lobbying organization in Washington, D.C. Its CEO is Jim DeMint. It describes itself as the leader of the conservative movement. It rose to prominence during the administration of President Ronald Reagan, when it issued its "Mandate for Leadership," which became the blueprint of the conservative agenda of the Reagan presidency. It was a leading opponent of the Obama administration's immigration policy, DACA and DAPA, and is a leading proponent of President Trump's approach to homeland security and immigration policy. It favors the travel ban, building the border wall, and expedited removal of illegal immigrants as logical steps to ensure national security.

Hudson Institute

The Hudson Institute was founded in 1961 by Herman Kahn, a noted strategist. It is a 501 (c) (3) organization (a think tank) financed by tax-deductible donations from private individuals, corporations, foundations, and government grants. It challenges conventional thinking and helps manage strategic transitions to the future through interdisciplinary analyses and studies specializing in defense, international relations, economics, health care, technology, culture, and law. It is headquartered in Washington, D.C. It regularly publishes books and hosts conferences and events, such as the July 6, 2017, event: "Russian Interference: Past, Present, and Future."

Human Rights First

Human Rights First is an independent advocacy and action organization that is a nonpartisan, a nonprofit, and an international human rights organization based in New York, Washington, D.C., Houston, and Los Angeles. It accepts no government funding. It challenges the United States to live up to its ideals—vigorously opposing, for example, the Trump administration's plans to restore waterboarding. It promotes American leadership in the global struggle for human rights, pressing the U.S. government and private companies to respect human rights and the rule of law and demanding reform, accountability, and justice. It exposes and protests injustice, advocating policy solutions to ensure consistent respect for human rights. It protects the rights of refugees, combats the use of torture, and defends persecuted minorities.

It conducts campaigns to pursue specific goals so that policy makers in Washington, D.C., hear from citizen champions of human rights. For more than 35 years it has built a bipartisan coalition of frontline activists and lawyers to tackle global challenges to human rights and to demand American leadership in protecting human rights. Human Rights First believes that supporting human rights is a moral obligation but is also a vital national interest and that America is strongest when its policies and actions match its national values.

National Conference of State Legislatures

The National Conference of State Legislatures (NCSL) was founded in 1975 to champion state legislatures by helping states to remain strong and independent and by providing information and tools to craft the best solutions to difficult problems. It has vigorously opposed the federal government's use of unfunded mandates. It annually conducts workshops for state legislators and legislative staff in every state. It seeks to improve the quality and effectiveness of state legislatures. It promotes policy innovation and communication among state legislatures and works to ensure that state legislatures have a strong, cohesive voice in the federal system. It promotes its "The States' Agenda," a blueprint for the NCSL's advocacy work on Capitol Hill. It has nine standing committees that adopt recommended policies to fight unwarranted federal preemption of state laws, unfunded mandates, and federal legislation that threaten state authority and autonomy. It has headquarters in Denver, Colorado, and in Washington, D.C.

National Immigration Forum

Founded in 1982, the National Immigration Forum (NIF) advocates to embrace and uphold America's tradition as a nation of immigrants and to build public support for public policies that welcome immigrants and refugees and that are fair and supportive to newcomers. As such it opposes President Trump's travel ban. NIF works to unite families torn apart by what it considers unreasonable and arbitrary restrictions. It advocates for fair treatment of refugees who have fled persecution and for legalization of unauthorized immigrants and promotes a pathway to full political incorporation and equitable access to social protections. It advocates for fundamental constitutional rights, no matter the legal status of immigrants. It advocates for policies that strengthen the U.S. economy by working with a diverse coalition of allies—immigrant, ethnic, religious, civil rights, labor union, business groups, and state and local governments—to forge a new vision of immigration policy consistent with global realities. It fosters economic growth, attracting needed workers to the United States, and protects the rights of workers and their families. It helps newcomers to settle into their communities and helps them to improve their socioeconomic status. It seeks to help localities to weave immigrants into the fabric of community life by building bonds of mutual understanding between residents and newcomers. It supported President Obama's executive orders of DACA and DAPA. Its headquarters is located in Washington, D.C.

National Immigration Law Center

The National Immigration Law Center is a national support center dedicated to protect and promote the rights and opportunities of low-income immigrants and their families. It specializes in immigration law and immigrant welfare. It conducts policy analysis and impact litigation and provides publications, technical services, and training to a broad constituency of legal aid agencies, community groups, and pro bono attorneys. It has offices in Los Angeles, Oakland, and Washington, D.C. It lobbies and works in coalition with other organizations favoring legalization and similar approaches to the illegal immigration problem. It opposes what it considers the civil liberties and privacy abuses of the Patriot Act and the DHS.

National Institute for Public Policy

The National Institute for Public Policy assesses U.S. foreign and defense policies in the post–Cold War environment. It was founded in 1981 as a nonprofit, public education organization focusing on a wide spectrum of rapidly evolving foreign policy and international issues. It is headquartered in Fairfax, Virginia. Its staff of 17 scholars and analysts conduct research. The institute publishes books and monographs on international security issues, such as missile and weapons of mass destruction, the effectiveness of deterrence theory, policy to counter proliferation, NATO and allied security, arms control regimes, the role of the intelligence community in a new security environment, air power and ballistic missile defense security policy, terrorism and emerging transnational threats, and space power and policy studies. It sponsors the refereed, scholarly journal, *Comparative Strategy*.

National Rifle Association

Founded in 1871, the National Rifle Association is one of the most powerful lobbies in national politics and exemplifies the 501 (c) (4) organizations. It was founded by George Wood Wingate and William Conant Church. In the past it was largely nonpartisan or bipartisan and emphasized gun safety training. Since 1975 it advocates strenuously for gun rights and has directly lobbied for pro-gun legislation at the state and national levels. It advocates for strict enforcement of immigration laws and the crackdown on illegal immigration and enhanced border control. Some of its members have joined "vigilante groups" like the Minutemen. Claiming more than 5 million members, it is headquartered in Fairfax, Virginia, and its CEO is Wayne LaPierre.

National Security Council

The National Security Council (NSC) was formed in 1947 (PL 235, 61 Stat. 496, U.S.C. 402). It is part of the Executive Office of the President. It is the primary advisor to the president on national security and foreign policy matters. It was established to ensure coordination between the various military intelligence agencies and the Central Intelligence Agency. In 2004, the position director of national intelligence (DNI) was created. In 2009, President Obama merged the White House staff supporting the Homeland Security Council and the NSC into one National Security Staff. The NSC is chaired by the president. Its members are the vice president, secretary of state, secretary of defense, secretary of energy, national security advisor, and the secretary of the Treasury. The chairman of the Joint Chiefs of Staff is the statutory military advisor to the NSC, and the DNI is the statutory intelligence advisor.

Office of Management and Budget

The Office of Management and Budget is a major office within the Executive Office of the President. It serves the president in overseeing the implementation of his agenda across the entire executive branch. Its mission is to assist the president in meeting his policy, budget and management, and regulatory objectives, and to fulfill its statutory responsibilities. These include (1) budget development and execution; (2) management, including oversight of agency performance, human capital, federal procurement, financial management, and information technology; (3) regulatory policy coordination; (4) legislative clearance and coordination; and (5) executive orders and presidential memoranda.

PEW Hispanic Center

Founded in 2001, the Pew Hispanic Center is a nonpartisan research organization supported by the Pew Charitable Trust. It strives to improve understanding of the U.S. Hispanic population and to chronicle Latinos' growing impact on the United States. Timeliness, relevance, and scientific rigor are characteristics of its work. A classic example of a think tank, it does not advocate for or take positions on policy issues. Demography, immigration, and remittances are its major research foci on unauthorized immigration matters. The Pew Forum, Hispanic Center, and Research Center are located in the headquarters in Washington, D.C.

RAND Corporation

RAND is a contraction of the terms "research and development." It was the first organization to be called a think tank. Established in 1946 by the U.S. Air Force, today RAND is a nonprofit institution that helps improve the policy and decision making of government through research and analysis whose areas of expertise include child policy, civil and criminal justice, community and U.S. regional studies, drug policy, education, health, homeland security, immigration, infrastructure, international policy, methodology, national security, population and aging, science and technology, and terrorism. On occasion its findings are considered so compelling that it advances specific policy recommendations. It serves the public interest by widely disseminating its research findings. The RAND Corporation headquarters is located in Santa Monica, California.

September 11 Commission

Senators Joseph Lieberman (I-CT) and John McCain (R-AZ) sponsored legislation to establish the National Commission on Terrorist Attacks upon the United States (9–11 Commission) as a bipartisan, independent commission created by Congress and signed into law by President George W. Bush in 2002. The 10-member commission was charged with creating a full and complete assessment of the 2001 attacks, including preparedness for it and to assess the immediate responses to the attacks and to make recommendations designed to guard against future attacks. In July 2004, it released its public report, and in August 2004 it released two staff reports/monographs. The commission announced creation of the 9/11 Discourse Project. The commission closed on August 21, 2004. Its recommendations led to the creation of the DHS in November 2002 and the Intelligence Reform and Terrorism Prevention Act of 2004. That act established the director of national intelligence. The Senate expanded the committee on government oversight, in S. 445, changing its name to Homeland Security and

Government Affairs Committee. In 2006, Congress established the SAFE Port Act of 2006. In 2011, on the 10th anniversary of the attacks, the committee launched a series of hearings to review the efficacy of the law and to assess future needs.

United States Customs and Border Protection

The United States Customs and Border Protection is one of the world's largest law enforcement organizations, with more than 60,000 employees. It was established with the creation of the DHS in 2002. It is charged with keeping terrorists and their weapons out of the United States while facilitating lawful international travel and trade. As the nation's unified border entity, CBP takes a comprehensive approach to border management and control, combining customs, immigration, border security, and agricultural protection into one coordinated and supportive activity. CBP is responsible for enforcing hundreds of U.S. laws and regulations, screening nearly a million visitors per day, as well more than 67,000 cargo containers. It arrests more than 1,100 persons at the borders daily and seizes nearly 6 tons of illegal drugs. Annually, it facilitates more than $3 trillion in legitimate trade, while enforcing U.S. trade laws. The CBP's mission is to safeguard the borders by protecting the public from dangerous people and materials, yet enhancing the global economic competitiveness of the United States by enabling legitimate trade and travel.

People

The following section presents short biographical sketches of individuals active in the arena of homeland security policy making and implementation. Some are elected officials (presidents, congressmen), some are appointed officials (bureaucratic leaders, judges), some are political activists (lobbyists) on the issue, and some are scholars/analysts heading major think tank organizations that study and advocate on the issue from a more bipartisan or nonpartisan perspective. Their profiles are presented in alphabeti-cal order.

Ashcroft, John (1942–)

John Ashcroft was born in Chicago, Illinois, in 1942. He attended Yale College and graduated from the University of Chicago and the University of Chicago Law School. He married Janet Ashcroft in 1967, and they have three children. He served as the attorney general of Missouri (1976–1985) and in 1984 was elected governor of Missouri and reelected in 1988. He chaired the Governors Association 1989–1990. In 1994 he was elected to the U.S. Senate but defeated in his bid for reelection in 2000. He was nominated by President George W. Bush to be U.S. attorney general and was confirmed by the Senate. He served as attorney general until he resigned in 2005. As attorney general, he was a notable proponent of the war on drugs and supported the U.S. Patriot Act and creation of the DHS. Throughout his political career he was known as a staunch fiscal and social conservative. After his term as attorney general, he was a lobbyist and consultant. He is the author of several books: *College Law for Business,* 10e (a textbook coau-thored with his wife, Janet); *On My Honor: The Beliefs That Shaped My Life* (1998); *Lessons from a Father to a Son* (2002); and *Never Again: Securing America and Restoring Justice* (2006).

bin Laden, Osama (1957–2011)

Osama bin Laden was born in 1957. His father was from South Yemen, and his mother was Syrian. He was the 7th son among 50 brothers and sisters. His father was a wealthy build-ing contractor and a devout Muslim but had a very dominat-ing personality. He died when Osama was 13. Osama attended college in Jeddah, earning a degree in public administration in 1981. He joined the jihad and raised money to fund the fight against the Soviet Union's invasion of Afghanistan. In 1982 he went to Afghanistan to fight and built six camps. He founded

Al Qaeda ("The Base") in 1988. After the Soviets withdrew from Afghanistan in 1989, he opened a new jihad in South Yemen. After the Iraq invasion by the United States, he issued a fatwa against the West and the United States. In 1991 he went to Sudan. After supporting bombings and terrorist attacks in Saudi Arabia, Sudan, and South Yemen, he fled to Afghanistan for a third time, in 1996, given refuge by the Taliban government. From there he plotted the Al Qaeda attacks on the United States, culminating in the 9/11 attacks. He had three wives and 15 children. He was killed in a U.S. Seal team raid in Pakistan on May 2, 2011.

Bush, George W. (1946–)

George W. Bush served as the 43rd president (2001–2009), a wartime president after the terrorist attacks on September 11, 2001. He was born in New Haven, Connecticut, and was enrolled at Phillips Academy in Andover, Massachusetts, in 1961. He worked in his father's Senate bid in 1964. The family moved to Midland, Texas. Bush graduated from Yale University in 1968 and then enlisted in the Texas Air National Guard. In 1973 he entered the Harvard Business School, took an MBA degree from Harvard in 1975, and then returned to Midland and also entered the oil business, founding an oil and gas exploration company. He married Laura Welch, and they have twin daughters. His first foray into elective office politics was an unsuccessful run for the House of Representatives in 1978. In 1978 he also worked on his father's campaign for the presidency. He later joined a group of investors buying the Texas Rangers baseball team in 1989. He ran for and was elected governor of Texas, serving as its 46th governor from 1995 to 2000. He was elected president in 2000, after a closely contested race against Al Gore, who won the popular vote but lost the White House when the U.S. Supreme Court, in *Bush v. Gore* (2000), awarded the Electoral College votes of Florida to Bush (Bush–Cheney won 271 Electoral College votes to 266 for Gore–Lieberman). After the attacks of September 11, 2001, President Bush declared a "war on terrorism," and his administration authored and Congress passed the USA Patriot Act, granting the executive branch sweeping powers to deal with terrorism. Congress also passed the administration-backed law to create the new cabinet-level Department of Homeland Security. He appointed former Pennsylvania governor Tom Ridge as the first secretary of Homeland Security and later Michael Chertoff as his second secretary of DHS. The administration was noted for its crackdown on illegal immigrants and efforts to enforce expedited removal. He appointed the first director of national intelligence in an effort to control international terrorism. He pushed, unsuccessfully, for comprehensive immigration reform and a bill that would have established a guest-worker program.

Card, Andrew, Jr. (1947–)

Andrew Card, Jr., served as President George W. Bush's White House chief of staff from 2000 through April 2006, making him one of the longest-serving White House chief of staffs. During his tenure in that position, Card was instrumental in crafting the Bush administration's creation of the Homeland Security Office in the White House and then the administration's input in establishing the Department of Homeland Security. Card married Kathleen Card, and they have three children. He is a graduate of the University of South Carolina, with a BS degree in engineering. He attended the United States Merchant Marine Academy, 1966–1967, and the John F. Kennedy School of Government at Harvard University. From 1993 through 1996, Andrew Card was president and chief executive officer of the American Automobile Manufacturers Association, which dissolved in December 1998. He served in the Massachusetts House of Representatives, 1975–1983, during which time, in 1982, he was named Legislator of the Year by the National Republican Legislators Association. He also received the Distinguished Legislator Award from the Massachusetts

Municipal Association. From 1992 to 1983 he served as the U.S. secretary of Transportation, at which time he led the administration's disaster relief effort after Hurricane Andrew. He then directed the Bush Transition team from the George H. W. Bush to the William Clinton presidential administrations. He served in President Bush's administration as assistant to the president, from 1988 through 1992, and deputy chief of staff, managing daily operations of the White House staff. He served in President Reagan's administration as special assistant to the president for intergovernmental affairs and then deputy assistant to the president and director of intergovernmental affairs. He was General Motors' (GM) vice president for government relations and represented GM before Congress. In 2011, Card became acting dean of the Bush School of Government and Public Service at Texas A & M University. From 2014 to 2016 he served as the fifth president of Franklin Pierce University in New Hampshire.

Cheney, Richard "Dick" (1941–)

Dick Cheney, former vice president of the United States (2000–2008), served six terms in the House of Representatives and four Republican presidents, including as the youngest White House chief of staff (at age 34, for President Gerald Ford). He was born in Lincoln, Nebraska, in 1941. He grew up in Casper, Wyoming. He studied at Yale University and then at the University of Wyoming, where he received a BA in political science in 1965 and an MA in political science in 1966. He applied for and received five draft deferments during the Vietnam War. He married Lynne Cheney (née Vincent) in 1964, and they have two daughters. Lynne and Dick Cheney both enrolled in PhD programs at the University of Wisconsin, which Lynne completed, but Dick did not as he went into active politics. He became a protégé of Donald Rumsfeld and was chief of staff to Gerald Ford. He became a six-term Republican congressman and served as House minority whip in 1988. He was selected as secretary of defense by incoming President George H. W. Bush and oversaw Operation Desert Storm. With William Clinton's election, Cheney left politics and joined the conservative think tank, American Enterprise Institute. In 1995 he became CEO of Halliburton, an oil conglomerate and multinational corporation. In 2000, Texas governor George W. Bush asked him to lead the search for his vice president. He recommended himself. He ran with Bush, and their ticket won the 2000 election. Cheney became one of the most powerful voices in the Bush administration, particularly after the 9/11 attacks, and was its leading voice for the USA Patriot Act, for creation of the DHS, and for the invasion of Iraq. During Bush's first term, he was known as the "shadow president." Since 2009, he has been a regular and outspoken critic of the Obama administration and remains a prominent Republican "hawk" on foreign and defense policy and on homeland security policy. He advocated enhanced interrogation, arguing waterboarding was not torture and was an effective intelligence tool. He strongly advocated expedited removal, border control, and a crackdown on illegal immigration.

Chertoff, Michael (1953–)

Michael Chertoff was born in New Jersey in 1953. He graduated magna cum laude from Harvard College in 1973 and magna cum laude from Harvard Law School in 1978. He was clerk to Supreme Court justice William Brennan, 1979–1980. Chertoff was a federal prosecutor for more than a decade, investigating political corruption (he was appointed special counsel for the Senate Whitewater Committee investigating possible impeachment of President William Clinton), organized crime, corporate fraud (the Enron Case), and terrorism, He was one of the investigators of the 9/11 terrorist attacks. He was U.S. attorney for the district of New Jersey, 1990–1994. He served as a federal judge on the U.S. Court of Appeals for the Third Circuit. He was nominated for secretary of the Department of Homeland Security in 2005 by President George W. Bush, confirmed by the Senate by a vote of 88–1, and he served until

January 2009. As secretary of the DHS he strengthened the borders, adding many border patrol agents. While he was secretary, the DHS cracked down on sanctuary cities and illegal immigration and began construction of the border fence. He stressed intelligence analysis and infrastructure protection and pushed for development of full body scanners to be used by the TSA (Transportation Security Administration). After the Hurricane Katrina disaster, Secretary Chertoff worked to improve FEMA into an effective organization. After his term as secretary of DHS, he cofounded The Chertoff Group, of which he is chairman, focusing on risk identification, analysis, mitigation, and crisis management and providing strategic counsel on global security solutions. He is a senior counsel at Covington and Burling, OOP, and is a member of that firm's White Collar Defense and Investigations group. His spouse is Meryl Justin, with whom he has two children. He cochairs the Bipartisan Policy Center's Immigration Task Force.

Clancy, Joseph (1953–)

Joseph Clancy was the 24th director of the U.S. Secret Service, serving from October 2014 to March 2017. He previously headed the agency's presidential protection service during which time he became close to President Barack Obama, who appointed him director of the Secret Service. Clancy was born in Indiana but grew up in the Philadelphia area. He attended the U.S. Military Academy and then transferred to and graduated from Villanova University. He taught high school for several years before joining the Secret Service in the 1980s, working in its New York field office, and was in charge of security at national special events before joining the president's protective detail. He was appointed head of the Secret Service within the DHS on the resignation of Julia Pierson in October 2014 and served until his retirement in March 2017. He led the Secret Service during the period of the agency's sex-related scandals and security breaches. He was succeeded by Randolph Alles, who was President Trump's pick to head the Secret Service.

Clarke, Richard (1950–)

Richard Clarke was born in 1950 in Massachusetts. He is a leading authority on security, counterterrorism, and cyber security. He graduated from Boston Latin School in 1968, received a BA from the University of Pennsylvania in 1972 and an MA in management from the Massachusetts Institute of Technology in 1978.

Clarke began his public service in 1973 in the Office of the Secretary of Defense. He served in the White House from 1992 through 2003, serving three presidents: as senior White House advisor, as Special Assistant to the President for Global Affairs, and as National Coordinator for Security and Counter-Terrorism and Special Assistant to the President for Cyber Security. He served for 19 years in the Pentagon, the intelligence community, and the State Department. He was deputy assistant secretary of state for intelligence during the Reagan administration and assistant secretary of state for political military affairs in the Bush-Quayle administration (1989–1992) and in 1990–1991 supported the Gulf War. Since leaving government he has served in various business capacities related to security and is an on-air consultant on global terrorism for ABC television and ABC News. He has also taught at Harvard University's Kennedy School of Government and is a key player in both national security and counterterrorism arenas. He is the author of nine books, four of which are novels. His nonfiction books are *Defeating Jihadism* (2004), *Against All Enemies: Inside America's War on Terror* (2004), *Your Government Failed You* (2008), *Cyber War* (2010, with Robert Knake), and *Warnings: Finding Cassandras to Stop Catastrophies* (2017, with R. R. Eddy).

Clinton, William (1946–)

William Jefferson Clinton was the 42nd U.S. president, serving from 1993 through 2001. He was the first president of the boomer generation. He was born in Hope, Arkansas. He graduated from Georgetown University, taking a degree in foreign service in 1968. He was class president in 1964–1965.

He was a congressional intern with Senator William Fulbright (D-AR) from 1964 through 1967 and was a Rhodes Scholar at University College, United Kingdom, studying philosophy, politics, and economics.

Clinton earned his JD degree from Yale Law School in 1973, where he met his future wife, Hillary Rodham, in 1980, the year in which he ran unsuccessfully for Congress. He served as Arkansas attorney general, 1979–1981 and then ran for and won the governorship of Arkansas, serving as the 42nd governor from 1983 through 1992. While governor, he helped establish the Democratic Leadership Council, 1990–1991. He secured the Democratic Party nomination for the presidency in 1992 and won the White House, with Al Gore as his vice-presidential candidate, defeating incumbent president George H. W. Bush. He sent a peacekeeping force to Bosnia, was a strong proponent of expanding the North Atlantic Treaty Organization, and negotiated the world trade agreement, the North American Free Trade Agreement. He launched a worldwide campaign against drug trafficking. His centrist approach to budget policy helped spur an economic recovery from the "Bush recession" and oversaw the U.S. economy to its best record in decades, which lasted until he left office, with a budget surplus, the first such surplus in decades. He won reelection but was soon embroiled in a sex scandal. He was impeached by the House of Representatives but not convicted in the Senate. His most notable legislation related to homeland security and immigration are the two 1996 acts: the Personal Responsibility and Work Opportunity Act and the Illegal Immigration Reform and Immigrant Responsibility Act. He is the author of five books: *Between Hope and History* (1996), *Clinton Foreign Policy Reader* (2000), *My Life* (2004), *Giving* (2007), and *Back to Work* (2011).

Comey, James (1960–)

James Comey was born in New York in 1960. He met his wife, Patrice Failor, while a freshman at William and Mary

University, and they were married in 1987. They have six children. In 2011, the William and Mary Law School honored Comey by naming him a Carter O. Lowance fellow, and he was honored with a fellowship from Columbia University. Comey has served as adjunct professor at the University of Richmond School of Law. Comey graduated from the University of Chicago School of Law in 1985. He clerked for a New York District judge before joining a law firm. He served as assistant U.S. attorney for the Southern District of New York, under Rudolph Giuliani, becoming the lead prosecutor against the crime boss, John Gambino. He joined a Virginia-based law firm in 1993, rising to partner in 1996. He was named deputy special counsel of a committee investigating the Whitewater real estate dealings of President William Clinton. He was assistant U.S. attorney for the Eastern District of Virginia, leading the investigation into the 1996 Khobar Tower Bombing in Saudi Arabia. He was appointed U.S. attorney for the Southern District of New York in 2002. Comey was named deputy to Attorney General John Ashcroft in 2003. In 2005, he left government to become senior vice president and general counsel at Lockheed Martin Corporation. In 2013, President Barack Obama nominated him to succeed Robert Mueller as FBI director, and Coney was confirmed 93–1 by the U.S. Senate. In 2016, the FBI became involved in the presidential campaign investigation of the use of a private e-mail server by Senator Hillary Clinton and, as it turned out, of the Russian interference in the election to support Donald Trump and of any possible collusion of the Trump campaign in that interference. On May 9, 2017, President Trump fired Comey as FBI director.

Conyers, John (1929–)

John Conyers (D-MI) is the ranking member of the House Judiciary Committee, which considers all legislative bills dealing with immigration matters. Conyers serves on its Subcommittee on the Constitution, Civil Rights, and Civil Liberties and is a leading critic of the privacy and civil liberties policies and procedures of the Patriot Acts and of the DHS's procedures for expedited removal. He is the coauthor of several books on civil rights matters: *The Politics of Cancer Revisited* (1998, with Samuel Epstein), *Warrior-King: The Case for Impeaching George W. Bush* (2003, with John Bonifaz), *Charting Your Course: Lessons Learned during the Journey toward Performance Excellence* (2003, with Robert Ewy), *What Went Wrong in Ohio: The Conyers Report on the 2004 Presidential Election* (2005), *George W. Bush versus the U.S. Constitution* (2006, with Anita Miller), and *The Constitution in Crisis* (2007, with Elizabeth Holtzman). Conyers was educated at Wayne State University. He was first elected to Congress in 1965 and is the oldest, longest-serving member of Congress—the "Dean of the House of Representatives." He has sponsored numerous bills on crime and law enforcement and on civil rights, civil liberties, and minority issues. He recently fought a congressional Republican-led attack on the Council on American-Islamic Relations. John Conyers is a founding member of the Congressional Black Caucus and the Congressional Progressive Caucus. He served in the National Guard and the United States Army Corps of Engineers in the Korean War. In 1957, he earned his BA degree and in 1958 his JD degree at Wayne State University. He appeared in the 2011 documentary film *War on Terror*, about the George W. Bush War on Terror and in the 2004 Michael Moore documentary film *Fahrenheit 9/11*.

Dinh, Viet (1968–)

Viet Dinh was born in 1968 in Ho Chi Minh City, Vietnam. He escaped in 1978 and came to the United States as a refugee. He served as assistant attorney general (to John Ashcroft) for legal policy 2001–2002, during which time he played a key role in writing the USA Patriot Act and in developing legal policy initiatives to combat terrorism, and represented the DOJ in selecting and confirming federal judges—100 district judges and 23 appellate judges. He has successfully argued cases before the U.S. Supreme Court, representing the government in *Nevada v. Hibbs* (538 U.S. 721, 2003). He graduated magna cum laude from Harvard College and from Harvard Law. He clerked for a D.C. Circuit Court judge and for Supreme Court judge Sandra Day O'Connor. Since leaving the DOJ he has been a founding partner of Bancroft PLLC and has served on the board of directors for 21st Century Fox, for the Revlon Corporation, and for LPL Financial Holdings. He is codirector of Georgetown Law, Asia, and is professorial lecturer in constitutional law at Georgetown Law.

Durbin, Richard "Dick" (1944–)

Dick Durbin (D-IL) is one of the Senate's "Gang of Eight," who crafted the bipartisan comprehensive immigration reform bill, S.744, the measure that passed the Senate in 2013. He is the 47th senator from Illinois and has served in the Senate since 1996, having been reelected in 2002, 2005, and 2014. He is a member of the Senate Judiciary Committee and of the Appropriations Committee and is ranking member on the Subcommittee on Constitution, Civil Rights, and Human Rights. He is the assistant Democratic leader in the Senate (a.k.a. the minority whip). He is leader of the Democrats in the Senate and their chief vote counter. He is an outspoken critic of President Trump's travel ban and of the Senate Republican approach to reforming immigration policy. He supported President Obama's DACA and DAPA orders and is a cosponsor of the various Dream Act bills.

Gonzales, Alberto (1955–)

Alberto Gonzales was born in San Antonio, Texas, in 1955. He served as U.S. attorney general from 2005 to 2007, succeeding John Ashcroft, and as White House counsel to President George W. Bush (2001–2005), where he was instrumental in preparing legal briefs justifying enhanced interrogation techniques. Gonzales was educated at the U.S. Air Force Academy (1973–1975) and earned his BA degree in political science from Rice University in 1979 and his JD from Harvard Law in 1982. He and his wife, Rebecca Turner Gonzales, have three sons. Gonzales joined the law firm of Vinson & Elkins, LLP, in Houston, in 1982. He also taught law as an adjunct professor at the University of Houston Law Center. Gonzales was elected to the American Law Institute in 1999. He was on the board of trustees of the Texas Bar Association from 1996 to 1999 and on the board of directors of the United Way of Texas Gulf Coast from 1993 to 1994. Gonzales was special legal counsel to the Houston Host Committee for the 1990 Summit of Industrialized Nations. Gonzales served as Texas's 100th secretary of state (1997–1999), where he was senior advisor to Governor George Bush and lead liaison on Mexico and border issues. He served as associate justice of the Supreme Court of Texas, 1999–2001. He served as general counsel to Governor George W. Bush for three years. Since leaving the attorney general's office in 2007, he has been dean and distinguished professor of law at Belmont University College of Law in Nashville, Tennessee. He has coauthored, with David Strange, *A Conservative and Compassionate Approach to Immigration Reform* (2014) and authored *True Faith and Allegiance* (2016).

Goodlatte, Bob (1952–)

Representative Bob Goodlatte (R-VA) took his BA in 1974 from Bates College and his JD from Washington and Lee Law School in 1977. He began his political career working from Congressman Caldwell Butler (R-VA) in 1988. He practiced law from 1970 to 1992, when he was first elected to the House of Representatives. He became chair of the House Judiciary Committee in 2017 and on its Crime, Terrorism, and Homeland Security Subcommittee, as well as serving on its Select Committee on Homeland Security and its Subcommittee on Infrastructure and Border Security. He has sponsored a law imposing tougher penalties on commercial counterfeiters. He has compiled a strongly conservative voting record. He has notably sponsored the Secure Our Borders First bill (2015).

Gore, Al (1948–)

Al Gore served as the 45th vice president of the United States, with President William Clinton, from 1993 through 2001. He is a noted environmentalist and recipient of an Academy Award for his documentary film *An Inconvenient Truth* (2006) and of the Nobel Peace Prize (2007) and the National Defense Service Medal. Al Gore was born in Washington, D.C., in 1948, the son of Senator Gore of Tennessee. Al Gore married Mary Elizabeth "Tipper" Aitcheson, to whom he was married for 40 years and with whom he has four children. They divorced in 2010, and he is now dating another prominent environmental activist, Mary Elizabeth Keadle. Gore graduated magna cum laude from Harvard University in 1969. He volunteered for the U.S. Army in 1969 and served in Vietnam from 1969 through 1971, with the 20th Engineer Brigade. He attended Vanderbilt University Law School but dropped out to run for the U.S. House of Representatives (D-TN), where he served from 1977 to 1983. He served as U.S. senator from Tennessee from 1985 to 1993. He campaigned for the nomination of the Democratic Party for president in 1988 but lost to Michael Dukakis. In 1992, he was picked by William Clinton to be his vice-presidential running mate and served as vice president from 1993 to 2001. He campaigned for president in 2000, when he won the popular vote by about a half-million votes but lost the Electoral College vote when the U.S. Supreme Court, in the controversial decision of *Gore v. Bush,* awarded Florida's votes to the Bush-Cheney ticket. Since leaving electoral politics he has become a noted environmental activist. In 2005, he founded the liberal news channel, Current TV, which broadcast to 60 million households. He starred in and produced the sequel to his Academy Award–winning documentary *An Inconvenient*

Sequel: Truth to Power (2017). Al Gore is the author of two environmental-related nonfiction books: *The Future: Six Drivers of Global Change* (2013) and *Earth in the Balance: Forging a New Common Purpose* (2013).

Graham, Lindsey (1955–)

Senator Lindsey Graham (R-SC) was one of the Senate's "Gang of Eight." They helped pass S.744, the 2013 bill that was a bipartisan comprehensive immigration reform bill. He is known as a military and international policy "hawk." He serves on the Senate Judiciary Committee and is on the Senate Armed Services Committee. He was born in Central, South Carolina. He graduated with a BA degree from the University of South Carolina in 1977 and took his JD from the South Carolina School of Law in 1981. He served in the U.S. Air Force from 1982 to 1988 and was an Air Force Reserve officer, retiring in 2015 as a colonel. He served in the House of Representatives from 1995 to 2002 and was elected to the Senate in 2002 and reelected in 2008 and 2014. He briefly sought the Republican Party's nomination for president in 2016 but was one of the first of the field of 17 to withdraw from the race. He has been a notable voice on the Judiciary Committee's investigation into the Russian cyberattack to influence the 2016 presidential election.

Gutierrez, Luis (1953–)

Luis Gutierrez (D-IL) is a key member of the House of Representative's "Gang of Eight," who sponsored the House version of the S.744 bill for comprehensive immigration reform. He has served in the House since 1992. He graduated from Northwestern Illinois University. He is a leading member of the House Hispanic Caucus and served as chairman of its Immigration Task Force. He has played an instrumental role in President Obama's decision to use executive action regarding DACA and DAPA and has sponsored the various Dream

Act bills introduced in the House of Representatives. He is a leading spokesman for Latino American issues. He serves on the House Judiciary Committee and on its Subcommittee on Immigration and Border Security.

Hanen, Andrew (1953–)

Andrew Hanen is a federal judge for the U.S. District Court for the Southern District of Texas. He was appointed to the federal bench by President George W. Bush in 2002. Judge Hanen took his undergraduate degree from Denison University in 1975 and his JD from Baylor University School of Law in 1978. He was confirmed by the Senate in May 2002, by a vote of 97–0. In February 2015, he placed an injunction (a judicial hold) to halt implementation of key elements of the immigration initiative of President Obama's Department of Justice regarding the president's executive action known as DAPA. Judge Hanen ruled that President Obama lacked the authority to implement the new immigration program regarding the granting of a deferred status to illegal immigrants who are the parents of U.S. citizens or legal residents. The administration filed a suit challenging the ruling with the Federal Circuit Court, but in the meantime, President Trump was elected and he issued an executive order reversing that of President Obama on both the extension of DACA and the DAPA programs. Subsequently, he rescinded the initial DACA program as well, although he announced his DHS and DOJ would not act to deport any of the Dreamers for six months, during which time President Trump urged the Congress to enact a Dreamer bill.

Hatch, Orrin (1934–)

Senator Orrin Hatch (R-UT) is a key member and chair of the Senate Judiciary Committee and is the most senior Republican member in the Senate, having been elected in 1977. Senator Hatch is noted for his sponsorship of the Americans with

Disabilities Act. He failed in his bid for the Republican Party's presidential nomination in 2000. Senator Hatch attended Brigham Young University. As the longest-serving member of the Senate, he is president pro tempore of the Senate and thereby third in succession to the presidency.

Hetfield, Mark (1967–)

Since 2013, Mark Hetfield has served as president and CEO of the Hebrew Immigrant Aid Society and is on the forefront of activists to protect and advocate for Syrian Refugee Relief. He is an immigration lawyer, having practiced immigration law in Washington, D.C., in the prestigious law firm of Fulbright & Jaworski, LLP. He graduated cum laude with a JD degree from Georgetown University Law, from which he also received a BS in foreign service. He adjudicated appeals at the INS. In 1994, he was posted to the U.S. Embassy in Haiti, while the country was under rule of the military junta. He processed in-country refugee applications, offering the equivalent of asylum while discouraging Haitians from attempting to escape in vessels that were not seaworthy. His quality assurance process increased approvals from 5 percent to 25 percent. He began his career with HIAS in 1989, serving as a caseworker in Rome assisting Jewish refugee applicants from the Soviet Union. He later joined HIAS at its Washington, D.C., office as representative and director of international operations. While at HIAS, Hetfield served as senior advisor on refugee issues at the U.S. Commission on International Religious Freedom, where he directed a congressionally authorized study on the treatment of asylum seekers. He authored its 2005 report, still widely used and assessed as the most comprehensive study on expedited removal to date. He and his team were presented with the Arthur Helton Award for the Advancement of Human Rights, presented by the American Immigration Lawyers Association. Prior to his appointment as president and CEO of HIAS, he was its senior vice president of policy and programs.

An expert on refugee and immigration law, policy, and programs, he transformed HIAS from an organization focused on Jewish immigrants to a global agency assisting refugees of all faiths and ethnicities. HIAS is a major implementing partner of the UN Refugee Agency and the U.S. Department of Justice. HIAS assists all who flee ethnic cleansing, violence, and other forms of persecution without regard to ethnic, racial, or religious affiliation.

Jackson-Lee, Sheila (1950–)

Congresswoman Sheila Jackson-Lee (D-TX) is an influential member of the House of Representatives, who sits on three congressional committees—a senior member of the House Committee on the Judiciary, on Homeland Security, and newly appointed by the leadership as a member of the Budget Committee. She is the ranking member of the Judiciary Subcommittee on Crime, Terrorism, Homeland Security, and Investigations. She has sponsored legislation, including the Sentencing Reform Act, Law Enforcement and Trust and Integrity Act, the RAISE Act, the Fair Chance for Youth Act, Kaleif's Law, and the American Rising Act of 2015. As ranking member of the Homeland Security Subcommittee on Maritime and Border Security, she coauthored HR 1417, a bipartisan bill for comprehensive immigration reform. As past chairwoman of the Homeland Security Subcommittee on Transportation Security and Infrastructure Protection, she led to passage of the Transportation Security Act of 2007, which dramatically increased funding for transportation security. She supported enhanced technology, better intelligence, increased cargo inspections, increased security for railroads, and implementation of the 9/11 Commission Report. *Congressional Quarterly* rated her one of the 50 most effective members of Congress, and the *U.S. News and World Report* named her one of the 10 most influential members of the House. She is chair of the Congressional Black Caucus Energy Brain Trust and cochair of the Justice Reform Task Force. She is senior whip of the Democratic Caucus, chairs the Texas Congressional Democratic Delegation, and is current chair of the Congressional Black Caucus Foundation Board. She earned a BA in political science from Yale University cum laude in the first graduating class that included females. She earned a JD from the University of Virginia Law School. She is married to Dr. Elwyn Lee, also a Yale graduate and an administrator at the University of Houston. They have two children.

Johnson, Jeh (1957–)

Jeh Johnson served as secretary of the Department of Homeland Security from 2013 to 2017. Johnson was appointed by President Barack Obama in 2013. He succeeded Janet Napolitano. As secretary of DHS, he oversaw the implementation of all laws, policies, and procedures pertaining to homeland security and to both legal and illegal immigration. He implemented President Obama's DACA executive order. He is an American civil and criminal trial lawyer. He is a graduate of Morehouse College and took his JD from Columbia Law School. He served as the Air Force general counsel and then, in 2009, as the general counsel in the Department of Defense. He also served as U.S. assistant attorney in the Southern District of New York.

Kelly, John F. (1950–)

John Kelly was born in Boston, Massachusetts, in 1950. He enlisted in the Marine Corps in 1970 and was discharged as a sergeant in 1972. Following graduation from the University of Massachusetts in 1976, he was commissioned as officer of Marines, serving in a number of command, staff, and school assignments. In 1976 he married Karen Hemest, and they have three children. His son, also a marine, was killed in action in Afghanistan. Kelly attended the National War College and served on Capitol Hill as the Marine Commandant's liaison to the U.S. Congress. He also served as special assistant to the Supreme Allied Commander, Europe, in Mons, Belgium. From 2001 to 2003, he was assistant chief of staff G-3 and ranked as brigadier general. He then served as assistant division commander, 1st Marine Division. He was legislative assistant to the commandant from 2004 to 2007. He was promoted to major general and commanding general, First Marine Expeditionary Force in Iraq. He was promoted to lieutenant general and commanded Marine Forces Reserve and Marine Forces North from 2009 to 2011. He was senior military assistant to two secretaries of defense, Bill Gates and Leon Panetta. In 2012, he received a fourth star and command of the U.S. Southern Command until his retirement in 2016. After less than a year in retirement, he was appointed secretary of Homeland Security by President Donald Trump, confirmed by a vote of 88–11, serving as its fifth secretary, until being appointed White House chief of staff on July 31, 2017, replacing Reince Priebus.

Kerry, John (1943–)

John Kerry was the U.S. Senator from Massachusetts when he was appointed, in 2013, as the 68th U.S. secretary of state, the first to be so appointed as sitting chairman of the Senate Foreign Relations Committee. John Kerry was born in Aurora, Colorado, in 1943, the son of a foreign service officer. He graduate from Yale University and then served in the United States Navy for two tours of duty as a combat swift boat skipper patrolling the rivers of the Mekong Delta during the Vietnam War. He was a true war hero, having been awarded a Silver Star, a Bronze Star with Combat V, and three Purple Hearts. On his return to the United States from service in Vietnam, he became a vocal critic of the war, testifying before the Senate Foreign Relations Committee. In 1976, he earned his law degree from Boston College School of Law. He worked as a prosecutor in Massachusetts, against organized crime, and fought for victims' rights and created a rape-counseling program. He served as lieutenant governor of Massachusetts in 1982 and was elected to the U.S. Senate in 1984, where he served for 28 years. Kerry became chairman of the Senate Foreign Relations Committee in 2009 and chair of the Senate Select Committee on POW/MIA Affairs. As chair of the Senate Foreign Relations Committee, he was instrumental in the ratification of the new START Treaty, a nuclear arms reduction agreement with Russia. He was the Democratic Party's nominee for president in 2004, losing to the Bush-Cheney Republican ticket. He is author of several books, three of which were best sellers: *The New Soldier* (1971); *The New War* (1997); *A Call to Service* (2003); *My Vision for a Better America* (2004); and *This Moment on Earth* (2007), an environmental book that he coauthored with his wife, Teresa Heinz Kerry. John and Teresa Kerry have two daughters.

Koch, Charles (1935–)

Charles Koch was born in Wichita, Kansas. He is president of Koch Industries and has a personal estimated worth of more than $44 billion. Charles graduated from the Massachusetts Institute of Technology in 1959. He joined the family business and became its CEO and chairman in 1967. Like his father, Fred C. Koch, the founder of the family oil business, Charles supports conservative politics. His father was the founder of the ultraconservative John Birch Society. Charles donates millions of dollars annually to various conservative think tanks and causes. He founded the Cato Institute in 1977 and Americans for Progress in 1984. He is vigorously anti-climate change and has financially backed the Tea Party movement. He is the author of *The Science of Success: How Market-Based Management Built the World's Largest Private Company* (2007).

Koch, David (1940–)

David Koch is the executive vice president of Koch Industries. He was born in Wichita, Kansas. He earned his BS degree from the Massachusetts Institute of Technology. He joined the family oil business in 1970, which he and his brother then built into Koch Institutes, a diversified corporation of oil pipelines, refineries, building materials, paper towels, and Dixie Cups, valued at $115 billion. In 2015, David's personal net worth was estimated at $44.2 billion. He resides in New York City. In 1984 he founded Americans for Prosperity and Citizens for a Sound Economy. In 1980, David ran for vice president on the Libertarian ticket with Ed Clark for president. He is a philanthropist, giving millions to the Johns Hopkins University School of Medicine for cancer research, $100 million over 10 years to renovate New York State Theatre in the Lincoln Center for the Performing Arts, and $10 million to renovate the fountain outside the Metropolitan Museum of Art. David and Charles spent 500 million on political activity and lobbying in 2016. According to *Forbes Magazine* David ranks ninth among billionaires, number seven in the United States, and was ranked sixth in 2005.

Krikorian, Mark (1961–)

Mark Krikorian has a BA degree from Georgetown University and took a master's degree from the Fletcher School of Law and Diplomacy at Tufts University. He also studied for two years in Yerevan State University in the then Soviet republic of Armenia. He has held various editorial and writing positions, and in 1995, he joined the Center for Immigration Studies in Washington, D.C., and serves as its executive director. He frequently testifies before Congress and has published numerous articles in such periodicals as *The Washington Post, The New York Times, Commentary,* and *The National Review.* He has appeared on *60 Minutes, Nightline, The News Hour with Jim Lehrer,* CNN, National Public Radio, National Public Television, and similar radio and television programs. He is an ardent advocate of reduced legal immigration and of strict controls to reduce or eliminate illegal immigration. He supports the Trump travel ban and the DHS's efforts to tighten border security and expedited removal of illegal immigrants.

Levin, Brian (n/a–)

Professor Brian Levin is director of the Center for the Study of Hate and Extremism at California State University-San Bernardino. An attorney and criminologist, Levin studies terrorism, hate crime, and legal issues. He earned a BA, summa cum laude, in 1989 from Stanford and, in 1992, a JD from Stanford Law School. Brian Levin served as associate director-legal affairs of the Southern Poverty Law Center and as a corporate litigator for a law firm. During the 1980s he was a New York City police officer working in Harlem and Washington Heights and received several citations for academics and excellent police duty. Before joining CSUSB, Brian Levin was an associate professor at New Jersey's Stockton College and an adjunct lecturer in advanced constitutional law at Seton Hall School of Law. He is author, coauthor, and editor of various books, scholarly articles, training manuals, and studies of extremism and hate crime. He has written amicus curiae briefs for U.S. Supreme Court cases, such as *Wisconsin v. Mitchell* (1993), in which he presented criminological data establishing the severity and characteristics of hate crime, and his analysis has won various awards and has been referenced in numerous social science journals and major law reviews. He has appeared in international news media on six continents and has lectured around the world. He is a court-certified expert on extremism in the United States and the United Kingdom and has testified before both houses of Congress. He has consulted for numerous state and federal agencies such as the FBI and DHS and for universities and civil rights groups. He has appeared on national and cable network shows like *60 Minutes, Dateline NBC, The Today Show, Good Morning America, the O'Reilly Factor, AC 360, and Hardball*. He has appeared in many major American newspapers and writes front-page analysis for the *Huffington Post*.

Lieberman, Joseph (1942–)

Former senator Joseph Lieberman (D-CT and I-CT) took his BA from Yale University in 1964 and received an LLB from

Yale in 1967. He was a practicing attorney from 1964 to 1980. In his political career he served in the Connecticut State Senate, from 1970 to 1980, including serving as its majority leader from 1974 to 1980. He was attorney general of Connecticut from 1983 to 1988, from which office he went on to be elected to the U.S. Senate, where he served until 2014. In 2000, Senator Lieberman ran as the vice-presidential candidate with Al Gore and for reelection to the U.S. Senate. He lost the vice presidency but won reelection to the Senate. In terms of homeland security matters, he was the leading sponsor of the bill to establish the Department of Homeland Security in 2002 and for its broad restructuring of immigration and dissolving of the INS. In 2016, he was briefly considered by President Trump for nomination as the U.S. attorney general.

Loy, James (1942–)

Admiral James Loy was born in Pennsylvania in 1942. He served as commandant of the U.S. Coast Guard from 1998 to 2002. Admiral Loy entered the Coast Guard Academy in 1960. He graduated with a BS degree in general engineering and was commissioned an ensign in 1964. He commanded four cutters, including combat patrols in Vietnam. He served in a couple flag assignments. He was Coast Guard chief of staff (1996–1998). From 1994 to 1996, he was commander of the Coast Guard's Atlantic Area, commanding forces during the mass Haitian and Cuban refugee migrations, and led Coast Guard forces participating in Operation Restore Democracy. As commandant, he led the Coast Guard's readiness and shaped the future of the service, including development of the Integrated Deepwater System acquisition project to modernize the ships, aircraft, and sensors that the Coast Guard employs in its many missions. He attended postgraduate school at Wesleyan University and at the University of Rhode Island, earning MA degrees in history/government and in public administration. He attended the Industrial College of the Armed Forces and interned at the John F. Kennedy School of Government at Harvard University. He has received numerous military awards, medals, and ribbons, including unit and campaign awards. Loy has been recognized by the American Society of Public Administration. He was given the Government Executive Leadership Award, named SEATRADE Personality of 2000 in London, United Kingdom, and has a NAACP Meritorious Service Award, among others. He retired from the Coast Guard in 2002 and was appointed deputy Undersecretary for transportation security and chief operating officer of the TSA by Secretary of Transportation Norman Mineta. He is married to the former Kay McGirk.

McCain, John (1936–)

Senator John McCain (R-AZ) was born at the Coco Solo Naval Station, Panama Canal, as son of Admiral John S. McCain, Jr. Both his father and grandfather were four-star admirals. John McCain graduated from the Naval Academy in 1958 and its Naval Flight School in 1960. He volunteered for Vietnam and in 1967 was shot down on his 23rd mission. He was moved to the "Hanoi Hilton" in 1969 and spent more than five years in captivity there. A true war hero, he was awarded the Silver Star, the Bronze Star, a Purple Heart, the Legion of Merit, a Distinguished Flying Cross, and a Naval Commendation Medal.

In 1981 John McCain retired as a captain and moved to Arizona. He was elected to the House of Representatives in 1982 and reelected in 1984. Embroiled in a campaign finance scandal, he survived the controversy and went on to enact campaign finance reform, the McCain-Feingold Act of 2002. In 1987, he ran for the U.S. Senate, eventually serving four terms. He chairs the Armed Services Committee and currently and prominently serves on the Committee on Homeland Security, and is an ex officio member of the Committee on Intelligence. He co-chairs the Senate National Security Caucus. He ran unsuccessfully for the presidential nomination of the Republican Party in 2000 (losing to George W. Bush) and ran and won the nomination in 2008 but lost to then senator Barack Obama.

McConnell, Mike (1943–)

John Michael McConnell was born in 1943. He is a former vice admiral of the United States Navy and served as director of the National Security Agency (1992–1996), appointed by presidents George H. W. Bush and William Clinton. Admiral McConnell served as the second director of national intelligence from 2007 to 2009, appointed to that position by President George W. Bush and reappointed by President Barack Obama, replacing John Negroponte, the first DNI. He was born in South Carolina and earned a BA in economics from Furman University and an MPA from George Washington University. He is a graduate of the National Defense University and the National Defense Intelligence College. He is married to Terry McConnell with whom he has four children and nine grandchildren. He joined the navy in 1967, worked as an intelligence officer for the chairman of the Joint Chiefs of Staff and the secretary of defense during Operation Desert Shield/Storm and during the dissolution of the Soviet Union. He served as director of the National Security Agency (NSA) from 1992 to 1996 and as a member of the Director of Central Intelligence Senior Leadership team. Since leaving as DNI, he has returned to Booz Allen as its senior vice president. From 2005 to 2007, he was chairman of the board of the Intelligence and National Security Alliance, "the premier not-for-profit, nonpartisan, private sector professional organization providing a structure and interactive forum for leadership and networking within the intelligence and national security communities," comprised of leaders in industry, government, and academia (www.nationalsecurityalliance.net).

McConnell, Mitch (1942–)

Senator Mitch McConnell (R-KY) became the Senate majority leader after the 2014 Senate elections, only the second senator from Kentucky to serve as majority leader. As such, he plays the key role in all Senate legislative proceedings and led the Senate Republicans in strident opposition to comprehensive immigration reform and to the vigorous border control and other conservative policy positions of the majority on homeland security matters. He previously served as Senate minority leader in the 110th–113th congresses and as majority whip in the 108th–109th congresses. He served as chairman of the National Republican Senatorial Committee (1998–2000). He was first elected to the U.S. Senate in 1984. He graduated cum laude from the University of Louisville College of Arts and Sciences and took his JD from the College of Law, University of Kentucky, where he served as president of the Student Bar Association. Prior to his election to the U.S. Senate, he served as deputy assistant attorney general to President Gerald Ford and as judge-executive of Jefferson County, Kentucky, from 1978 to 1985. He served as a senior member of the Appropriations, Agriculture, and Rules Committees in the Senate.

Minihan, Ken (1943–)

Lieutenant General Kenneth Minihan was director of the Defense Intelligence Agency, 1995–1996 and as director of national intelligence, 1996–1999. He is a retired air force general with more than 33 years of active, commissioned service. He earned a BA degree from Florida State University in 1966 and a master's degree from the Naval Postgraduate School in 1979, attended the Air Command and Staff College in 1979, and completed executive development programs at the University of Illinois and at Harvard University (1993). He has numerous awards, decorations, and medals, including the National Security Medal and the National Intelligence Distinguished Service Medal. He was the 14th director of the NSA and the senior uniformed intelligence officer in the DOD. From 1999 to 2002 he was president of the Security Affairs and Support Association. He is currently managing director in the Paladin Capital Group. He is founder of the Intelligence and National Security Alliance in Washington, D.C., a flagship organization for industry, government, and academia partners to enhance effective intelligence development. He is a member of the Air Force Association and sits on a number of public and private boards, and often serves pro bono on government committees and panels to examine ways to enhance homeland and national security capabilities.

Napolitano, Janet (1957–)

Janet Napolitano was born in New York City in 1957. She has never married and has no children. She won a Truman Scholarship and graduated as Santa Clara University's first female valedictorian of her class in 1979, graduating summa cum laude with a degree in political science and a member of its chapter of Phi Beta Kappa. She took her JD degree in 1983 from the University of Virginia, School of Law. She holds honorary degrees from several universities and colleges. She served as a law clerk for Judge Mary Schroeder of the U.S. Court of Appeals for the Ninth Circuit before joining a law firm, becoming a partner in the firm in 1989. Janet Napolitano served as the U.S. attorney for the District of Arizona. As U.S. attorney, she helped lead the domestic terrorism investigation into the Oklahoma City Bombing. She served as attorney general, state of Arizona, from 1999 to 2003, where she helped write the law to break up human smuggling rings. Napolitano served as the 21st governor of Arizona, from 2003 to 2009. While governor, she implemented one of the first homeland security strategies in the country and opened the first counterterrorism center, and she became a pioneer in coordinating federal, state, local, and binational homeland security efforts. She also presided over large-scale disaster relief efforts and readiness exercises. She became the first woman to chair the National Governors Association, where she was instrumental in establishing its Public Safety Task Force and the Homeland Security Advisors Council. Napolitano also chaired the Western

Governors Association. She was appointed secretary of DHS by President Obama in January 2009 and served until September 2013. In 2010, she was awarded the prestigious Thomas Jefferson Foundation Medal (Law), the University of Virginia's highest external honor. She was named the 20th president of the University of California on July 18, 2013, and took office on September 30, 2013, where she leads a university system of 10 campuses, 5 medical centers, 3 affiliated national laboratories, and a statewide agriculture and natural resources program.

Obama, Barack (1961–)

Barack Obama was the 44th president of the United States (2009–2017). He was born in Hawaii and raised by his grandparents. After working his way through college on scholarships, he moved to Chicago, where he worked with a group of churches as a community organizer to help rebuild communities devastated by high unemployment because of the closure of local steel plants. He went on to Harvard Law School, becoming the first African American president of the *Harvard Law Review*.

Obama returned to Chicago to lead voter registration drives, taught constitutional law at the University of Chicago, and eventually ran for the state legislature. In the Illinois State Senate, he passed the first major ethics reform law in 25 years, cut taxes for the working-class families, and expanded health care. As U.S. senator from Illinois (D-IL), Obama worked on bipartisan lobbying reform and transparency in government by putting federal spending online. He burst on to the national political scene when giving the Democratic National Convention Keynote Address in 2004. He ran for president in 2008, and after a tough primary battle with then senator Hillary Clinton (D-NY), he was elected president and sworn into office on January 20, 2009. He was reelected in 2012. During his two terms in office he appointed two secretaries of Homeland Security, Janet Napolitano and Jeh Johnson, and issued two executive orders impacting unauthorized immigrants: DACA and

DAPA. But his administration also set a record for deporting unauthorized immigrants, by focusing on those with criminal convictions.

Obama and his wife, Michelle, are the parents of two daughters: Malia and Sasha. President Obama is the recipient of the Nobel Peace Prize, one of only four U.S. presidents so honored. Barack Obama is the author of three best-selling books: *Dreams of My Father* (2004), *The Audacity of Hope* (2007), and *Of Thee I Sing* (2010).

Peterman, Brian (n/a–)

Vice Admiral D. Brian Peterman (Ret.) is senior advisor at Command Group and president of Command at Sea International, specializing in comprehensive yacht security services and headquartered in Washington, D.C. He served as commander, U.S. Coast Guard, Atlantic Area. Brian Peterman served in the U.S. Coast Guard from 1973 to 2008. He was active in coping with the 9/11 attacks. He previously was commander of the Seventh Coast Guard District and served as Special Assistant to the President, Border and Transportation Security, White House Homeland Security Council. He was director of Defense Policy and Arms Control Directorate in the White House National Security Council and earlier was security officer at the U.S. European Command Headquarters. He is the recipient of the Defense Distinguished Service Medal, the Coast Guard Distinguished Service Medal, the Legion of Merit, the Joint Meritorious Service Medal, the Cutterman's Insignia, and the Presidential Service Insignia. He was raised in Pennsylvania. He earned a BS degree from West Chester University in 1972 and entered the Coast Guard through the Officer Candidate program. He earned an MS degree from the Naval War College.

Ridge, Tom (1945–)

Tom Ridge is a Pennsylvania politician who served as the first assistant to the president in the White House Office of

Homeland Security (2001–2003) and as the first secretary of the Department of Homeland Security (2003–2005). A stalwart Republican, prior to his White House and cabinet service, Ridge was a member of the House of Representatives (R-PA) from 1983 to 1995 and 43rd governor of Pennsylvania from 1995 to 2001. He was born and raised in Pennsylvania. Ridge graduated from Harvard University, cum laude, and then served in the Vietnam War as a sergeant in the U.S. Army, where he was awarded the Bronze Star for Valor. After his army service, he returned to Pennsylvania and completed his JD degree at the Dickinson School of Law, graduating in 1972, after which he entered private practice. Ridge was a district attorney in Erie and then ran for Congress. He was the first congressman to have served as an enlisted man in the Vietnam War. He was overwhelmingly reelected five times, serving six terms. He was elected governor in 1994 and reelected in 1998. Following the September 11, 2001, attacks, President George W. Bush named him the director of the newly created Office of Homeland Security. In January 2003, the office became an official cabinet-level Department of Homeland Security, with Ridge as its first secretary. He served in that role for President Bush's first term, succeeded by Michael Chertoff. Tom Ridge then returned to the private sector. He served on several boards of directors, for the Home Depot, Hershey Company, and Exelcon Corporation, and as senior advisor to Deloitte and Touche, PURE Bioscience, and TechRadium. He is also founder and CEO of Ridge Global LLC, a security consulting firm based in Washington, D.C. He worked in the 2008 presidential campaign of Senator John McCain. Tom and his wife Michele have two children.

Rogers, Mike (1959–)

Admiral Mike Rogers is the commander of U.S. Cyber Command, director of National Security Agency (NSA), and chief of Central Security Service. He was appointed director of NSA by President Barack Obama in 2014. Mike Rogers was born in

Chicago and attended Auburn University, earning a BA degree in 1981. He has an MS degree in National Security Strategy from the Naval War College graduating summa cum laude. He is also a Massachusetts Institute of Technology Seminar XXI fellow and an alumnus of Harvard University Executive in National Security. He received his commission via the Naval Reserve Officers Training Corps as a surface warfare officer and then was selected for reassignment to cryptology (now called Information Warfare) in 1986. He had several ship commands and served as senior cryptologist on the staff of commander, Carrier Group II/JFK Carrier Strike Group. He was on the staff of commander, U.S. 6th Fleet, fleet information officer, and fleet cryptologist, and led cryptologist support aboard U.S. submarines and surface units in the Arabian Gulf and Mediterranean. Mike Rogers was special assistant to the chairman of the Joint Chiefs of Staff and director of the Chairman's Action Group and a leader of the JCS Joint Strategic Working Group. He has numerous service medals and awards, including a Navy Distinguished Service Award.

Ryan, Mary (1940–2006)

Mary Ryan was notably the assistant secretary of state for consular affairs, first appointed in 1993 by President Clinton, who led consular affairs at the time of the 9/11 attacks and was something of a scapegoat for the State Department's approval of visas for the terrorist attackers. She was born in New York City and received a BA in 1963 and an MA in 1965, from St. John's University. She joined the U.S. Foreign Service in 1966 and was first posted in Naples, Italy, and was the personnel officer in Honduras, then consular officer in Mexico, and in such assignments as roving administrative officer for Africa, and was a foreign service inspector and later the executive director of the Bureau of European and Canadian Affairs. She was appointed Ambassador Extraordinary and Plenipotentiary (Swaziland) in 1988. In 1993, she was appointed assistant secretary of state for consular affairs. She was named Career Ambassador in 1999. She was the recipient of the Presidential Distinguished Service Award in 1998 and 1992, the Arnold L. Rachel Award in 1996, and the Award for Outstanding Public Service in 2001. She left the service in 2002, much admired and respected in the State Department but blamed by outside political forces for the perceived failure of the visa application program in preventing international terrorists from entering the country. She died in 2006 of myelofibrosis.

Sensenbrenner, James (1943–)

Jim Sensenbrenner (R-WI) was first elected to the House of Representatives in 1978. He was born in Chicago. He received an AB degree from Stanford University in 1965 and his JD degree from the University of Wisconsin in 1968. He practiced law from 1968 to 1969 before being elected to the Wisconsin Assembly (1968–1974). He was elected to the Wisconsin Senate in 1974, serving there until 1978. He serves as the chair of the powerful Judiciary Committee in the House and on the Select Committee on Homeland Security. He staunchly supported the use of force in Iraq and the creation of the Department of Homeland Security in 2002. He was critical of Attorney General Ashcroft's possible violation of civil liberties and calls for additional investigative powers for law enforcement. Representative Sensenbrenner insisted on strict provisions for the USA Patriot Act and Patriot Act II. He cosponsored a bill to split the INS into two separate agencies, and when they were moved to the DHS, he expressed strong concerns that internal problems in the INS would not be resolved. He has long opposed racial quotas and preferences and was vocal in his support of Milwaukee's school-choice program. He has won election and reelection by wide margins and has often been unopposed in the general election. He notably was sponsor of legislation to control illegal immigration, such as the REAL ID Act of 2005.

Sessions, Jeff (1946–)

Jeff Sessions was nominated for attorney general by President Trump in 2016 and confirmed by the U.S. Senate in 2017. He has been an ardent supporter of President Trump's agenda related to immigration and to homeland security concerns. He strongly advocated for President Trump's travel ban executive orders. He was elected to the U.S. Senate in 1997 and chaired the Senate Judiciary's Subcommittee on Immigration and National Interest. He was reelected to the U.S. Senate in 2008. In 2011, he was the ranking member of the Budget Committee and the Subcommittee on Banking. He is the sponsor of a bill to block any funding for amnesty. He served on the Senate Armed Forces Committee and on the Environment and Public Utility Committee. He took his BA degree from Huntington College in 1969 and his JD from the University of Alabama, School of Law, in 1973. Prior to his election to the U.S. Senate, he served as a President Reagan appointee to the U.S. Attorney, Alabama Southern District. While in the Senate he was an outspoken opponent of comprehensive immigration reform and on any sort of amnesty program. He was an ardent advocate of Patriot Acts I and II and supported creation of the DHS.

Sullivan, Mark (1956–)

Mark Sullivan was director of the U.S. Secret Service from May 2006 to March 2013. He was succeeded by Julia Pierson. The Secret Service was rocked by scandals during his tenure as director. He was first appointed by George W. Bush and then by President Barack Obama. He was born in Arlington, Massachusetts, one of six children. He received a BA in criminal justice from St. Anselm College in 1977. He married Laurie Bell, and they have three daughters. He began his Secret Service career in 1983, at the Detroit Field Office, after having served for five years as a special agent in the Office of the Inspector General for the U.S. Department of Housing and Urban Development. In 1990, he began working in the Fraud Division. In 1991, he was assigned to the Presidential Protective Operations. During 1997–1998, he was agent in charge of the Columbus, Ohio, office, and then as special agent in charge of the Counterfeit Division, 1998–1999. He returned to the Presidential Protective Division in 1999. In 2000, he was made deputy assistant director in the Office of Protective Operations and, in 2002, deputy special agent in charge of the Vice Presidential Protective Division. In 2003, he was reassigned as deputy assistant director of Human Resources and Training. In 2006, President George W. Bush appointed him director of the Secret Service. In April 2012, a scandal involving the president's security detail rocked the agency. After 30 years of service, he retired in February 2013. He and several partners founded Global Security and Innovative Strategies.

Thornberry, Mac (1958–)

Representative William "Mac" Thornberry (R-TX) serves as chairman of the House Armed Services Committee, since 2015, which oversees the Pentagon, all military services, and all Department of Defense agencies, their budgets, and policies. He is a leading voice in Congress on the need to confront terrorism. He previously served on the House Permanent Select Committee on Intelligence, as well as on the Budget Committee, Resources Committee, and the Select Committee on Homeland Security. He chaired the Task Force on Cybersecurity (2011–2012). He and his wife, Sally, married in 1986, and they have two children. He attended Texas Tech University and has a BA degree in history from the University of Texas. He earned his JD from the University of Texas, School of Law, in 1983. Thornberry was assistant secretary of state for legislative affairs under President Ronald Reagan. He is a member of the Council on Foreign Relations. He was elected to the House of Representatives in 1995. In 2002, he cosponsored the Federal Information Security Management Act on cyber security.

Trump, Donald (1946–)

Donald J. Trump is a billionaire real estate mogul, former reality television star, and the 45th president of the United States. Trump was born in Queens, New York. He was married several times to former models: Ivanka Winklmayr, 1977–1992; Marla Maples, 1993–1999; and Melania Knauss, 2005 to present. Donald Trump attended Fordham University in 1964 and received his degree in economics from the Wharton School of Finance, University of Pennsylvania. He took over his father's real estate business in 1971. In 1980, he opened the Grand Hyatt and a casino in Atlantic City. In 1989, he purchased Eastern Airlines Shuttle, renaming it Trump Shuttle. He is the founder of a number of businesses: the Trump Organization, the Trump Entrepreneur Institute, Trump Entertainment Resort, Trump Shuttle, and Trump Mortgage. Much disputed, his estimated net worth is $4.5 billion. In 2004, he appeared as host of *The Apprentice,* a reality television show. In 2012, he briefly considered running for president and was embroiled in and largely led the anti-Obama "birther" movement. On June 15, 2015, he announced his candidacy for the Republican Party nomination for president, running in a field of 17. On July 15, 2016, he clinched the nomination and announced his choice for vice president, Governor Mike Pence of Indiana. He accepted the GOP nomination on July 21, 2016, won the Electoral College vote, and was inaugurated president on January 20, 2017. He nominated John Kelly as secretary of the Department of Homeland Security and Jeff Sessions as attorney general, and they in turn issued departmental rules and regulations turning back President Obama's reform policies. He also issued several controversial executive orders that impacted homeland security, particularly the travel ban orders aimed primarily at Muslims and refugees from the Middle East.

Donald Trump is the author of nine books: *Trump: The Art of the Deal* (1987), *The America We Deserve* (2000), *Trump: How to Get Rich* (2004), *Why We Want You to Be Rich* (2996),

Think Big and Kick Ass in Business (2007), *Trump 101: The Way to Success* (2007), *Trump: Never Give Up* (2008), *Think Like a Champion* (2009), and *Time to Get Tough* (2011).

Watson, Derrick (1966–)

Judge Derrick Kahala Watson is a U.S. district judge of the U.S. District Court of Hawaii. He was born in 1966 in Honolulu. He received his BA cum laude from Harvard College in 1988 and his JD from Harvard Law School in 1991, in the same graduating class as Barack Obama and Neil Gorsuch. He began his legal career in California as an associate in a San Francisco law firm, 1991–1995. He served as assistant U.S. attorney in the Northern District of California from 1995 to 2000, including serving as deputy chief of the Civil Division from 1999 through 2000. He then worked in private practice, becoming a partner in a San Francisco firm in 2003. He did pro bono work for the San Francisco Lawyers Committee for Civil Rights and pro bono work involving human trafficking. He served as assistant U.S. attorney for the District of Hawaii from 2007 to 2013 and chief of the Civil Division, 2009–2013. From 1998 to 2006, Judge Watson served in the U.S. Army Reserve in the Judge Advocate General's Corps, with the rank of captain. He was honorably discharged in 2013. In November 2012, President Barack Obama nominated Watson to serve as a U.S. district judge for the U.S. District Court for the District of Hawaii and was confirmed in the Senate by a vote of 94–0 on April 18, 2013. He is the fourth Native Hawaiian to serve on the federal bench and the only currently serving one. In March 2017, Judge Watson granted a temporary restraining order blocking President Trump's revised executive order banning entry of nationals from six majority-Muslim countries into the United States from going into effect. In June 2017, the U.S. Court of Appeals upheld the majority of the injunction, unanimously determining that President Trump had exceeded his authority under the Immigration and Nationality Act of

1965. In June, the U.S. Supreme Court partially reinstated the travel ban, setting oral arguments for October 2017. It canceled the oral arguments on September 25, 2017, asking lawyers for both sides to address the issue as to whether the case was moot (http://www.abajournal.com/news/article/supreme_court_cancels_oral_arguments_on_travel_ban_asks_lawyers_to_address).

Yates, Sally (1960–)

Sally Yates served as U.S. attorney and deputy attorney general and briefly acting attorney general until President Trump fired her following her refusal to defend his travel ban executive order in federal courts and the Supreme Court in 2017. She was acting attorney general from January 20, 2017, through January 30, 2017. She was preceded by Attorney General Loretta Lynch (both appointed by President Barack Obama) and was succeeded as acting attorney general by Dana Boente. She was deputy attorney general from January 10, 2015, through January 30, 2017, and was succeeded by Rod Rosenstein. Previous to that office, Yates was the U.S. attorney for the Northern District of Georgia, March 2010 to January 10, 2015, again appointed by President Obama, and from July 2004 to December 2004 by President George W. Bush. She was born in Atlanta, Georgia, and earned her BA in journalism from the University of Georgia in 1982 and her JD from the University of Georgia, School of Law, in 1986, graduating magna cum laude. She was executive editor of the *Georgia Law Review*. In 1989 she was hired as assistant U.S. attorney by Bob Barr for the Northern District of Georgia. In 1994, Yates became chief of the Fraud and Public Corruption Section and was the lead prosecutor in the case of Eric Rudolph, the domestic terrorist who committed the Centennial Olympic Park bombing. She rose to first assistant U.S. attorney in 2002 and then acting U.S. attorney in 2004, holding leadership positions under both Republican and Democratic administrations. While a U.S. attorney,

Attorney General Eric Holder appointed her to serve as vice chair of the Attorney General's Advisory Committee. She was confirmed as deputy attorney general, the second-highest ranking position in the Justice Department, by the Senate by a vote of 84–12. She oversaw the day-to-day operations of the Justice Department, including its 113,000 employees. In late January, Acting Attorney General Yates warned White House counsel that the then serving national security advisor, Michael Flynn, had lied about his contacts with Russia related to sanctions and that he was therefore vulnerable to blackmail by Russian intelligence. For 18 days, nothing was done about the warning. When *The Washington Post* published her reported warning, on February 13, 2017, Flynn was forced to resign within hours. Acting Attorney General Yates ordered the DOJ not to defend Trump's executive order on travel and immigration, upholding her stated position during her Senate confirmation hearing, when questioned by then Senator Jeff Sessions, that she would disobey a president's unlawful order. Her decision not to defend in court the travel ban order as unconstitutional was essentially upheld by several federal district courts and the Appellate Court. Her action was praised by several Democratic U.S. senators as "a profile in courage."

Ziglar, Jim (n/a–)

James Ziglar served as commissioner of the Immigration and Naturalization Service under President George W. Bush from January 2001 through December 2002, when the INS was dissolved and its functions merged into the Department of Homeland Security. While INS commissioner, the agency faced its greatest challenge after the attacks of September 11, 2001. Prior to serving as INS commissioner, he was the 35th Sergeant of Arms of the U.S. Senate, where he served as chief administrative officer, chief protocol officer, and chief security officer. In 1987 he served as assistant secretary of the Interior for Water and Science. He served on the staff of the U.S. Senate

Judiciary Committee and as a legislative and public affairs officer in the Department of Justice. He served as law clerk to Supreme Court justice Harry A. Blackmun in 1972, during which term the Supreme Court rendered its landmark decision regarding abortion rights in *Roe v. Wade*. Ziglar also was in investment banking for 16 years and for 7 years in private law practice. He was a resident fellow at the Harvard University John F. Kennedy School of Government Institute of Politics in 2003. He is distinguished visiting professor of law at Georgetown University School of Law and a member of the bars of New York, Washington, D.C., Virginia, and Arizona. He earned a BA and a JD from George Washington University. Jim Ziglar is a senior fellow at the Migration Policy Institute (MPI) focusing on U.S. immigration policy, border control, and security initiatives. Prior to joining MPI, he served as president and CEO of Cross Match Technologies. He serves on several boards, as director of the National Immigration Forum and the Dui Hua Foundation; he is a member of the Independent Task Force on Immigration and America's Future and is a member of the Board of Human Rights First and ImmigrationWorks USA.

References

http://www.abajournal.com/news/article/supreme_court_cancels_oral_arguments_on_travel_ban_asks_lawyers_to_address. Accessed March 2, 2018.

www.nationalsecurityalliance.net. Accessed March 2, 2018.

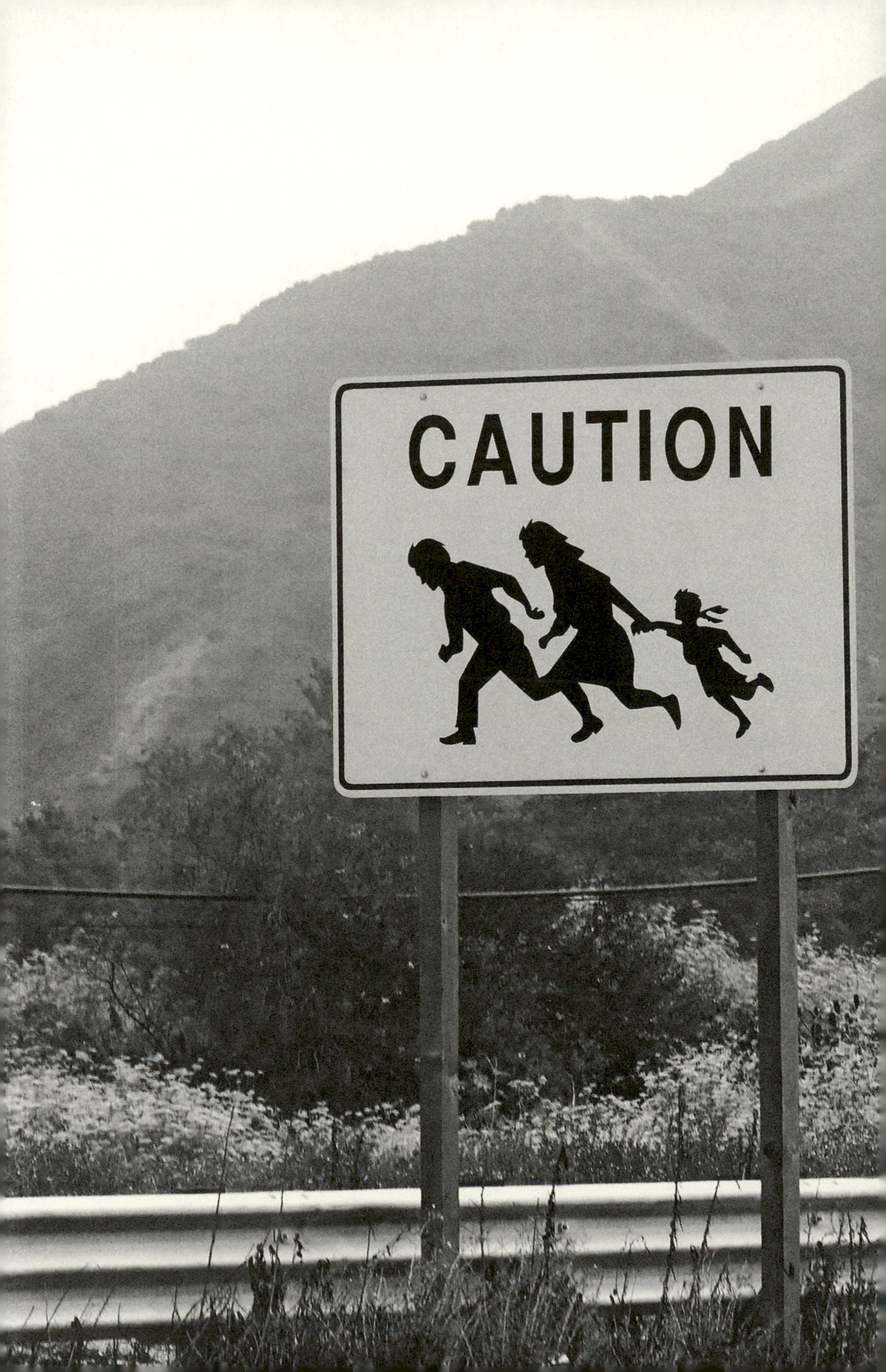
CAUTION

5 Data and Documents

Introduction

This chapter presents some primary source data and documents related to the Department of Homeland Security (DHS) and efforts to implement security policy. It first presents details on the structure of the; it then reviews data and documents on some of the topics DHS deals with: disasters, hate crimes, terrorism, immigration, and border control.

Structure of the Department of Homeland Security

Table 5.1 lists the component units that comprise the DHS and specifies the agency or department from which they came to be merged into DHS.

Table 5.1   Component Units of the Department of Homeland Security and the Department/Agency from Which They Came to DHS

Current DHS Department	Previous Department/Agency
U.S. Citizenship and Immigration Services (USCIS)	Immigration and Naturalization Service (Department of Justice); U.S. Customs Service (Department of Treasury); Federal Protective Service

(continued)

A road sign warns motorists to watch for families crossing the highway into the United States from Mexico. Since 2000, the United States has experienced an exponential increase in the migration of unauthorized immigrants across the Southwestern border. (Shutterstock)

Table 5.1 (*continued*)

U.S. Customs and Border Protection (CBP)	Immigration and Naturalization Service (Department of Justice); U.S. Customs Service (Department of Treasury); Animal and plant Health Inspection Service (Department of Agriculture)
U.S. Coast Guard (USCG)	U.S. Coast Guard
Federal Emergency Management Agency (FEMA)	Office for Domestic Preparedness (Department of Justice); Nuclear Incident Response Team (Department of Energy); Domestic Emergency Support Teams (Department of Justice); National Domestic Preparedness Office (FBI)
Federal Law Enforcement Training Center (FLETC)	FLETC (Department of Treasury)
U.S. Immigration and Customs Enforcement (ICE)	Federal Protective Service; Immigration and Naturalization Service (Department of Justice)
Transportation Security Administration (TSA)	Department of Transportation
U.S. Secret Service (USSS)	Department of Treasury
Directorate for Management	NA
National Protection and Programs Directorate	NA
Science and Technology Directorate	CBRN Countermeasures Programs (Department of Energy); Environmental Measurements Laboratory (Department of Energy); National BW Defense Analysis Center (Department of Defense); Plum Island Animal Disease Center (Department of Agriculture)
Countering Weapons of Mass Destruction Office	NA
Office of Intelligence and Analysis	Department of Defense
Office of Operations Coordination	Protection Center, FBI

Sources: https://www.dhs.gov/operational-and-support-components; and https:// www.dhs.gov/who-joined-dhs.

Figure 5.1 presents the latest organizational chart for the DHS, as of December 17, 2017.

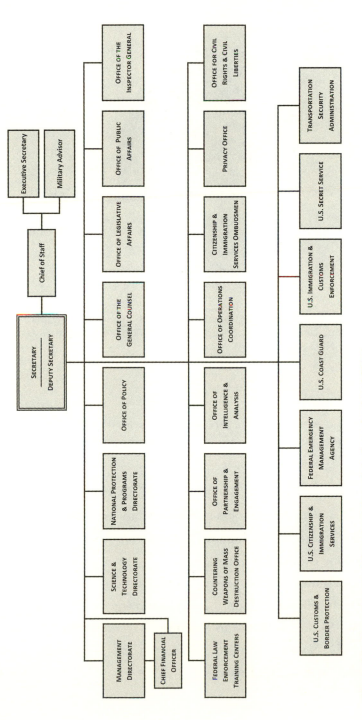

Figure 5.1 Department of Homeland Security's Organizational Chart
Source: https://www.dhs.gov/organizational-chart.

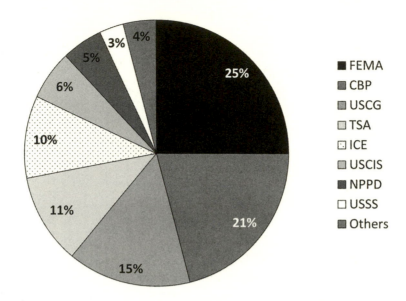

Figure 5.2   The DHS Budget, Fiscal Year 2016, by Agencies/Programs
Source: https://www.dhs.gov/sites/default/files/publications/FY_2016_DHS_
Budget_in_Brief.pdf.

*Figure 5.2 presents a pie chart showing the percentage of the fiscal
year 2016 budget of the DHS by its organizational components.*

Total FY 2016 DHS Budget = $64,858,484,000
FEMA: Federal Emergency Management Agency
CBP: Customs and Border Protection
USCG: U.S. Coast Guard
TSA: Transportation Safety Administration
ICE: Immigration Control and Enforcement
USCIS: U.S. Citizenship and Immigration Service
NPPD: National Protection and Programs Directorate
USSS: U.S. Secret Service

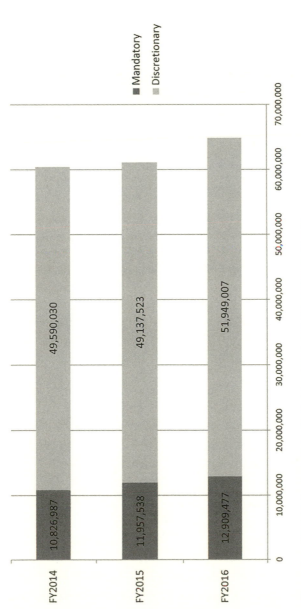

Figure 5.3 DHS FY Budget, 2014–2016, Mandated and Discretionary Funds

Source: https://www.dhs.gov/publication/fy-2016-budget-brief.

Figure 5.3 shows the fiscal year budgets of the DHS from 2014 to 2016, clearly depicting its steady increase in billions of dollars, and showing the mandated versus discretionary portion of the DHS budgets.

Table 5.2 shows the DHS offices in states, territories, and tribal agencies across the United States.

Table 5.2   States, Territories, and Tribal Agencies for Departments of Homeland Security/Emergency Management

State	Agency/Department
Alabama	Alabama Emergency Management Agency
Alaska	Alaska Division of Homeland Security and Emergency Management
Arizona	Arizona Department of Homeland Security
Arkansas	Arkansas Department of Emergency Management
California	California Governor's Office of Emergency Services
Colorado	Colorado Division of Homeland Security and Emergency Management
Connecticut	Connecticut Division of Emergency Management and Homeland Security
Delaware	Delaware Department of Safety and Homeland Security
Florida	Florida Division of Emergency Management
Georgia	Georgia Emergency Management Agency/Homeland Security
Hawaii	Hawaii Emergency Management Agency
Idaho	Idaho Bureau of Homeland Security
Illinois	READY Illinois
Indiana	Indiana Department of Homeland Security
Iowa	Iowa Homeland Security and Emergency Management
Kansas	Kansas Division of Emergency Management
Kentucky	Kentucky Office of Homeland Security
Louisiana	Louisiana Governor's Office of Homeland Security and Emergency Preparedness
Maine	Maine Homeland Security
Maryland	Maryland Governor's Office of Homeland Security

Massachusetts	Massachusetts Executive Office of Public Safety and Security (EOPSS)
Metropolitan Washington Council of Governments	Homeland Security and Public Safety
Michigan	Michigan State Police: Emergency Management and Homeland Security
Minnesota	Minnesota Department of Public Safety: Homeland Security and Emergency Management
Mississippi	Mississippi Office of Homeland Security
Missouri	Missouri Department of Public Safety: Office of Homeland Security
Montana	Montana Disaster and Emergency Services
Nebraska	Nebraska Emergency Management Agency
Nevada	Nevada Division of Emergency Management-Homeland Security
New Hampshire	New Hampshire Department of Safety: Homeland Security and Emergency Management
New Jersey	New Jersey Office of Homeland Security and Preparedness
New Mexico	New Mexico Department of Homeland Security and Emergency Management
New York	New York Division of Homeland Security and Emergency Services (DHSES)
North Dakota	North Dakota Department of Emergency Services
Ohio	Ohio Homeland Security
Oklahoma	Oklahoma Office of Homeland Security
Oregon	Oregon Office of Emergency Management
Pennsylvania	Pennsylvania Governor's Office of Homeland Security
Rhode Island	Rhode Island Emergency Management Agency (RIEMA)
South Carolina	South Carolina Law Enforcement Division
South Dakota	South Dakota Office of Homeland Security
Tennessee	Tennessee Office of Homeland Security
Utah	Utah Department of Public Safety: Division of Emergency Management
Vermont	Vermont Division of Emergency Management
Virginia	Virginia Department of Emergency Management

(continued)

Table 5.2 *(continued)*

Washington	Washington Military Department: Emergency Management Division
West Virginia	West Virginia Division of Homeland Security and Emergency Management
Wisconsin	Wisconsin Emergency Management
Wyoming	Wyoming Office of Homeland Security
Territories	
Northern Mariana Islands	Commonwealth of the Northern Mariana Islands Homeland Security and Emergency Management
Guam	Guam Homeland Security/Office of Civil Defense Pacific Disaster Management Information Platform
Virgin Islands	Virgin Islands Territorial Emergency Management Agency (VITEMA)

Tribal Agencies

National Tribal Emergency Management Council (NTEMC)

Northwest Portland Area Indian Health Board

Northwest Tribal Emergency Management Council

Oneida Tribe of Indians of Wisconsin: Emergency Management

St. Croix Chippewa Indians of Wisconsin: Emergency Management

Tribal Risk & Emergency Management Association

Source: https://www.hsdl.org/?collection&id=1176.

Document 5.1: The Homeland Security Act (November 19, 2002)

On November 19, 2002, Congress enacted the Department of Homeland Security (DHS) Act. It is in excess of 400 printed pages in the U.S. Code. It merged 22 federal agencies, the most extensive reorganization of the federal government since the creation of the Department of Defense after World War II. It creates the DHS. This excerpt of the table of contents for the bill gives an idea of its breadth.

TITLE I—DEPARTMENT OF HOMELAND SECURITY

Sec. 101. Executive department; mission.

Sec. 102. Secretary; functions.

Sec. 103. Other officers.

TITLE II—INFORMATION ANALYSIS AND INFRA-STRUCTURE PROTECTION

Subtitle A—Directorate for Information Analysis and Infrastructure Protection; Access to Information

Subtitle B—Critical Infrastructure Information

Subtitle C—Information Security

Subtitle D—Office of Science and Technology

TITLE III—SCIENCE AND TECHNOLOGY IN SUP-PORT OF HOMELAND SECURITY

TITLE IV—DIRECTORATE OF BORDER AND TRANSPORTATION SECURITY

Subtitle A—Under Secretary for Border and Transportation Security

Subtitle B—United States Customs Service

Subtitle C—Miscellaneous Provisions

Subtitle D—Immigration Enforcement Functions

Subtitle E—Citizenship and Immigration Services

Subtitle F—General Immigration Provisions

TITLE V—EMERGENCY PREPAREDNESS AND RESPONSE

TITLE VI—TREATMENT OF CHARITABLE TRUSTS FOR MEMBERS OF THE ARMED FORCES OF THE UNITED STATES AND OTHER GOVERNMENTAL ORGANIZATIONS

TITLE VII—MANAGEMENT

TITLE VIII—COORDINATION WITH NON-FED-ERAL ENTITIES; INSPECTOR GENERAL; UNITED STATES SECRET SERVICE; COAST GUARD; GEN-ERAL PROVISIONS

Subtitle A—Coordination with Non-Federal Entities

Subtitle B—Inspector General

TITLE XVI—CORRECTIONS TO EXISTING LAW RELATING TO AIRLINE TRANSPORTATION SECURITY

TITLE XVII—CONFORMING AND TECHNICAL AMENDMENTS

Source: 107th Congress, Public Law 296. Washington, DC: Government Printing Office. Available online at https://www.gpo.gov/fdsys/pkg/PLAW-107publ296/html/PLAW-107publ296.htm.

Document 5.2: Reform of the Intelligence Community (2004)

In 2004, Congress passed the National Security Intelligence Reform Act. This act's major provision was to create the position of director of national intelligence (DNI) and an attempt to better coordinate the intelligence data and findings from the various intelligence agencies comprising the intelligence community. The DNI was charged with briefing the president on intelligence. This document excerpts key provisions of the act.

National Security Intelligence Reform Act of 2004, 50 USC 401, 118 Stat. 3644, Public Law 108–458, December 17, 2004, President, Congress, 50 USC 403.

Subtitle A—Establishment of Director of National Intelligence

Sec. 102 (a) DIRECTOR OF NATIONAL INTELLIGENCE

(1) There is a Director of National Intelligence who shall be appointed by the President, by and with the advice and consent of the Senate. Any individual nominated for appointment as Director of National Intelligence shall have extensive national security expertise.

(2) The Director of National Intelligence shall not be located within the Executive Office of the President.

(b) Principal Responsibility, Subject to the authority, direction, and control of the President, the Director of National Intelligence shall—

    (1) serve as head of the intelligence community;

    (2) act as the principal adviser to the President, to the National Security Council, and the Homeland Security Council for intelligence matters related to the national security;

    (3) consistent with section 1018 of the National Security and Intelligence Reform Act of 2004, oversee and direct the implementation of the National Intelligence Program.

    C. Prohibition of Dual Service—the individual serving in the position of Director of National Intelligence shall not, while so serving, also serve as the Director of the Central Intelligence Agency or the head of any other element of the intelligence community.

Source: https://www.gpo.gov/fdsys/pkg/PLAW-108publ458/pdf/PLAW-108publ458.pdf.

Disasters

Table 5.3 from the FEMA website shows the types and durations of declared disasters in 2017.

Table 5.3   Declared FEMA Disasters (2017)

State	Declaration Date	Incident Type	Incident Start Date	Incident End Date
VT	1/2/2018	Severe Storm(s)	10/29/2017	10/30/2017
NH	1/2/2018	Severe Storm(s)	10/29/2017	11/1/2017
ME	1/2/2018	Severe Storm(s)	10/29/2017	11/1/2017
CA	1/2/2018	Fire	12/4/2017	

NM	12/20/2017	Flood	10/4/2017	10/6/2017
AK	12/20/2017	Severe Storm(s)	9/28/2017	9/30/2017
CA	12/8/2017	Fire	12/4/2017	
MS	11/22/2017	Hurricane	10/6/2017	10/10/2017
AL	11/16/2017	Hurricane	10/6/2017	10/10/2017
NY	11/14/2017	Flood	5/2/2017	8/6/2017
KS	11/7/2017	Severe Storm(s)	7/22/2017	7/27/2017
SC	10/16/2017	Hurricane	9/6/2017	9/13/2017
LA	10/16/2017	Hurricane	8/28/2017	9/10/2017
CA	10/10/2017	Fire	10/8/2017	10/31/2017
FL	10/8/2017	Hurricane	10/7/2017	10/11/2017
AL	10/8/2017	Hurricane	10/6/2017	10/10/2017
MS	10/7/2017	Hurricane	10/6/2017	10/10/2017
WI	10/7/2017	Severe Storm(s)	7/19/2017	7/23/2017
ID	10/7/2017	Flood	3/29/2017	6/15/2017
LA	10/6/2017	Hurricane	10/5/2017	10/8/2017
FL	9/27/2017	Hurricane	9/4/2017	10/4/2017
VI	9/20/2017	Hurricane	9/16/2017	9/22/2017
PR	9/18/2017	Hurricane	9/17/2017	11/15/2017
VI	9/18/2017	Hurricane	9/16/2017	9/22/2017
GA	9/15/2017	Hurricane	9/7/2017	9/20/2017
AL	9/11/2017	Hurricane	9/8/2017	9/14/2017
FL	9/10/2017	Hurricane	9/4/2017	10/18/2017
PR	9/10/2017	Hurricane	9/5/2017	9/7/2017
FL	9/8/2017	Hurricane	9/4/2017	10/4/2017
GA	9/8/2017	Hurricane	9/7/2017	9/20/2017
SC	9/7/2017	Hurricane	9/6/2017	9/13/2017
VI	9/7/2017	Hurricane	9/5/2017	9/7/2017
FL	9/5/2017	Hurricane	9/4/2017	10/18/2017
PR	9/5/2017	Hurricane	9/5/2017	9/7/2017
VI	9/5/2017	Hurricane	9/5/2017	9/7/2017
LA	8/28/2017	Hurricane	8/27/2017	9/10/2017
ID	8/27/2017	Flood	5/6/2017	6/16/2017
IA	8/27/2017	Severe Storm(s)	7/19/2017	7/23/2017

(continued)

Table 5.3   (*continued*)

TX	8/25/2017	Hurricane	8/23/2017	9/15/2017
WV	8/18/2017	Severe Storm(s)	7/28/2017	7/29/2017
VT	8/16/2017	Severe Storm(s)	6/29/2017	7/1/2017
NH	8/9/2017	Severe Storm(s)	7/1/2017	7/2/2017
OR	8/8/2017	Severe Storm(s)	1/7/2017	1/10/2017
WY	8/5/2017	Flood	6/7/2017	6/22/2017
MI	8/2/2017	Severe Storm(s)	6/22/2017	6/27/2017
NE	8/1/2017	Severe Storm(s)	6/12/2017	6/17/2017
OK	7/25/2017	Tornado	5/16/2017	5/20/2017
ND	7/12/2017	Flood	3/23/2017	4/29/2017
NY	7/12/2017	Snow	3/14/2017	3/15/2017
NE	6/26/2017	Severe Storm(s)	4/29/2017	5/3/2017
TN	6/23/2017	Severe Storm(s)	5/27/2017	5/28/2017
KS	6/16/2017	Snow	4/28/2017	5/3/2017
AR	6/15/2017	Severe Storm(s)	4/26/2017	5/19/2017
MO	6/2/2017	Flood	4/28/2017	5/11/2017
NH	6/1/2017	Severe Storm(s)	3/14/2017	3/15/2017
OK	5/26/2017	Severe Storm(s)	4/28/2017	5/2/2017
MS	5/22/2017	Severe Storm(s)	4/30/2017	4/30/2017
ID	5/18/2017	Flood	3/6/2017	3/28/2017
CA	5/2/2017	Severe Storm(s)	2/8/2017	2/11/2017
UT	4/21/2017	Flood	2/7/2017	2/27/2017
WA	4/21/2017	Flood	1/30/2017	2/22/2017
ID	4/21/2017	Flood	2/5/2017	2/27/2017
CA	4/1/2017	Flood	2/1/2017	2/23/2017
NV	3/27/2017	Severe Storm(s)	2/5/2017	2/22/2017
WY	3/21/2017	Severe Storm(s)	2/6/2017	2/7/2017
CA	3/16/2017	Flood	1/18/2017	1/23/2017
KS	2/24/2017	Severe Ice Storm	1/13/2017	1/16/2017
NV	2/17/2017	Severe Storm(s)	1/5/2017	1/14/2017
CA	2/14/2017	Severe Storm(s)	1/3/2017	1/5/2017
CA	2/14/2017	Dam/Levee Break	2/7/2017	2/23/2017
CA	2/14/2017	Severe Storm(s)	1/3/2017	1/12/2017
LA	2/11/2017	Tornado	2/7/2017	2/7/2017

OK	2/10/2017	Severe Storm(s)	1/13/2017	1/16/2017
SD	2/1/2017	Severe Storm(s)	12/24/2016	12/26/2016
GA	1/26/2017	Tornado	1/21/2017	1/22/2017
MS	1/25/2017	Tornado	1/20/2017	1/21/2017
GA	1/25/2017	Severe Storm(s)	1/2/2017	1/2/2017
OR	1/25/2017	Severe Storm(s)	12/14/2016	12/17/2016

Source: https://www.fema.gov/media-library/assets/documents/28318.

Document 5.3: President Bush's Remarks on Hurricane Katrina Recovery Efforts (September 8, 2005)

After Hurricane Katrina, President Bush gave the following speech to review the efforts made by FEMA and other organizations toward recovery.

I want to thank the members of my Cabinet who have joined me today. Today I'm going to take this opportunity to speak directly to our citizens who have been displaced by Hurricane Katrina.

Many of you have been evacuated from the flooded and destroyed areas and now find yourselves far from home, without proper identification or even a change of clothes. So today I'm announcing two important steps that we are taking to provide you the help you need, steps that will cut through the red tape so that we get that help into your hands as quickly and easily as possible.

The first step is providing every household with $2,000 in emergency disaster relief that can be used for immediate needs such as food or clothing or personal essentials. For those of you who are living in the large shelters, such as the Houston Astrodome, I know that you don't have cars or transportation and cannot get yourself to the centers to collect these funds. I also know that some of you do not have access to a savings or checking account or ways to cash a check. FEMA and Red Cross teams are either—are working or soon will be working with your shelters to meet your challenges and to get assistance into your hands as soon as possible. By registering for the first $2,000, you will begin the process of arranging for the delivery of other, longer term assistance that will be made available in the coming weeks for eligible households. For those of you who are staying with family members or in a rented room or a hotel or apartment, FEMA is also working to get these funds in your hands.

Now, here are two ways that you can register for this assistance. You can call 1–800–621-FEMA. That's 1–800–621-FEMA. Or, if you have the capability to use the Internet, you can log on to www.fema.gov. A FEMA representative will arrange for your assistance to be delivered by mail or deposited into your bank account. If you have special needs, the FEMA representative can help arrange to get the money to you in another way.

Now, we have 3,000 people who are working around the clock to take the calls. We're in the process of training more, and that number will be increasing dramatically. More than 400,000 families have already been registered. We still have tens of thousands more people who need to be processed, so I ask for your patience if you experience problems in trying to contact FEMA.

To those of you in our faith-based and community groups who have opened up your hearts and homes, I want to thank you for your service to our fellow Americans. If you've not been in contact with a FEMA representative, please do so to help the people in your shelters. And, again, you can call 1-800-621-FEMA. By calling a FEMA representative, you can assure that the people you've taken in are registered and able to receive the emergency assistance funds.

As we work to deliver this emergency relief, we're also working to ensure that those of you who have received Federal benefits administered by the States of Alabama, Mississippi, and Louisiana will continue to get those benefits in the States where you're now staying.

So the second step we're taking today is designed to make it easier for you to register and collect these benefits in any State in the country. We will start by granting evacuee status for all of you who have lived in counties that have been declared disaster areas. We know that many of you no longer have the legal documents or the records to prove your eligibility for the benefits you've been getting. We understand that. And so, with this evacuee status, you will be able to register for your benefits without many of the traditional administrative requirements for verification and enrollment.

The special evacuee status applies to the full range of Federal benefits administered by the States. These programs include: Medicaid; temporary assistance for needy families; child care; mental health services and substance abuse treatment; food stamps; housing; foster care; women, infants, and children nutrition; school lunch; unemployment compensation; and job training.

The States that have opened up their doors should not be penalized for coming to the aid of Americans in distress. And so I'm going to work with the Congress to reimburse the States that are taking in evacuees from the affected areas along the gulf coast.

I want to thank the Governors and the leaders of the States that have taken in so many of our fellow citizens. I want to thank you for your compassion. And we understand that this is going to strain your budgets, so the Federal Government, as I just said, will operate under this principle: You should not be penalized for showing compassion. State enrollment teams are already set up in many shelters, and many have 1–800 numbers that people can call. Any evacuee can contact the nearest State or local benefits office to get the information about enrolling.

And those of you who are staying in a home or church that has access to the Internet can find out how to receive these benefits by going to www.govbenefits.gov. These are just some of the many steps we'll be taking in what will be a long relief effort. We have much more work to do. But the people who have been hurt by this storm know that—need to know that the Government is going to be with you for the long haul.

In all the steps we take, our goal is not to simply provide benefits but to make them easy and simple as possible to collect. The responsibility of caring for hundreds of thousands of citizens who no longer have homes is going to place many demands on our Nation. We have many difficult days ahead, especially as we recover those who did not survive the storm. I've instructed all agencies to honor their memory by treating the dead with the dignity and respect they deserve.

Throughout our history, in times of testing, Americans have come together in prayer to heal and ask for strength for the tasks ahead. So I've declared Friday, September the 16th, as a National Day of Prayer and Remembrance. I ask that we pray, as Americans have always prayed in times of trial, with confidence in His purpose, with hope for a brighter future, and with the humility to ask God to keep us strong so that we can better serve our brothers and sisters in need.

Source: George W. Bush: "Remarks on Hurricane Katrina Recovery Efforts," September 8, 2005. Online by Gerhard Peters and John T. Woolley, *The American Presidency Project*. http://www.presidency.ucsb.edu/ws/?pid=64141.

Hate Crimes

Table 5.4 details the number of hate crime incidents reported by the FBI for selected years, 2000 to 2014, targeting Muslim and Jewish minorities.

Table 5.4   FBI Hate Crime Data, by Year/Group

Year	Total	Religious-Based	Anti-Muslim	Anti-Jewish
2000	8,063	1,472	28	1,109
2001	9,730	1,828	481	1,043
2012	6,513	1,329	148	868
2013	5,228	1,031	135	625
2014	5,479	1,014	154	609

Source: www.huffingtonpost.com/brian-levin-jd/study-in-wake-of-terror-a_b_883 8670.html.

Table 5.5 lists the number of hate groups identified by the Southern Poverty Law Center annually from 1999 to 2016 found throughout the United States.

Table 5.5   Number of Organized Hate Groups, 1999–2016

Year	Number of Groups
1999	457
2000	602
2001	676
2002	708
2003	751
2004	762
2005	803
2006	844
2007	888
2008	926
2009	932
2010	1,002
2011	1,018
2012	1,007
2013	939
2014	784
2015	892
2016	917

Source: https://www.splcenter.org/hate-map.

Figure 5.4 presents a pie chart depicting the top five triggers of anti-Muslim bias incidents occurring in 2016, by number and percentage of total.

Terrorism

Table 5.6 shows the number of Americans killed or wounded during the War on Terrorism.

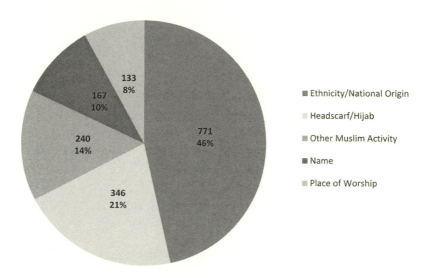

Figure 5.4   Top Five Triggers of Anti-Muslim Incidents
Source: Council on American-Islamic Relations, Report, May 2017, http://islam
ophobia.org/images/2017CivilRightsReport/2017-Empowerment-of-Fear-Final.pdf.

Table 5.6 Total American Casualties of the War on Terrorism

	Killed	Wounded
U.S. military	7,008	50,422
U.S. civilians	3,000+	6,000+
Total Americans	10,008+	56,422+

*Source: "Operation Iraqi Freedom, U.S. Casualty Status," Armed
Forces Press Service, DoD, January 18, 2013.*

Document 5.4: REAL ID Act (2005)

*In 2005, Congress passed the REAL ID Act, Title II, H.R. 1268.
It is designed to improve state-issued driver's licenses and identi-
fication cards. Its official title was the Emergency Supplemental
Appropriations Act for Defense, the Global War on Terrorism, and
Tsunami Relief, 2005. Some of its key provisions are excerpted in
this document.*

Title II—Improved Security for Driver's Licenses and Personal Identification Cards

Sec. 202—MINIMUN DOCUMENT REQUIRE-MENT AND ISSUANCE STANDARDS FOR FEDERAL RECOGNITION

Minimum Standards for Federal Use

(1) IN GENERAL—beginning 3 years after the date of enactment of this division, a Federal agency may not accept, for any official purpose, a driver's license or identification card issued by a State to any person unless the State is meeting the requirements of this section.

(2) STATE CERTIFICATIONS—The Secretary shall determine whether a State is meeting the requirements of this section based on certification made by the State to the Secretary. Such certification shall be made at such times and in such manner as the Secretary, in consideration with the Secretary of Transportation, may prescribe by regulations.

(a) Minimum Document Requirements—To meet the requirements of this section, a State shall include, at a minimum, the following information and features on each driver's license and identification card issued to a person by the State:

(1) The person's full legal name.

(2) The person's date of birth.

(3) The person's gender.

(4) The person's driver's license or identification card number.

(5) A digital photograph of the person.

(6) The person's address of principal residence.

(7) The person's signature.

(8) Physical security features designed to prevent tampering, counterfeiting, or duplication of the document for fraudulent purposes.

(9) A common machine-readable technology, with defined minimum data elements.

(c) Minimum Issuance Standards—

(1) IN GENERAL—To meet the requirements of this section, a State shall require, at a minimum, presentation and verification of the following information before issuing a driver's license or identification card to a person:

(A) A photo identification document, except that a non-photo identity document is acceptable if it includes both the person's full legal name and date of birth.

(B) Documentation showing the person's date of birth.

(C) Proof of the person's Social Security account number or verification that the person is not ineligible for a social security account number.

(D) Documentation showing a person's name and address of physical residence.

(2) SPECIAL REQUIREMENTS—

(A) IN GENERAL—To meet the requirements of this section, a State shall comply with the minimum standards of this paragraph:

(B) EVIDENCE OF LAWFUL STATUS—A State shall require, before issuing a valid driver's license or identification card to a person, valid documentary evidence that the person:

(1) is a citizen of the United States;

(2) is an alien lawfully admitted for permanent residence status or temporary residence in the United States;

(3) has conditional permanent resident status in the United States;

(4) has an approved application for asylum in the United States, or has entered into the United States in refugee status;

(5) has a valid, unexpired nonimmigrant visa or nonimmigrant visa status for entry into the United States;

(6) has a pending application for asylum in the United States;

(7) has a pending or approved application for temporary protected status in the United States;

(8) has a pending application for adjustment of status to that of an alien lawfully admitted for permanent resident status in the United States.

(3) VERIFICATION OF DOCUMENTS—to meet the requirements of this section, a State shall implement the following procedures:

(A) Before issuing a driver's license or identification card to a person, the State shall verify with the issuing agency, the issuance, validity, and completeness of each document required to be presented by the person under paragraph (1) or (2).

(B) The State shall not accept any foreign documents, other than an official passport, to satisfy a requirement of paragraph (1) or (2).

(C) Not later than September 11, 2005, the State shall enter into a memorandum of understanding with the Secretary of Homeland Security to routinely utilize the automated system, known as Systematic Alien Verification of Entitlement, as provided for by section 404 of the Illegal Immigration Reform and Immigrant Responsibility Act of 1996 (110 Stat. 3009–664), to verify the legal presence status of a person, other than a United States citizen, applying for a driver's license or identification card.. .

(1) Employ technology to capture a digital image of identity source of documents so that the images may be retained in electronic storage in a transferable format.

(2) Retain paper copies of source documents for a minimum of 7 years or images of source documents presented for a minimum of 10 years.

(3) Subject each person applying for a driver's license or identification card to mandatory facial image capture.

(4) Establish an effective procedure to confirm or verify a renewing applicant's information.

(5) Confirm with the Social Security Administration a social security account number presented by a person using the full social security number. In the event that a social security account number is already registered to or associated with another person to which any State has issued a driver's license or identification card, the State shall resolve the discrepancy and take appropriate action.

(6) Refuse to issue a driver's license or identification card to a person holding a driver's license issued by another State without confirmation that the person is terminating or has terminated the driver's license.

(7) Ensure the physical security of locations where driver's licenses and identification cards are produced and the security of document materials and papers from which driver's licenses and identification cards are produced.

(8) Subject all persons authorized to manufacture or produce driver's licenses and identification cards to appropriate security clearance requirements.

(9) Establish fraudulent document recognition training programs for appropriate employees engaged in the issuance of driver's licenses and identification cards. . . .

Source: https://www.eff.org/files/filenode/realid/real_id_final_rule_part1_2008-01-11.pdf.

Document 5.5: Executive Order: Protecting the Nation from Foreign Terrorist Entry into the United States

This document summarizes President Trump's "travel-ban" (also known as the Muslim travel ban) executive order of 2017, entitled "Protecting the Nation from Foreign Terrorist Entry into the United States." The ban was ruled unconstitutional by federal district court judges in several states and by an appellate court decision, but partially reinstated by a Supreme Court temporary order issued in July 2017.

By authority vested in me as President by the Constitution and laws of the United States of America, including the Immigration and Nationality Act (INA), 8 U.S.C.1101 et seq., and section 301 of title 3, United States Code, and to protect the American people from terrorist attacks by foreign nationals admitted to the United States, it is hereby ordered as follows:

Section 1. Purpose. The visa-issuance process plays a crucial role in detecting individuals with terrorist ties and stopping them from entering the United States. Perhaps in no instance was that more apparent than the terrorist attacks of September 11, 2001, when State Department policy prevented consular officers from properly scrutinizing the visa applications of several of the 19 foreign nationals who went on to murder nearly 3,000 Americans. And while the visa-issuance process was reviewed and amended after the September 11 attacks to better detect would-be terrorists from receiving visas, these measures did not stop attacks by foreign nationals who were admitted to the United States.

Numerous foreign-born individuals have been convicted or implicated in terrorism-related crimes since September 11, 2001, including foreign nationals who entered the United States after receiving visitor, student, or employment visas, or who entered through the United States refugee resettlement program. Deteriorating conditions in certain countries due to war, strife, disaster, and civil unrest increase the likelihood that terrorists will use any means possible to enter the United States. The United States must be vigilant during the visa-issuance process to ensure that those approved for admission do not intend to harm Americans and that they have no ties to terrorism.

In order to protect Americans . . . the United States cannot, and should not, admit those who do not support the Constitution, or those who would place violent ideologies over American law . . . the United States should not admit those who engage in acts of bigotry or hatred (including "honor" killings, other forms of violence against women, or the persecution of those who practice religions different from their own) or those who would oppose Americans of any race, gender, or sexual orientation.

Sec. 2. Policy. It is the policy of the United States to protect its citizens from foreign nationals who intend to commit terrorists attacks in the United States, and to prevent from the admission of foreign nationals who intend to exploit United States immigration laws for malevolent purposes.

Sec. 3. Suspension of Issuance of Visas and Other Immigration Benefits to Nationals of Countries of Particular Concern. (a) The Secretary of Homeland Security, in consultation with the Secretary of State and the Director of National Intelligence, shall immediately conduct a review to determine the information needed from any country to adjudicate any visa, admission, or other benefit under the INA (adjudications) in order to determine that the individuals seeking the benefit is who the individual claims to be and is not a security or public safety threat. . . .

(c) To temporarily reduce investigative burdens on relevant agencies during the review period described in subsection (a) of this section, to ensure the proper review and maximum utilization of available resources for the screening of foreign nationals, and to ensure that adequate standards are established to prevent infiltration by foreign terrorists or criminals . . . I hereby proclaim that the immigrant and nonimmigrant entry into the United States of aliens from countries referred to in section 217 (a) (12) . . . would be detrimental to the interests of the United States and I hereby suspend entry into the United States, as immigrants and nonimmigrants, of such persons for 90 days from the date of this order . . . (f) At any point after submitting the list described in subsection (e) of this section, the Secretary of State or the Secretary of Homeland Security may submit to the President the names of any additional countries recommended for similar treatment. . .(h) The Secretaries of State and Homeland Security shall submit to the President a joint report on the progress in implementing this order within 30 days of the date of this order, a second report within 60 days of the date of this order, a third report within 90 days of the date of this order, and a fourth report within 120 days of the date of this order.

Sec. 4. Implementing Uniform Screening Standards for All Immigration Programs. (a) The Secretary of State, the Secretary of Homeland Security, the Director of National Intelligence, and the Director of the Federal Bureau of Investigation shall implement a program, as part of the adjudication process for immigration benefits, to identify individuals seeking to enter the United States on a fraudulent basis with the intent to cause harm, or who are risk of causing harm subsequent to their admission. This program will include the development of a uniform screening standard or procedure, such as in-person interviews; a database of identity documents proffered by applicants to ensure that duplicate documents are not used by multiple applicants; amended application forms that include questions aimed at identifying fraudulent answers and malicious intent; a mechanism to ensure that the applicant is who the applicant claims to be; a process to evaluate the applicant's likelihood of becoming a positively contributing member of society and the applicant's ability to make contributions to the national interest; and a mechanism to assess whether or not the applicant has the intent to commit criminal or terrorist acts after entering the United States . . .

Sec. 5. Realignment of the U.S. Refugee Admission Program for Fiscal Year 2017. (a) The Secretary of State shall suspend the U.S. Refugee Admission Program (USRAP) for 120 days. During the 120-day period, the Secretary of State, in conjunction with the Secretary of Homeland Security and in consultation with the Director of National Intelligence, shall review the USRAP application and adjudication process to determine what additional procedures may be taken to ensure that those approved for refugee admission do not pose a threat to the security and welfare of the United States, and shall implement such additional procedures. . . . Upon the date that is 120 days after the date of this order, the Secretary of State shall resume USRAP admissions only for nationals from countries for which the Secretary of State, the Secretary of Homeland Security, and the Director of National Intelligence have jointly determined that such additional procedures are adequate to ensure the security and welfare of the United States. (b) Upon the resumption of USRAP admissions, the Secretary of State, in consultation with the Secretary of Homeland Security, is further directed to make changes, to the extent permitted by law, to prioritize refugee claims made by individuals on the basis of religious-based persecution, provided that the religion of the individual is a minority religion in the individual's country of nationality . . .(c) Pursuant to section 212 (f) of the INA . . . I hereby proclaim that the entry of nationals from Syria as refugees is detrimental to the interests of the United States and this suspend any such entry until such time as I have determined that sufficient changes have been made to the USRAP to ensure that admission of Syrian refugees is consistent with the national interest. (d) Pursuant to section 212(f) . . . I hereby proclaim that the entry of more than 50,000 refugees in fiscal year 2017 would be detrimental to the interests of the United States, and thus suspend any such entry until such time as I determine that additional admissions would be in the national interest . . . (f) The Secretary of State shall submit to the President an initial report on the progress of the directive in subsection (b) of this section regarding prioritization of claims made by individuals on the basis of religious-based persecution within 100 days of the date of this order and shall submit a second report within 200 days of the date of this order . . .

Sec. 7. Expedited Completion of the Biometric Entry-Exit Tracking System. (a) The Secretary of Homeland Security shall expedite the completion and implementation of a biometric entry-exit tracking system for all travelers to the United States, as recommended by the National Commission on Terrorist Attacks Upon the United States . . .

Sec. 8. Visa Interview Security. (a) The Secretary of State shall immediately suspend the Visa Interview Waiver Program and ensure compliance with Section 222 of the INA . . . which requires that all individuals seeking a nonimmigrant visa undergo an in-person interview, subject to specific statutory exceptions . . .

Source: https://www.whitehouse.gov/presidential-actions/exe cutive-order-protecting-nation-foreign-terrorist-entry-united-states/.

Document 5.6: Summary Excerpts of the Supreme Court Ruling on the Travel Ban (June 26, 2017)

This document presents a summary of the Supreme Court ruling on June 26, 2017, that partially upheld the travel ban and scheduled full oral arguments of the travel ban order for the fall of 2017.

The United States Supreme Court decided that the United States can ban entry by persons from Muslim countries, partially and temporarily upholding the Executive Order travel ban. Travelers from Iran, Syria, Sudan, Libya, Somalia, and Yemen are barred from coming to the United States unless they have a bona fide, well-documented connection to a United States person or entity. The timeframe appears to be from June 29, 2017 for 90 days to September 27, 2017. For refugees, the timeframe appears to be 120 days, to October 27, 2017.

There does not appear to be any basis for revoking previously approved visas. However, the ruling could cause confusion in particular for those with plans to come to the United States on tourism or for business visits. B-1 and B-2 visa applications for business or tourism may be denied, and B-1/B-2 travelers may be refused entry at United States airports and ports of entry if the Immigration Officer is not convinced the traveler meets the "bona fide connection" standard. But foreign workers from countries with approved visas, such as H-1B workers, F-1 students; J-1 exchange visitors; K-1 fiance's; L-1 intracompany executive, manager, and specialized knowledge transferees; O-1 extraordinary ability personnel; P-1 performers; R-1 religious workers; and E-2 investors; should be allowed entry. It is unclear how dual citizens, such as dual Iranian-Canadian citizens will be treated under the ruling. Green card holders should not be affected.

Source: https://www.jdsupra.com/legalnews/muslim-country-travel-ban-upheld-in-part-70428/.

Immigration

Since 2009, the United States has received a growing number of illegal immigrants arriving as children unaccompanied by an adult, sent by their families in a desperate attempt to get them out of harm's way in the hope they will be given asylum in the United States. Table 5.7 lists the annual number of such arrivals from their country of origin.

Critics of the Obama administration have labeled him the "Deporter-in-Chief." One reason why can be seen by the data in Table 5.8. It reports the number of deportations from the United States for the years 2011 to 2016.

Table 5.7 Unaccompanied Immigrant Children Encountered, by Fiscal Year and Country of Origin, 2009–2014

Country	2009	2010	2011	2012	2013	2014
El Salvador	1,221	1,910	1,394	3,134	5,990	16,404
Guatemala	1,115	1,517	1,516	3,835	8,068	17,057
Honduras	968	1,017	974	2,997	6,747	18,244
Mexico	16,114	13,724	11,768	13,974	17,240	15,634
Total	19,418	18,168	15,701	24,120	38,045	67,339

Source: Data from U.S. Customs and Border Patrol, https://www.cbp.gov/new sroom/stats/southwest-border-unaccompanied-children/fy-2014.

Table 5.8 Trends in Removals: 2011–2016

Year	2011	2012	2013	2014	2015	2016
Total	387,134	418,397	438,421	577,295	462,463	450,954

Sources: https://www.dhs.gov/news/2014/12/19/dhs-releases-end-year-statistics; https://www.dhs.gov/news/2015/12/22/dhs-releases-end-fiscal-year-2015-statistics; https://www.dhs.gov/news/2016/12/30/dhs-releases-end-year-fiscal-year-2016-statistics.

Document 5.7: Immigration Act (1996)

In the 1996 immigration act, provisions for categories of inadmissible immigrants and for expedited removal were enacted. This document excerpts related regulations from the Federal Register promulgated in 1997 that were applied to Citizenship and Immigration Service, Immigration Control and Enforcement, and Customs and Border Protection defining inspection and expedited removal of immigrants, the detention and removal of immigrants, and conduct of removal proceedings.

235.3 Inadmissible Aliens and Expedited Removal

(a) Detention prior to inspection. All persons arriving at a port of entry in the United States by vessel or aircraft shall be detained aboard the vessel or at the airport of arrival by the owner, agent, master, commanding officer, person in charge, purser, or consignee of such vessel or aircraft until admitted or otherwise permitted to land by an officer of the Service. . . . The Service will not be liable for any expenses related to such detention or presentation or for any expenses of a passenger who has not been presented for inspection and for whom a determination has not been made concerning admissibility by a Service officer.

(b) Expedited removal. (1) Determination of inadmissibility. An alien who is arriving in the United States or other alien as designated pursuant to paragraph (b)(2)(ii) of this section who is determined to be inadmissible . . . shall be ordered removed from the United States in accordance with section 235 (b)(1) of the Act. The examining immigration officer shall serve the alien with Form I-860, Notice and Order of Expedition Removal. Except as otherwise provided in this section, such alien is not entitled to a hearing before an immigration judge in proceedings pursuant to section 240 of the Act, or to an appeal of the expedited removal order by the Board of Immigration Appeals . . .

(2) Applicability. The expedited removal provisions shall apply to the following classes of aliens who are determined to be inadmissible under section 212(a)(6)(c) or (7) of the Act:

(1) Arriving aliens, as defined in &1.1(q) of this chapter, except for citizens of Cuba arriving at a United States port-of-entry by aircraft;

(ii) As specifically designated by the Commissioner, aliens who arrive in, attempt to enter, or have entered the United States without having been admitted or paroled following inspection by an immigration officer at a designated port-of-entry, and who have not established to the satisfaction of the immigration officer that they have been physically present in the United States. The Commissioner shall have the sole discretion to apply the provisions of section 235 (b)(1) of the Act, at any time, to any class of aliens described in this section. . . . Any absence from the United States shall serve to break the period of continuous physical presence. An alien who has not been inspected and admitted or paroled into the United States but who establishes that he or she has been continuously physically present in the United States for the 2-year period immediately prior to the date of determination of inadmissibility shall be detained in accordance with section 235(b)(2) of the Act for a proceeding under section 240 of the Act.

(3) Additional charges of inadmissibility. In the expedited removal process, the Service may not charge an alien with any additional grounds other than section 212(a)(6)(C) or 212(a)(7) of the Act. . . . Nothing in this paragraph shall preclude the Service from pursuing such additional grounds of inadmissibility against the alien in any subsequent attempt to reenter the United States, provided the additional grounds of inadmissibility still exist.

(4) Claim of asylum or fear of persecution. If an alien subject to the expedited removal provisions indicates an intention to apply for asylum, a fear of persecution, or a fear of return to his or her country, the inspecting officer shall, before proceeding further with the case, detain the alien and refer him or her for an interview by an asylum officer in accordance with &208.30 of this chapter to determine if the alien has a credible fear of persecution. . . . Pending the credible fear determination, the alien shall be detained. Parole of such alien in accordance with section 212(d)(5) of the Act may be permitted only when the Attorney General determines, in the exercise of discretion, that parole is required to meet a medical emergency or is necessary for a legitimate law enforcement objective.

(5) Claim to lawful permanent resident, refugee, or asylee status. (i) Verification of status. If an applicant for admission who is subject to expedited removal pursuant to section 235(b)(1) of the Act claims to have been lawfully

admitted for permanent residence, admitted as a refugee under section 207 of the Act, or granted asylum under section 208 of the Act, the immigration officer shall attempt to verify the alien's claim. Such verification shall include a check of all available Service data systems and any other means available to the officer. . . . Whenever practicable, a written statement shall be taken from the alien. The immigration officer shall issue an expedited order of removal under section 235(b)(1)(A)(i) of the Act and refer the alien to the immigration judge for review of the order in accordance with paragraph (b)(5)(iv) of this section and &235.6(a)(2)(ii).

(iii) Claimed refugees and asylees. If a check of Service records or other means indicates that the alien has been granted refugee status or asylee status, and such status has not been terminated in deportation, exclusion, or removal proceedings, the immigration officer shall not order the alien removed pursuant to section 235(b)(1) of the Act. . .

(7) Review of expedited removal orders. Any removal order entered by an examining immigration officer pursuant to section 235(b)(1) of the Act must be reviewed and approved by the appropriate supervisor before the order is considered final. . .

(8) Removal procedures relating to expedited removal. An alien ordered removed pursuant to section 235(b)(1) of the Act shall be removed from the United States in accordance with section 241(c) of the Act and 8 (CFR) part 241.

(d) Service custody. The Service will assume custody of any alien subject to detention under paragraph (b) or (c) of this section. In its discretion, the Service may require any alien who appears inadmissible and who arrives at a land border or port-of-entry from Canada or Mexico, to remain in that country while awaiting a removal hearing. Such alien shall be considered detained for a proceeding with the meaning of section 235(b) of the Act and may be ordered removed in absentia by an immigration judge if the alien fails to appear for the hearing.

Source: https://www.uscis.gov/sites/default/files/ocomm/ilink/0-0-0-10948.html.

Document 5.8: Changes to National Security Entry-Exit Registration System

On December 1, 2003, the Department of Homeland Security released the following fact sheet regarding changes to National Security Entry-Exit Registration System (NSEERS) 202–282–8010. It presents statistical data on the NSEERS program as well as specifies the changes made to the program, its processes, and the sending nations covered by NSEERS. The new procedures were published in the Federal Register. The fact sheet is presented in its entirety in this document.

The Department of Homeland Security has decided to suspend the National Security Entry-Exit Registration System (NSEERS) re-registration requirement that mandated aliens to re-register after 30-days and one year of continuous presence in the United States. The new process is outlined in the interim rule published in the Federal Register.

NSEERS established a national registry for temporary foreign visitors (non-immigrant aliens) arriving from certain countries, or who meet a combination of intelligence-based criteria, and are identified as presenting an elevated national security concern. The program has collected detailed information about the background and purpose of an individual's visit to the United States, the periodic verification of their location and activities, and departure confirmation. NSEERS was the first step taken by the Department of Justice and then DHS in order to comply with the development of the congressionally-mandated requirement for a comprehensive entry-exit program by 2005.

The domestic registration program included citizens or nationals from Afghanistan, Algeria, Bahrain, Bangladesh, Egypt, Eritrea, Indonesia, Iran, Iraq, Jordan, Kuwait, Libya, Lebanon, Morocco, North Korea, Oman, Pakistan, Qatar, Somalia, Saudi Arabia, Sudan, Syria, Tunisia, United Arab Emirates, and Yemen. However, to date, individuals from more than 150 countries have been registered in the NSEERS program.

Most of the foreign visitors registered are students, individuals in the U.S. on extended business travel, or individuals visiting family members for lengthy periods. The requirement to register does not apply to U.S. citizens, lawful permanent residents (green card holders), refugees, asylum applicants, asylum grantees, and diplomats or others admitted under "A" or "G" visas.

At the time of initial registration, all individuals were given instructions that they had to re-register in one year, or after thirty days if initially registered at a port-of-entry. The numbers who were to re-register were expected to vary from last year because some individuals may have left the country; traveled outside and back into the country (changing their one-year anniversary date to the most recent entry registration date); or adjusted their status, eliminating the need for re-registration.

Previous Re-Registration Requirements:

• All individuals registered under NSEERS were required to re-register after thirty days if initially registered at a port-of-entry, and annually if they are remaining in the United States past one year. This notice was given to individuals at the time of registration, either at a designated port of entry or a Bureau of Citizenship and Immigration Services office.

• The annual anniversary date for re-registration is based on the last time that an individual registered. The annual interview requirement of those individuals subject to the first call-in registration, which began on November 15, 2002, began November 5, 2003. The annual interviews of those individuals who registered at a port of entry beginning September 11, 2002, began on the one-year anniversary of their date of registration.

- Individuals have a ten-day window in which to show up for their annual interview. In other words, they can report for their interview within ten days after their anniversary dates.

- Those individuals required to report for their yearly interview were expected to return to the same office at which they registered last year. If they had moved, they would go to the nearest ICE or CIS office or sub-office. The willful failure to do so is a criminal violation of the Immigration and Nationality Act, and the willful failure to register would also render an alien deportable.

- The NSEERS program is a valuable first step towards a more comprehensive entry-exit system—USVISIT. Congress mandated that a comprehensive entry-exit program be developed by 2005.

Changes Made by the New Rule:

- There will no longer be a 30-day or one-year re-registration requirement, effective with the publishing of the new rule in the Federal Register.

- In place of the previous requirement, the new rule will allow DHS, as a matter of discretion, to notify individual nonimmigrant aliens subject to NSEERS registration to appear for one or more additional continuing registration interviews in those particular cases where it may be necessary to determine whether the alien is complying with the conditions of his or her nonimmigrant visa status and admission.

- The rule also provides that when an alien who is monitored under Student and Exchange Visitor Information System (SEVIS) notifies DHS of a change of address or change of educational institution through SEVIS, it also constitutes a notification for the purposes of NSEERS registration.

NSEERS Background:

- On September 11, 2002, the United States began implementation of NSEERS at U.S. ports of entry. On November 5, 2002, the domestic all-in registration began. Congress required the Immigration and Naturalization Service (INS) to implement a comprehensive entry-exit program in 1996. That system must be in place by 2005. NSEERS is the first step in fulfilling that congressional mandate.

- NSEERS promotes several national security objectives: (1) NSEERS allows the United States to run the fingerprints of aliens who may present elevated national security concerns against a database of wanted criminals and known terrorists; (2) NSEERS enables DHS to determine instantly when such an alien has overstayed his visa, which was the case with three of the 9/11 hijackers; (3) NSEERS enables DHS to verify that an alien in the United States on a temporary visa is doing what he said he would be doing, and living where he said he would live.

- The countries prioritized for special registration were selected because: (1) All of these countries are places where Al-Qaeda or other terrorist organizations have been active, or where the United States has other national security concerns; (2) This was not an exclusive list—all non-immigrant visitors from other countries eventually will be included as the US-VISIT program is implemented.

NSEERS General Information:

- The majority of those required to register under NSEERS complied and fulfilled this requirement successfully. It is the individual's responsibility to comply with U.S. immigration law and maintain legal status while in the United States.

- There were a small number of individuals who temporarily were kept in detention while they were processed for immigration violations during the domestic enrollment portion of the program.

- As of September 30, 2003, individuals from 150 countries have complied with the NSEERS registration requirements for a total of 290, 526 registrations, which includes those registering both a Ports-of-Entry (POEs) and the former INS district offices nationwide. The registrations performed are broken down in the following ways: 207,007 registrations (93,741 individuals) at the POEs, and 83,519 individuals at the former INS offices.

- NSEERS requirements applied only to certain non-immigrant aliens. These requirements do NOT include U.S. citizens, lawful permanent residents (green card holders), refugees, asylum applicants (who applied before November 22, 2003), asylum grantees, and diplomats or others admitted under A or G visas.

- European countries have had similar registration systems in place for decades.

NSEERS Statistics through September 30, 2003:

Total Number of Registrations: 290,526.
   Total Number of Individuals Registered: 177,260
   Port-of-Entry Registration
   Total Port of Entry Registration: 207,007
   Number of Individuals: 93,741
   Domestic Registration. Total Domestic Registration: 83,519
   Referred to Investigation: Notices to Appear Issued: 13,799
   Total Number Detained: 2,870; Total Number in Custody: 23; Total Number of Criminals: 143.

Source: web.cache.googleusecontent.com/search?q=cache:11 RQPS

Document 5.9: The Deferred Action for Childhood Arrivals (DACA) and the Deferred Action for Parents of Americans and Lawful Permanent Residents (DAPA)

This document excerpts a summary of the eligibility requirements specified in President Obama's two executive deferred actions programs, Deferred Action for Childhood Arrivals (DACA) and Deferred Action for Parents of Americans and Lawful Permanent Residents (DAPA). They were announced in 2012 and 2014, respectively. DACA took place and enrolled thousands. A court-ordered injunction stopped the Department of Homeland Security from implementing DAPA. Both executive actions were overturned by executive orders from President Trump.

DACA APPLICANTS MUST:

- Have come before their 16th birthday.
- Lived in the United States continuously since January 1, 2010.
- Be present in the United States on June 15, 2012 and every day since.
- Have graduated or obtained a GED certificate, or be in school on the date the person submits an application.
- Pay an application fee of $465, which consists of a $380 fee for employment authorization, and an $85 fee for fingerprints.

PERSONS ELIGIBLE FOR DAPA INCLUDE:

- A parent of a United States Citizen or lawful permanent resident.
- Have continuously lived in the United States since January 1, 2010.
- Have been present in the United States on November 20, 2014.
- Not have a lawful immigration status as of November 20, 2014—meaning one entered the country undocumented or if lawfully entered, must have stayed beyond the expiration of the temporary visa.

- Have not been convicted of certain criminal offenses, including felonies, acts of terrorism, and some misdemeanors.

Source: Summaries of both actions by author; data from https://www.uscis.gov/immigrationaction.

Border Control

Table 5.9 summarizes the various Border Patrol forces in 2017.

Table 5.9: U. S. Border Patrol Summary Data, FY 2017

Sector	Number of Agents	Apprehen- sions	Deaths
Coastal Border Sector	212	3,588	NA
Northern Border Sector	2,048	3,027	NA
Southwest Border Sector	16,605	303,916	294
Nationwide Total	19,437	310,531	294

Source: Adapted from https://www.cbp.gov/sites/default/files/assets/documents/2017-Dec/USBP%20Stats%20FY2017%20sector%20profile.pdf.

Document 5.10: USA Patriot Act of 2001

In response to the 9/11 international terrorist attacks, Congress enacted the USA Patriot Act, a bill of 288 pages. Some key provisions of the act broadened the definition of terrorism, expanded grounds for inadmissibility to include immigrants suspected of terrorist activity or those who publicly endorsed such activity, and required the attorney general to detain immigrants whom he certified as threats to national security. This document presents some of its key provisions.

Title IV—Protecting the Border

SUBTITLE A—PROTECTING THE NORTHERN BORDER

Sec. 401—Ensures adequate personnel on the northern border.

Sec. 403—Grants access by the Department of State and the INS to certain identifying records of visa applicants and applicants for admission to the United States.

Sec. 405—Establishes an integrated automated fingerprint identification system for ports of entry and overseas consular posts.

SUBTITLE B—ENHANCED IMMIGRATION PROVISIONS

Sec. 412—Mandates detention of suspected terrorists; suspends habeas corpus under certain conditions, and limits judicial review.

Sec. 413—Ensures multilateral cooperation against terrorism.

Sec. 414—Provides for increased integrity and security of visas.

Sec. 415—Mandates participation by the Office of Homeland Security in the Entry-Exit Task Force.

Sec. 416—Establishes a foreign student monitoring program.

Sec. 417—Calls for machine-readable passports.

Title X-Miscellaneous

Sec. 1006—Provides for the inadmissibility of aliens engaged in money laundering.

Source: PL107–56, https://www.congress.gov/bill/107th-congress/house-bill/3162; and http://www.usapatriotact.com.

Document 5.11: FEMA's Operation Liberty Shield

On March 17, 2003, FEMA released the following press release describing what it referred to as "Operation Liberty Shield." It details the administrative actions taken by FEMA to increase border protections for the flow of people and goods across the thousands of miles of U.S. border. This document presents the press release about Operation Liberty Shield.

Operation Liberty Shield is a comprehensive national plan to increase protections for American citizens and infrastructure while maintaining the free flow of goods and people across our border with minimal disruption to our economy and way of life. Operation Liberty Shield is a multi-department, multi-agency, national team effort. It includes:

1) Increased security at borders—**More Patrols.** Security has been increased at major U.S. ports and waterways with more Coast Guard patrols by aircraft, ships and boats. **Major escorts of passenger ships**. The Coast Guard has increased its escorts of ferries and cruise ships. **More Sea Marshals.** Every high interest vessel arriving or departing from American ports will have armed Coast Guard Marshals onboard, closely watching the ship's crew and ensuring that it makes its port call safely. These merchant ships have cargoes, crewmembers, or other characteristics that warrant closer examination. **Selective Maritime Restrictions.** The Coast Guard will enforce security zones in and around critical infrastructure sites in key ports. This information will be published and announced for those using U.S. waterways.

2) **Land Borders.** Increasing border surveillance and monitoring of the borders will be increased with more agents and patrol assets. These forces will cover areas between major ports of entry. **Increased Border Screening.** Customs and Border Protection officers will increase screenings of vehicles and cargo crossing our land borders. Officers will conduct more interviews and detailed screenings as people transit in and out of the United States. The actions at land borders are not expected to significantly impact the movement of people and cargo across the border.

3) **Asylum Modifications**. Asylum applicants from nations where al-Qaeda, al-Qaeda sympathizers, and other terrorist

groups are known to have operated will be detained for the duration of their processing period. This reasonable and prudent temporary action allows authorities to maintain contact with asylum seekers while we determine the validity of their claim. DHS and the Department of State will coordinate exceptions to this policy.

4) **Stronger Transportation Protections.** The Transportation Security Agency will implement airport security measures that are proactive, sustainable, and focused, based on intelligence information. One of the most visible changes will be increasing the presence of law enforcement officers on patrol and in airport facilities. TSA has advised air carriers to review and ensure the validity of all personal ID's for those personnel who have an airport ID.

Source: www.fema.gov/news-releases/2003/03/17/operation-liberty-shield.

Document 5.12: The Intelligence Reform and Prevention Act of 2004

The Intelligence Reform and Terrorism Prevention Act of 2004 runs hundreds of pages comprised of eight titles, each of which has numerous subtitles and many sections. This document cites the titles and sections related to border protection, immigration and visa matters, and terrorism prevention.

Title V—Border Protection, Immigration, and Visa Matters

SUBTITLE A—ADVANCED TECHNOLOGY NORTHERN BORDER SECURITY PILOT PROGRAM

Sec. 5102. Program requirements.

Sec. 5103. Administrative provisions.

Title VIII—Other Matters

Source: https://www.gpo.gov/fdsys/pkg/PLAW-108publ458/pdf/PLAW-108publ458.pdf.

Document 5.13: The Secure Border Initiative

In 2005, Department of Homeland Security (DHS) secretary Michael Chertoff announced the Secure Border Initiative. This document excerpts the DHS press release describing the Secure Border Initiative.

The Secure Border Initiative (SBI) is a comprehensive, multi-year plan to secure America's borders and reduce illegal immigration. Homeland Security Secretary Michael Chertoff has announced an overall vision for the SBI which includes:

- More agents to patrol our borders, secure our ports of entry, and enforce immigration laws.
- Expanded detention and removal capabilities to eliminate "catch and release" once and for all.
- A comprehensive and systematic upgrading of the technology used in controlling the border, including increased manned aerial assets, expanded use of UAVs, and next-generation detection technology.
- Increased investment in infrastructure improvements at the borders—providing additional physical security to sharply reduce illegal border crossings, and
- Greatly increased interior enforcement of our immigration laws—including more robust worksite enforcement.

Staffing: Under SBI, our goal is to have operational control of both the northern and southern borders within five years.

- An 11% increase in U.S. Customs and Border Protection, bringing funding to $7 billion . . . by hiring an additional 1,000 Border Patrol agents. . . . Border Patrol will increase by nearly 3,000 since 9/11.
- Homeland Security Appropriations will include roughly $3.9 billion in total funding for ICE this fiscal year, a 9% increase over last year.

- Increased funding will allow ICE to add roughly 250 new criminal investigators to better target human smuggling organizations. . . . It will allow ICE to add 400 new Immigration Enforcement Agents and 100 new Deportation Officers.

Detention and Removal: The vision for re-engineering the detention and removal process is to create an effective system that will always have available detention capacity and a streamlined process to minimize the length of detention prior to removal of the alien. Detention Capacity: .. . add 2,000 new beds, bringing the total to 20,000. . . Effective Removal (ER) . . . by policy, DHS has chosen to exercise its authority at all ports of entry and between ports of entry only along the Southwest border for aliens apprehended within 100 miles of the border and within 14 days of entry.

Technology and Infrastructure. DHS will field the most effective mix of current and next generation technology with appropriately trained personnel. Our goal is to ultimately have the capacity to integrate multiple state of the art systems and sensor arrays into a single comprehensive detection suite. . . .

Source: https://www.gao.gov/products/GAO-10-651T.

Document 5.14: The Secure Fence Act

Congress passed the Secure Fence Act of 2006 (H.R. 6061). This document excerpts sections 2, 3, and 4 of the act. It defines "operational control of the border," and authorizes construction of a fence along the southern border, and a study of the Northern Border.

SECTION 2: ACHIEVING OPERATIONAL CONTROL OF THE BORDER.

(a) IN GENERAL—not later than 18 months after the date of the enactment of this Act, the Secretary of Homeland shall take all actions the Secretary determines necessary and appropriate to achieve and maintain operational control over the entire international land and maritime borders of the United States to include the following:

(1) systematic surveillance of the international land and maritime border of the United States through more effective use of personnel and technology such as unmanned aerial vehicles, ground-based sensors, satellites, radar coverage, and cameras; and;

(2) physical infrastructure enhancements to prevent unlawful entry by aliens into the United States and facilitate access to the international land and maritime borders by U.S. Customs and Border Protection, such as additional checkpoints, all weather access roads, and vehicle barriers.

(b) OPERATIONAL CONTROL DEFINED. In this section, the term "operational control" means the prevention of all unlawful entries into the United States, including entry by terrorists, narcotics, other unlawful aliens, instruments of terrorism, and other contraband. . . .

SECTION 3. CONSTRUCTION OF FENCING AND SECURITY IMPROVEMENTS IN BORDER AREAS FROM PACTIFIC OCEAN TO GULF OF MEXICO.

Section 102 (b) of the Illegal Immigration Reform and Immigrant Responsibility Act of 1996 . . . is amended—

(a) REINFORCED FENCING—In carrying out subsection (a), the Secretary of Homeland Security shall provide for at least 2 layers of reinforced fencing, the installation of additional barriers, roads, lighting, cameras, and sensors—

(i) extending from 10 miles west of the Tecate, California port of entry to 10 miles east of Tecate, California, port of entry;

(ii) extending from 10 miles west of Calexico, California port of entry to 5 miles east of the Douglas, Arizona port of entry;

(iii) extending from 5 miles west of Columbus, New Mexico, port of entry to 10 miles east of El Paso, Texas;

(iv) extending from 5 miles northwest of the Del Rio, Texas, port of entry to 5 miles southwest of the Eagle Pass, Texas, port of entry; and

(v) extending from 15 miles to the Brownsville, Texas port of entry. . . .

SECTION 4. NORTHERN BORDER STUDY

(A) IN GENERAL—The Secretary of Homeland Security shall conduct a study on the feasibility of a state-of-the-art infrastructure security system along the northern international border and maritime border of the United States and shall include in the study—(1) the necessity of implementing such a system; (2) the feasibility of implementing such a system; (3) the economic impact implementing such a system will have along the northern border.

(B) REPORT—Not later than one year after the date of the enactment of this Act, the Secretary of Homeland Security will submit to the Committee on Homeland Security of the House of Representatives and the Committee on Homeland Security and Government Affairs of the Senate a report that contains the results of the study conducted under subsection (A). . . .

Source: www.congress.gov/bill/109th-congress/house-bill/6061.

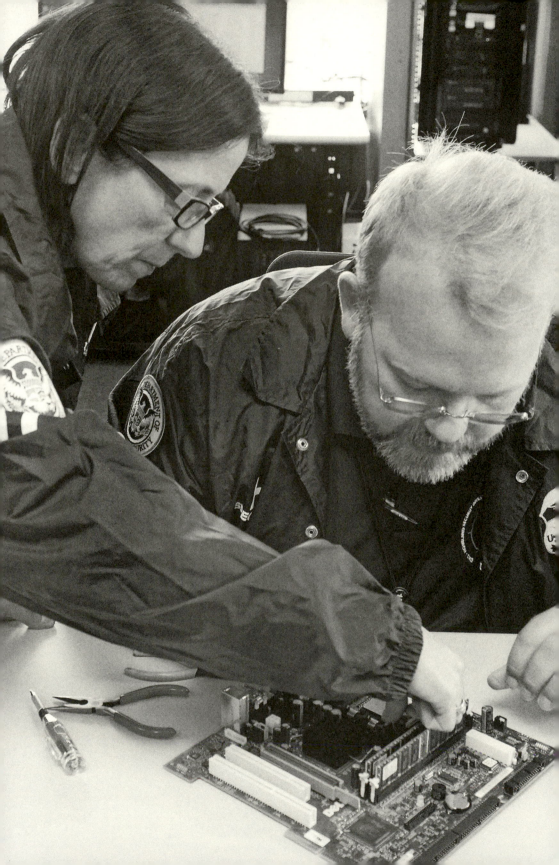

Introduction

This chapter lists and discusses briefly some major sources of information the reader is encouraged to consult. It begins with print sources: 73 scholarly books on the subject are cited and annotated. It then lists and discusses 27 scholarly refereed journals that publish articles pertinent to the subject. Finally, it lists and discusses nonprint sources: 12 feature-length films and seven videos that give "life" and faces to the subject, illustrating the discourse and the politics of attempting to "secure" the homeland.

Books

Al-Bayati, T. Hamid. 2017. *A New Counterterrorism Strategy: Why the World Failed to Stop Al Qaeda and ISIS/ISIL and How to Defeat Terrorists.* Santa Barbara, CA: Praeger Press.

> Ambassador Al-Bayati explains why current policies failed to stop Al Qaeda and ISIS/ISIL. He concludes that they focus too much on military and security measures and have shortcomings that allow terrorists to continue their

---

Employees of the U.S. Immigration and Customs Enforcement's Homeland Security Investigations work in a state-of-the-art computer forensics laboratory in Boston on October 12, 2011. The facility assists federal, state, and local law enforcement authorities in New England with a wide range of forensic investigative support systems. (Department of Defense)

operations. He identifies these policy shortcomings and presents a comprehensive and sustainable strategy of counterterrorism.

Alden, Edward. 2008. *Closing the American Border: Terrorism, Immigration, and Security since 9/11*. New York: Harper Perennial. Alden's book is a provocative and behind-the-scenes look at the country's efforts to secure its borders since the 9/11 attacks. Based on extensive interviews with Secretary of State Collin Powell, Secretary of Homeland Security Tom Ridge, other Bush administration officials, and many innocent citizens whose lives have been upended by new security and visa policy and rules, he offers a compelling assessment of the dangers for the United States that results from the United States cutting itself off from the rest of the world.

Andreas, Peter, and Timothy Snyder, eds. 2000. *The Wall around the West: State Borders and Immigration Controls in North America and Europe*. Lanham, MD: Rowman and Littlefield. A balanced but critical examination of the increasing barriers being enacted in response to increasing international terrorism to control immigration and refugee flows into Canada, the United States, and the major immigration-receiving nations of Europe, particularly the European Union countries.

Ashcroft, John. 2006. *Never Again: Securing America and Restoring Justice*. New York: Hachette Book Group. The highly controversial former attorney general tells the story, from his viewpoint, behind the War on Terror post 9/11. Ashcroft shares his unique perspective on the dangers to and within the United States from outside forces and what the Department of Justice did to repair the serious breaches in the security of the United States. His book dwells on the security problems and concerns and addresses, but treats lightly, the civil liberty and privacy concerns raised by the policy attempts to "secure the homeland."

Bergen, Peter L. 2006. *The Osama Bin Laden I Know: An Oral History of Al Qaeda's Leader*. New York: Free Press.

Written by an American journalist who met, interviewed, and followed the career of Osama bin Laden, then the world's most sought-after terrorist, Bergen's book provides insight into the life and character of Osama bin Laden, drawing on his own never-before-published interviews with the terrorist, with Osama's close associates, and with the experiences of bin Laden's close acquaintances. It is an enduring look at the man who declared war on the West.

Bolden, Jane, and Thomas Weiss, eds. 2004. *Terrorism and the UN: Before and after September 11*. Bloomington: Indiana University Press.

Terrorism and the UN is a scholarly examination of international terrorism whose authors focus on how the United Nations responded to the global challenge. It is one of the few books that look at the role of the international community writ large. An edited volume, it brings together various essays of an academically diverse collection of scholars from the theoretical to the practical aspects of dealing with terrorism. It is an important and insightful book for students of international organizations and of terrorism.

Brill, Stephen. 2003. *After: How America Confronted the September 12 Era*. New York: Simon and Schuster.

Brill is an award-winning journalist whose narrative reads like a thriller novel, but is real. The book focuses on how Americans cope with the aftermath of the 9/11 attacks. He draws on 317 interviews including a customs inspector searching cargo containers from all over the world;

a young widow with three children who challenges the head of a federal victims fund; a Silicon valley entrepreneur who makes screening devices; Attorney General John Ashcroft, a recently hired director of the ACLU, and DHS secretary Tom Ridge, to paint a gritty story of coping with the post-9/11 era in America.

Brisard, Jean Charles, and Damien Martinez. 2005. *Zarqawi: The New Face of Al Qaeda.* New York: Other Press.
Jean-Charles Brisard is an international expert on terrorism and terrorism financing. The book traces the career of the leader of Al Qaeda who came after Osama bin Laden, detailing the threat he poses to the world. The book reveals details from inside intelligence sources, documents, and witness testimonials.

Burke, Jason. 2004. *Al Qaeda: The True Story of Radical Islam.* New York: Penguin Books.
Burke is an award-winning reporter who shows how the threat of Islamic terrorism comes from a broad movement with profound roots in politics, societies, and history in the Islamic world. He shows that Al Qaeda is a diverse, disorganized global movement leading what Al Qaeda members perceive of as a "cosmic battle" with the West. It is a compelling account of a mysterious organization that challenges myths that threaten the foundations of the War on Terror.

Bush, Jeb, and Clint Bolick. 2013. *Immigration Wars: Forging an American Solution.* New York: Threshold Edition.
Jeb Bush, former Florida governor and candidate for the Republican Party's nomination for president in 2016, and Clint Bolick, vice president of Litigation at the Goldwater Institute, both long-time advocates of immigration policy reform, break a bit with their past positions by arguing that there should be two penalties for illegal entry:

fines/community service and ineligibility for citizenship. They argue, however, in favor of a path to citizenship for Dreamers. They advocate changing immigration policy to a demand-driven immigration system, responding more to the needs of the American economy than to family reunification.

Cainkar, Louise. 2009. *Homeland Insecurity: The Arab American and Muslim American Experience after 9/11*. New York: Russell Sage Foundation.

Cainkar details the intense scrutiny many Arab and Muslim Americans came under post-9/11—portraying even native-born as outsiders. She traces anti-Muslim attitudes that preceded the 9/11 attacks. The book combines ethnography and analysis. Based on hundreds of interviews, it draws an intimate image of what it means to be Arab or Muslim American after the terrorist attacks.

Clarke, Richard. 2004. *Against All Enemies: Inside America's War on Terror*. New York: Free Press.

An award-winning book by a former counterterrorist presidential advisor, Clarke criticizes past and present administrations for the way they handled the War on Terrorism. He is particularly critical of President George W. Bush for failing to prevent 9/11, and for the 2003 invasion of Iraq, which took resources away from the fight against Al Qaeda in Afghanistan. Insiders within the Bush administration were highly critical of some of the details in the book.

Clarke, Richard, and Robert Knake. 2010. *Cyber War*. New York: HarperCollins.

Clarke and Knake sound a timely and chilling warning about America's vulnerability to cyber warfare. It defines the term and elaborates on the concept and the need for a defensive strategy to cope with cyberattacks. It describes the actions taking place on the front lines of America's cyber defense.

Clarke, Richard A., and Randolph Post Eddy. 2017. *Warnings: Finding Cassandras to Stop Catastrophes*. New York: HarperCollins. The authors warn of the future of national security, threatening technologies, the threat to the U.S. economy, and the possible fate of civilization as we know it. They describe modern-day Cassandras who warned of Katrina, Fukushima, the rise of ISIS, and similar catastrophes but were ignored. The authors are successful CEOs and White House National Security Council veterans.

Cole, David. 2003. *Enemy Alien: Double Standards and Constitutional Freedoms in the War on Terrorism*. New York: New Press. Cole describes the anti-immigrant hysteria in the immediate aftermath of the 9/11 attacks. He then reviews court cases that have found the Bush administration's tactic of secrecy and assumptions of guilt as unconstitutional. Cole's book offers a prescient and critical indictment of the double standards applied to the War on Terror. Cole shows why it is a moral, constitutional, and practical imperative to provide every person in the United States the protection from government excess.

Commission Report-9/11. *Final Report of the National Commission on Terrorist Attacks on the United States*. New York: W.W. Norton. In late 2002, Congress passed legislation that the president signed into law establishing an independent, bipartisan commission to study the 9/11 attacks. It prepared a final report that included the preparedness (and lack thereof) for the attack, problems of the lack of coordination within the intelligence community, and the immediate response to the attacks. It provided many specific recommendations of actions to take in order to better guard against future attacks.

Cooper, Barry. 2004. *New Political Religions, or an Analysis of Modern Terrorism*. Columbia: University of Missouri Press.

Cooper applies the insights of political scientist Eric Vogelin to the phenomenon of modern terrorism. He faults most analyses of contemporary terrorists for omitting the spiritual motivation central to the actions of the terrorists today—what he terms the disease of the spirit. He focuses on Osama bin Laden's "second reality." He provides a penetrating analysis of the 9/11 attacks and shows how the spiritual perversity enables the terrorists to go on a campaign of mass destruction, which, in their minds, is justified as God's will.

Cordesman, Anthony H. 2002. *Terrorism, Asymmetric Warfare, and Weapons of Mass Destruction: Defending the U.S. Homeland*. Westport, CT: Praeger Press.

The potential threats to the U.S. homeland do not involve overt attacks by states using long-range missiles or conventional military forces. Rather, the threat is from covert attacks by state actors or state-sponsored proxies, and from independent terrorists and from the "lone-wolf" terrorist already residing in the United States. Cordesman argues the new threats require new thinking. He offers a range of recommendations that are a valuable contribution to the debate over homeland security.

D'Appollonia, Ariane Chabel, and Simon Reich. 2008. *Immigration, Integration, and Security*. Pittsburgh, PA: University of Pittsburgh Press.

The authors discuss the "securitization" of immigration, examining the identity discourse in Western Europe and the United States in the aftermath of the 9/11 attacks. They review religious legacies and the politics of multiculturalism. They discuss European security and counterterrorism, and the changes in immigration policy in Europe and the United States. They explore what they call the "Security Myth," and the relation of national security and political asylum. They focus on security, immigration, and integration in the EU, and on Muslims and the state in Western Europe. They highlight the challenges to EU border control enforcement by looking especially at France, Britain, and Italy.

Donohue, Laura. 2008. *The Cost of Counterterrorism: Power, Politics, and Liberty*. New York: Cambridge University Press.
In reaction to the 9/11 attacks, legislators and the courts have granted sweeping powers to the executive branch with little debate. The courts have narrowed the checks on the executive in all but the margins. The "Security or Freedom" debate fails to capture the shifts in the balance between the branches of government. Donohue re-calculates the cost of counterterrorist law to the United Kingdom and the United States, arguing the damage is greater than it first appears. She warns extremists may drive each country to take drastic measures with the resultant shift in the basic structure of both nations.

Emerson, Steven. 2002. *American Jihad: The Terrorists among Us*. New York: Free Press.
Emerson is the former FBI assistant director in charge of counterterrorism. He argues the America is "rampant" with Islamic terrorist networks and sleeper cells. He warns how close such internal terrorists are to each of us. The book is an audacious and sobering look at "American jihadists."

Etzioni, Amitai, ed. 2004. *How Patriotic Is the Patriot Act: Freedom versus Security in the Age of Terrorism*. London: Routledge.
Etzioni argues that when it comes to national security we face two profound commitments: (1) protecting our homeland and (2) safeguarding our rights. He demonstrates that extremism in defense of either security or

liberty is not a virtue. He charts a middle course between those committed to the preservation of liberty but blind to the needs of public safety with those willing to sacrifice our freedoms for the sake of preventing terrorism.

Etzioni, Amitai, and Jason H. Marsh, eds. 2003. *Rights vs. Public Safety after 9/11: America in the Age of Terrorism*. Lanham, MD: Rowman and Littlefield.

> After the 9/11 attacks, tension between civil rights and public safety dominated public discourse, raising questions and issues ranging from racial profiling to the use of military tribunals, to questions as to whether the United States can defend itself against terrorism without violating the values and principles at the heart of the democratic order. The authors bring together a collection of thoughtful essays to such topics as the ethical dilemmas of an emergency response to bioterrorist attack, the role of the government in promoting public service, the need to expand authority to combat terrorism, where government is overreaching, and how the new era might strengthen U.S. society.

Ferguson, Charles D., William C. Potter, Amy Sands, Leonard Spector, and Fred L. Wahling. 2005. *The Four Faces of Nuclear Terrorism*. New York: Routledge.

> This book, from the Center for Nonproliferation Studies, assesses the motivations and capabilities of terrorist organizations to acquire and use nuclear weapons, to fabricate crude nuclear devices, to strike nuclear power plants and other nuclear facilities, and to build a so-called dirty bomb. They maintain that there is greater likelihood today than at any time in the past three decades that such weapons will be used. They recommend specific steps to prevent a catastrophic form of nuclear terrorism and to reduce the consequences of the most likely nuclear terror attacks. They stress the need to educate the public on the

real risks of radiation exposure and contamination to help immunize citizens psychologically against such attacks, which they conclude are not only possible, but are likely in the coming years.

Flynn, Stephen. 2004. *America the Vulnerable: How Our Government Is Failing to Protect Us from Terrorism.* New York: HarperCollins.

Flynn is a senior fellow in national security studies at the Council on Foreign Relations and a commissioned United States Coast Guard officer. He served in the White House Military Office during the Bush administration, and was director of global issues for the National Security Council staff. His book is an urgent call to action, offering a startling picture of the shortcomings of America's plan for homeland security. He describes the likely results of what the next major terrorist attack might bring, the seismic political consequences for Washington, and how to better prepare for such a disaster. He offers a plan for achieving security in a way that is safe, smart, effective, and manageable.

Fouda, Josri, and Nick Fielding. 2003. *Masterminds of Terror.* New York: Arcade Publishing.

Josri Fouda, an Al Jazeera TV reporter, and Nick Fielding have written a book based on in-depth interviews with Al Qaeda leaders in Pakistan: Khalid Shaikh Mohammad and Ramzi Binalshibh, the masterminds of the 9/11 attacks. The book covers the two-year period of their planning and executing the attacks. It is a dramatic account of their seizure, and it analyzes Al Qaeda's attempt to justify its actions on what it calls "Holy Tuesday."

Givens, Terri, Gary A. Freeman, and David L. Leal, eds. 2009. *Immigration Policy and Security: U.S., European, and Commonwealth Perspectives.* New York: Routledge.

The editors bring together a collection of essays that carefully examine the terror attacks of 9/11 and subsequent events in London, Madrid, and elsewhere. It examines a broad range of issues in order to better understand them, the significant changes in the numbers of immigrants allowed to enter, and in the asylum policies of a number of nation-states. It examines how and why immigration and asylum policies have changed in response to the threat of terrorism. It presents a thorough analysis of border policies, and how the intensification of immigration politics has had severe consequences for the social and economic circumstances of minorities based on immigrant origins.

Gonzales, Alberto. 2016. *True Faith and Allegiance*. New York: Thomas Nelson/HarperCollins.

This book is a revealing autobiography of the former attorney general and White House Counsel to President George W. Bush. Gonzales served at the center of the administration and had a pivotal role in some of the most highly charged decisions of the first term—such as the USA Patriot Act, the DHS Act, and intelligence reform acts. He provided legal justification for enhanced interrogation, for granting sweeping powers to the attorney general, the Department of Justice and Department of Homeland Security. The book is an "insider's view" of the first term. It defends his conservative values and the administration's response to the crucible event of 9/11, and their subsequent attempts to protect the homeland that had such far-reaching effects.

Hoffman, Frank G. 2002. *Homeland Security: A Competitive Strategies Approach*. Washington, DC: Center for Defense Information.

Hoffman presents a theoretical examination of homeland security policy. He offers a holistic framework for thinking about homeland security using a strategic approach. His book examines what he terms are its three fundamental elements: the context in which a strategy is operative,

the capabilities of potential adversaries, and the anticipated interactions of alternative strategies.

Kean, Thomas H., and Lee H. Hamilton. 2006. *Without
Precedent: The Inside Story of the 9/11 Commission.* New York:
Alfred A. Knopf.

In this somewhat dry and colorless book, Kean, a former
governor of New Jersey, and Hamilton, a former congressman from Indiana, offer little new information about
the 9/11 attacks, but do provide an insiders' "keyhole"
view of the 9/11 Commission's bureaucratic conflict with
a White House and administration obsessed with secrecy
and control. They note that both the administration and
Congress often held up documents the Commission
needed to do its work. They conclude that throughout its
life, the real power resided not with the Commission, but
with the families of the victims whose relentless pressure
forced the White House to loosen its restrictions.

LeMay, Michael C. 2006. *Guarding the Gates: Immigration and
National Security.* Westport, CT; and London: Praeger Security
International.

This book traces how immigration policy and national
security policy interwove and influenced one another
over the entire history of the United States. It is the first
book in the post-9/11 period to focus specifically on the
role national security considerations play in determining
immigration policy. It provides readers with the historical
perspective necessary to assess the pros and cons of what
is happening today. It analyzes the problems of moving
the responsibilities of the Immigration and Naturalization Service to the Department of Homeland Security.
It examines how the United States is handling the balance between homeland security and civil liberties compared to ways in which it was done during World Wars
I and II and the Cold War. It does not advocate a specific

immigration policy, but rather gives students and citizens the tools to make up their own minds about these enduring and controversial issues.

LeMay, Michael C. 2015. *Illegal Immigration*, 2nd ed. Santa Barbara, CA: ABC-CLIO.

This volume defines the concept and analyzes the flow of unauthorized immigration to the United States since 1970. It focuses on why immigration reform is such a vexing problem. It demonstrates the problems and issues resulting from bad policy, the gaps, failures and unanticipated consequences of provisions in legal immigration that contribute so significantly to the illegal immigration flow. It discusses the groups who advocate for or oppose immigration reform proposals. It emphasizes that legal and illegal immigration policy are intermestic—involving both domestic and international concerns. It details how immigration flows wax and wane in response to push and pull factors that make the problem increasingly difficult in complexity and scope, thereby making policy responses all the more difficult. It shows how, since the 9/11 attacks, a sense of "fortress America" has permeated the political debate regarding both legal and illegal immigration, and how the unauthorized immigration flow has become an important element in homeland security and defense policy making.

Leone, Richard, and Greg Anrig, eds. 2003. *The War on Our Freedoms: Civil Liberties in an Age of Terrorism*. New York: Public Affairs Books.

This collection of 14 essays by leading thinkers, scholars, journalists, and historians explains what is happening in the War on Terror. The book stresses why the implications of that war are ultimately destructive of American values and ideals. It shows how the judiciary is undermined, the press is intimidated, racial profiling is rampant, and privacy is invaded. It is a reasoned though passionate report on what homeland security policy has contrived against our liberty.

Light, Paul C. 2002. *Homeland Security Will Be Hard to Manage.* Washington, DC: Brookings Institution's Center for Public Service.

Written just after the enactment of the law establishing the Department of Homeland Security (DHS), this expert in bureaucratic management offers insights and accurate foresight as to the difficulties the DHS will face as its managers attempt to merge the operations, procedures, and political/ bureaucratic cultures of so many diverse agencies into the new mega department.

Lightblau, Eric. 2008. *Bush's Law: The Remaking of American Justice.* New York: Random House.

Lightblau makes a significant contribution to the literature by examining the role of legal advisors to the Bush administration's response to the War on Terror. Rich in detail, insightful in analysis, and well researched and written, it draws on government documents, court records, congressional testimony, and more than 120 interviews. It tells three interrelated stories: a brief account of antiterrorism policies, the FBI's extensive use of national security letters, and secret detentions.

Logan, Gregory, ed. 2017. *Homeland Security and Intelligence,* 2nd ed. Santa Barbara, CA: Praeger Press.

This fully updated and revised edition of a text covers all the major aspects of the topic: analysis, military intelligence, terrorism, emergency oversight, and domestic intelligence. It adds new chapters to expand the coverage of topics such as recent developments in cyber security, the use of drones, lone-wolf radicalization, whistleblowers, the U.S. Coast Guard, border and private security, and the role of first responders in homeland security.

Mackey, Chris, and Greg Miller. 2005. *The Interrogators: Task Force 500 and America's Secret War against Al Qaeda.* New York: Back Bay Books.

> Mackey and Miller discuss the interrogators of the 3,000 prisoners seized in the War on Terror in Afghanistan alone. They were captured, held, and interrogated in-country. The book lifts the veil, a bit, in this dramatic account of the "soldier spies" who engineered a breakthrough in interrogation strategy. It includes the "tricks of the trade." The team of five interrogators broke virtually every prisoner. It reads like a spy novel.

Mahle, Melissa Boyle. 2006. *Denial and Deception: An Insider's View of the CIA.* New York: Nation Books.

> The author is a counterterrorism expert who was the top-ranked female Arabist in the CIA when she retired. She sheds new light on intelligence failures leading up to the 9/11 attacks. Her account offers a detailed personal narrative of the CIA during the Reagan presidency through 2002. She criticizes big mistakes along the way. Since leaving the CIA, she works as a private consultant on Middle East political and security affairs.

Mayer, Jane. 2008. *The Dark Side: The Inside Story of How the War on Terror Turned into a War on American Ideals.* New York: Doubleday.

> Mayer's book is a dramatic, riveting, and definitive narrative on the self-destructive decisions made by U.S. policy makers in pursuit of terrorists around the world. These decisions, she maintains, violated the Constitution. Ironically, they hampered the very pursuit of Al Qaeda. She relates, in detail, the decisions by key players, especially Vice President Dick Cheney and his powerful, secretive advisor, David Addington, and how they exploited the 9/11 attacks to push a long-held agenda to strengthen presidential powers to an unprecedented degree. She

argues that they obliterated constitutional protections that define the very essence of the American experiment.

McDermott, Terry. 2005. *Perfect Soldiers: The 9/11 Hijackers, Who They Were, and Why They Did It.* New York: HarperCollins. McDermott is an award-winning journalist. His book is well researched. It examines the lives of the 9/11 terrorists. He details how they lived, what they believed, and how they became terrorists who could plan and take the lives of thousands of innocents. It focuses on Khalid Shaikh Mohammad, mastermind of the attacks, and on his 20-years of plotting to get even with Americans who he maintained hated Muslims. McDermott depicts how they were turned from apolitical and mildly religious men into devout Muslims who debated extensively how best to serve fundamentalist Islam in which religion and politics are inseparable, seeing themselves as "soldiers of God."

Mittlestadt, Michelle, Burke Speaker, Doris Meissner, and Muzaffare A. Chisti. 2011. *Through the Prism of National Security: Major Immigration Policy and Program Changes in the Decade since 9/11.* Washington, DC: Migration Policy Institute. This technical report from the Migration Policy Institute critically examines the decade since the 9/11 attacks, and how, in response, a new generation of interoperable databases and systems at the crossroads of intelligence and law enforcement has reshaped immigration enforcement at the federal, state, and local levels. It details the collection and sharing of information; a significant expansion in the use of immigrant detention; broad use of nationality-based interviewing, screening, and enforcement initiatives, and the growing state and local involvement in immigration enforcement and policy making. It shows how the security paradigm will remain the legacy of 9/11 for the foreseeable future.

Migration Policy Institute. 2003. *America's Challenge: Domestic Security, Civil Liberties, and National Unity after September 11.* Washington, DC: Migration Policy Institute.

This report is based on 18 months of extensive research and interviews with detainees, lawyers, senior government officials engaged in domestic security and immigration issues, and leaders of Arab- and Muslim American communities across the country. It is a comprehensive compilation and analysis of persons detained post-9/11. It concludes that the harsh measures enacted against immigrants since the attacks have had dire consequences for antiterrorism efforts, fundamental civil liberties, and national unity. The authors conclude that authorities have placed too much emphasis on immigration in their counterterrorism efforts, and that immigration enforcement is of limited effectiveness. It discusses the widespread discrimination experienced by Arab- and Muslim Americans since the 9/11 attacks and explains how rampant discrimination undermines national unity.

Miniter, Richard. 2007. *My Year Inside Radical Islam.* New York: Jeremy P. Tarcher/Penguin Group.

This is Richard Miniter's memoir of a spiritual and then political seduction. It chronicles the journey of Daveed Gartenstein-Ross, a Jew by birth in liberal Ashland, Oregon, who yearned for a religion that would suit his ideals. In college, he met a charismatic Muslim student who grounded his political activism with religious conviction. Daveed converted to Islam and eventually to radical politics. It is a story of how good faith can be distorted and a decent soul seduced away from its principles. It offers a rare glimpse at the personal interface of religion and politics.

Miniter, Richard. 2011. *Mastermind: The Many Faces of the 9/11 Architect, Khalid Sheikh Mohammad.* London: Penguin Books.

Miniter presents a biography of the mastermind of the 9/11 attacks, but also a concise history of terrorism from the first (1993) World Trade Center bombing through the 9/11 attacks to the present day. Miniter is an investigative reporter who has written for major publications in the United Kingdom, Europe, and the United States. It is a straightforward narrative using never-before reported events.

Mirescu, Alexander. 2008. *Balancing Federal, State, and Local Priorities in Police-Immigration Relations: Lessons from Muslim, Arab, and South Asian Communities since 9/11*. Washington, DC: Immigration Policy Center.

Mirescu traces changes in federal, state, and local law enforcement priorities and practices since the 9/11 attacks and details their profound impact on America's Muslims, Arabs, and South Asians. Some of those policies applied exclusively to these communities, such as special registration, selective enforcement of immigration law based on national origin or religion. It examines federal counterterrorism efforts that target these communities. It shows how a wide range of ethnic groups have been affected by the use of state and local police agencies to enforce federal immigration law. It details the use of detention and deportation authority for even minor infractions and technicalities. It criticizes the enactment and implementation of the USA Patriot Act and its wide range of surveillance of targeted communities.

Mowbray, Joel. 2003. *Dangerous Diplomacy: How the State Department Threatens America's Security*. Washington, DC: Regnery.

Investigative reporter and conservative journalist, Joel Mowbray examines the inner workings of the State Department in this exposé. Relying on interviews with State Department personnel and research of its publications, procedures, and recent history, he explores a pattern of short-sightedness and misguided policies, and an ingrained aversion to self-criticism and correction. He concludes that the State Department is in dire need of reform. He has been described as a "pit-bull" journalist. He concludes that the State Department's culture is corrupted and that it coddles terrorists, tyrants, and other "American-haters." It provides fodder for the "deep state" conspiracy theorists.

Nance, Malcolm, and Gregory Itzin. 2016. *The Plot to Hack America*. New York: Skyhorse Publishing.

New York Times' best-selling author, and career intelligence officer, Nance and his coauthor offer this fast-paced, real-life spy thriller that traces Putin's rise from the KGB to spymaster-in-chief who performed the ultimate political manipulation: to convince Donald Trump to abandon 70 years of American foreign policy, including undermining NATO, cheering the end of the EU, allowing Russian domination of Eastern Europe, and destroying the existing global order with America as its leader. It characterizes Trump's crew as unwitting assets of the Russian government.

Nance, Malcolm, and Michael Kramer. 2016. *Defeating ISIS: Who They Are, How They Fight, What They Believe*. New York: Skyhorse Publishing.

Nance and Kramer give a counterterrorist insider's view of ISIS, explaining its origins, its violent propaganda, and how it spreads its ideology throughout the Middle East and to disaffected youth deep in the heart of Western Europe. It offers a step-by-step analysis of the street-level tactics, its urban combat, and its terrorist operations in Europe. The book shows the dangers of ISIS as a heretical death cult that redefines Islam as a fight to the death against all comers.

Nance, Malcolm, and Christopher Sampson. 2017. *Hacking ISIS: How to Destroy the Cyber Jihad.* New York: Skyhorse Publishing.

Two leading antiterrorist experts explain in graphic detail how ISIS produces religious cultism, recruits vulnerable young people of all religions and nationalities, and disseminates their brutal social media to the world. It shows how ISIS uses cyberspace to spread its terrifying content, and how it distributes thousands of pieces of propaganda daily. It shows why they are winning the battle in cyberspace, and how to stop it.

National Commission on Terrorist Attacks upon the United States. 2004. *The 9/11 Commission Report.* Washington, DC: U.S. Government Printing Office.

This narrative is the unanimous final report of the Commission and its recommendations to the government. It is the result of the bipartisan (5 Democrats, 5 Republican elected leaders) study of the 9/11 attacks and their aftermath. It provides an impartial, independent, thorough, and nonpartisan examination of the terrorist attacks on the United States. The Commission held 19 hearings and took the testimony of 160 witnesses. It sought not to assign individual blame, but rather to provide the fullest possible account and assessment of the events surrounding 9/11 and to identify lessons learned. It proposed a balanced strategy for going forward for the long-haul. It sought to recommend policy to attack the terrorists, to prevent their ranks from swelling, and to protect the United States from future attacks.

Nguyen, Tram. 2005. *We Are All Suspects Now: Untold Stories from Immigrant Communities after 9/11.* Boston: Beacon Press.

Nguyen reveals the human costs of the domestic war of terrorism and examines the impact of post-9/11 policies on people targeted because of immigration status, nationality, race, and religion. It is a compelling narrative about the families, detainees, community advocates, and others living on the frontlines of the War on Terror, and of people who see and experience firsthand the unjust detention and deportation of family members, friends, and neighbors. It takes the reader inside a dark world where the American Dream is transformed into a nightmare. It suggests proactive responses to the growing climate of xenophobia, intimidation, and discrimination.

O'Hanlon, Michael. 2005. *Defense Strategy for the Post-Saddam Era*. Washington, DC: Brookings Institution Press.

The War on Terror and ongoing operations in Iraq and Afghanistan forced soaring budgets and unprecedented challenges in policy making. O'Hanlon, a leading foreign policy expert, offers policy recommendations for strengthening the ability of America's military to respond to international crises. He argues the United States will be involved in Iraq and Afghanistan for the foreseeable future, will remain involved in deterrence in Korea and the Taiwan Strait, and will be engaged in European security and the cohesion of NATO. He reviews national security priorities, asking tough questions and proposing a framework for answering them. In an era of apocalyptic terrorism, he deals with how the country will protect its citizens while maintaining fiscal responsibility.

O'Hanlon, Michael. 2015. *The Future of Land Warfare: Geopolitics in the 21st Century*. Washington, DC: The Brookings Institution Press.

O'Hanlon addresses what happens if the United States relies too heavily on unmanned systems, cyber warfare, and special operations. He analyzes the future of the world's ground forces, where large-scale conflicts are more plausible, and which are areas in which American ground forces will be significant in such operations. He offers a cautioning note against overconfidence. He considers several scenarios in which large, conventional force may be necessary against Russian expansion in the Baltic countries, China in the Korean Peninsula, asymmetric threat in the South China Sea and in South Asia, coping with severe Ebola outbreaks in Africa, and addressing a further meltdown in security in Central America.

O'Hanlon, Michael, Peter R. Orszag, Iro H. Daadler, I. M. Destler, David L. Gunter, Robert E. Laton, and James Steinberg, eds. 2002. *Protecting the American Homeland: A Preliminary Analysis*. Washington, DC: The Brookings Institution Press.

The authors offer a four-tier plan for efforts of the Bush administration and Congress to enhance homeland security policy. Their book includes a rationale for and recommendations on spending for increased security, on projected costs to the private sector, and on the impact to the various agencies merged into the Department of Homeland Security (DHS). Its recommendations include the restructuring of the INS and the Border Patrol as well as visa and naturalization policies and programs into the new.

Reeve, Simon. 2002. *The New Jackals: Ramzi Yousef, Osama Bin Laden, and the Future of Terrorism*. Boston: Northeastern University Press.

Drawing on previously unpublished reports, interrogation files, interviews with senior FBI agents who hunted them, and intelligence sources and government figures, Reeve presents a harrowing account of the "new jackals' terror bombings," details the hunt to capture and kill them, and explains the rise of Al Qaeda's international terror network. The book sheds light on two of the world's most notorious terrorists. Reeve warns that they are but the first of a new breed of terrorist men with no restrictions on mass killings, offering evidence that Al Qaeda may already have chemical, and possibly even nuclear, weapons of mass destruction.

Renshon, Stanley. 2005. *The 50% American: Immigration and National Identity in an Age of Terror*. Washington, DC: Georgetown University Press.

> Renshon is a political psychologist who offers unique insight into the political and national ramifications of personal loyalties held by persons with dual citizenship. In an age of terrorism, he argues that the concept that we are all Americans is essential to national security. The book is a comprehensive examination of present immigration trends and traces the assimilation process that immigrants undergo. It deals with such volatile issues as language requirements, voting rights, and schooling. He casts a critical eye on the challenges posed over the past four decades by multiculturalism, culture conflict, and global citizenship. He offers comprehensive proposals for dual citizenship and for helping immigrants and citizens alike to become more integrated into the American national community.

Ressa, Maria A. 2003. *Seeds of Terror: An Eyewitness Account of Al Qaeda's Newest Center of Operations in Southeast Asia*. New York: Free Press.

> Ressa sheds illuminating light on Muslim strongholds in the Philippines and Indonesia as Al Qaeda's newest but little known "terrorist HQs." She documents that every major Al Qaeda attack since 1993 has had connection to the Philippines. She breaks new major revelations about how the 9/11 attacks were planned, and an even more ambitious scheme aimed at Singapore. She shows how Al Qaeda's tactics are shifting under the pressures of the War on Terror. She details how its estimated 3,000 members are now enmeshed in local conflicts, co-opting Muslim independence movements, and helping locals to fund, plan, and execute terror attacks. She uncovers and uses classified investigative documents.

Reuter, Dean, and John Yoo, eds. 2011. *Confronting Terror: 9/11 and the Future of American National Security.* New York: Encounter Books.

> The 9/11 attacks killed nearly 3,000 persons, inflicted billions of dollars in damage, and caused drastic military and security measures in response—what is known as the War on Terror.
>
> This edited volume by Reuter and Yoo examines controversies over fundamental objectives, and the strategies and tactics of the War on Terror. It presents a reasoned, clear, and considered discussion of the future in a collection of essays written on the 10th anniversary of the attacks by both critics and supporters of the War on Terror, policy makers and commentators, insiders and outsiders, who collectively are among the leading voices on the war both inside and outside of government.

Rosenblum, Marc R. 2011. *U.S. Immigration Policy since 9/11: Understanding the Stalemate over Comprehensive Immigration Reform.* Washington, DC: Migration Policy Institute.

> Rosenblum was deputy director of the Migration Policy Institute (MPI). This book is a report of MPI's Regional Migration Study Group. It reviews the history of immigration legislation since the 9/11 attacks, focusing on the new enforcement mandates, and the unsuccessful attempts to pass comprehensive immigration reform. It finds that the history and asymmetries of the political process favor the enforcement responses and that the economic downturn stacks the deck against comprehensive reform.

Rudolph, Christopher. 2006. *National Security and Immigration: Policy Developments in the United States and Western Europe since 1945.* Stanford, CA: Stanford University Press.

> Global terrorism has emerged as a central security issue around the world. Effective immigration and border

control is now a necessary condition to maintain national security. Rudolph's book identifies the security-related implications and determinants of immigration and border policies in the United States and Western Europe since 1945. He shows how international migration presents nation-states with important choices that impact economic production, internal security, relations with other states, and national identity. He reveals how immigration and border policies are shaped by a nation-state's desire to maximize security interests along three dimensions: defense, wealth, and stability.

Sageman, Marc. 2008. *Leaderless Jihad: Terror Networks in the Twenty-First Century.* Philadelphia: University of Pennsylvania Press.

A former CIA operations officer in Islamabad, Sageman rejects the views that place responsibility for terrorism on society or a flawed, predisposed person. He argues the individual, outside influences, and group dynamics come together in a four-step process in which Muslim youth are radicalized. He offers a ray of hope by drawing on historical analysis, arguing that the zeal of jihadism is self-terminating and that eventually its followers will turn away from violence as the way to voice their discontent. He offers recommendations for law enforcement efforts to combat terrorism.

Schindler, John R. 2007. *Unholy Terror: Bosnia, Al Qa'ida and the Rise of the Global Jihad.* St. Paul, MN: Zenith Press.

Schindler traces how Al Qaeda has metastasized throughout the world's geopolitical body. He describes where the terrorists are today. He answers the puzzle of Al Qaeda's transformation from an isolated fighting force into a lethal global threat. He analyzes the role that radical Islam played in Al Qaeda's growth. He shows how Bosnia in the 1980s became the training ground for the mujahideen,

showing how Osama bin Laden exploited the Bosnia conflict for his own ends, and how the U.S. government gave
substantial support to the "unholy warriors."

Shenon, Philip. 2008. *The Commission: The Uncensored History of the 9/11 Investigation*. New York: Hachette Books.
Shenon's book helps show why, despite the 9/11 Com-
mission's report and recommendation, not much has
changed in America's intelligence services. An investigative reporter for the *New York Times*, he expertly examines
numerous documents and interviews, then weaves them
into a mesmerizing account, vividly portraying the key
players, and detailing the incessant maneuvering among
commissioners.

Stana, Richard M. 2003. *Homeland Security: Challenges to Implementing the Immigration Interior Enforcement Strategy*. GAO-03–660T, Washington, DC: U.S. Government Printing Office.
Stana was the director of homeland security and justice
for the Government Accounting Office. This report to
Congress details the management challenges to effective
implementation of the Immigration Interior Enforcement Strategy.

Stone, Geoffrey. 2004. *Perilous Times: Free Speech in Wartime from the Sedition Act of 1798 to the War on Terrorism*. New York: W.W. Norton.
A University of Chicago law professor and leading author-
ity on the First Amendment, Stone provides a history of
the actions by the U.S. government that have the potential to endanger fundamental rights during wartime. He
shows how exchanging liberty for security often leads to
ending up with neither. He details how the United States
balanced, and often unbalanced, the scale of freedom
versus the exigencies of self-defense. He describes the

"evolutionary learning curve" of the courts on the balance of these two fundamental values. Stone covers the history from the Alien and Sedition Acts, through the Civil War, World War I, and World War II on up to today's War on Terrorism.

Suskind, Ron. 2006. *The One Percent Doctrine: Deep Inside America's Pursuit of Its Enemies since 9/11*. New York: Simon and Schuster.

A Pulitzer Prize–winning journalist and best-selling author, Suskind uses his connections to get insiders' interviews and reviews of documents to write this riveting work of narrative nonfiction with historically significant disclosures of how the United States searches for its enemies at home and abroad. It exposes the deeply secretive core of America's playbook for the War on Terror, designed by Vice President Dick Cheney. It argues that policy approach separates America from its moorings in fighting the wars in Afghanistan and Iraq, and the global search for jihadists. It is a startling book that reframes the debates that roil the globe.

Thomas, Jeffrey L. 2015. *Scapegoating Islam: Intolerance, Security, and the American Muslim*. Santa Barbara, CA: Praeger Press.

This is a well-researched and referenced volume that explores the experience of Muslims in America following the 9/11 attacks. It assesses how anti-Muslim bias within the American government and the broader society undermine American security and democracy.

Tirman, John, ed. 2004. *The Maze of Fear: Security and Migration after 9/11*. New York: New Press.

The roster of security measures enacted in the panic that followed the 9/11 attacks have in common a concern about the link between migration and security. This edited volume raises vital questions about government policy and explores the many dimensions of the migration-security link, including essays about civil liberties, transnational organization, refugee populations, and politically active diasporas.

Torr, James D., ed. 2004. *Homeland Security*. San Diego, CA: Greenhaven Press.

This book provides a highly critical but comprehensive examination of the homeland security issue and its myriad ramifications. Torr is especially skeptical as to the effectiveness of the "super-agency" approach to a massive new department, focusing on the largely unanticipated managerial problems of a new mega department.

West, Darrell M. 2010. *Brain Gain*. Washington, DC: Brookings Institution Press.

West examines how gifted immigrants have led to advances in energy, information technology, international commerce, sports, arts, and culture: a "brain gain" that benefited American international competitiveness through its more open-door policy to attract unique talents from other countries. He asserts that the "vision" America has of immigration is one reason that immigration reform is so politically difficult. Public discourse emphasizes negative perceptions. Fear too often trumps reason and optimism. He describes a series of reforms to put America back on the track of a better course that enhances its long-term social and economic prosperity. He advocates "reconceptualizing" immigration as a way to enhance innovation and competitiveness to help America find its next Sergey Brin, Andrew Grove, and Albert Einstein.

Wright, Lawrence. 2006. *The Looming Tower: Al Qaeda and the Road to 9/11*. New York: Alfred A. Knopf.

This Pulitzer Prize–winning book is a gripping historical narrative spanning five decades to explain in great detail the growth of Islamic fundamentalism, the rise of

Al Qaeda, and the intelligence failures that ended in the attacks of 9/11. He re-creates firsthand the transformations of Osama bin Laden and Ayman al-Zawahiri from incompetent and idealistic soldiers in Afghanistan to leaders of the most successful terrorist group in history. He details FBI counterterrorism chief John O'Neill's efforts to uncover Al Qaeda and to track down the leaders of this new threat. It is a definitive history of the long road to the 9/11 attacks.

Wucker, Michele. 2006. *Lockout: Why America Keeps Getting Immigration Wrong When Our Prosperity Depends on Getting It Right.* New York: Public Affairs Press.

Wucker's narrative history reviews how we shut the door to immigration after World War I, only to realize the error of doing so and reopening the door in 1965. The current record-high foreign-born population, global turbulence, and economic instability have once again pushed Americans past a tipping point about immigration and the global role of the United States. She documents the mistakes that led to our predicament today, and clarifies why it would be a catastrophic error of judgment, and a colossal lack of self-knowledge for America to again turn its back on the rest of the world, and in doing so, on the best of itself.

Yount, Lisa, ed. 2004. *Fighting Bioterrorism.* San Diego, CA: Greenhaven Press.

Yount describes the post-anthrax attack of October 2001 and how the government and the health care system struggled to prepare for even more serious and deadly bioterrorist attacks in the future. This anthology discusses the potential links of bioterrorism to immigration, ways to handle a possible smallpox attack, attacks on agriculture and food, and other bioterrorist threats. It discusses methods of preventing such terrible possibilities from happening.

Scholarly Journals

Air and Space Power Journal

Begun in 1947, this is the U.S. Air Force's bimonthly professional, peer-reviewed journal and a leading forum for air power thought and dialogue. It is published in four languages besides English. Recent articles considered how to deal with the threat of Russian disinformation, cyber warfare, the threat-environment demanding modernization of nuclear weapons, assessing intelligence, surveillance, and reconnaissance.

American Demographics

Published 10 times per year, this peer-reviewed journal is an outlet for multidisciplinary articles dealing with all topics related to demography, as well as occasional articles and reflective essays on migration, legal and illegal immigration, and migration's impact on homeland security. It publishes an annual resource guide helpful to any reader studying demographics.

American Journal of Sociology

A scholarly, peer-reviewed quarterly journal of sociology, with frequent articles concerning immigration and integration, social trends, and policies regarding migration and both legal and illegal immigration, it has occasional articles related to homeland security issues. It has useful book reviews on immigration-related topics such as the social implications of homeland security policies and how they affect social minority groups in particular.

American Prospect

This monthly magazine covers politics, culture, and policy from a liberal perspective. It is based in Washington, D.C. It frequently has critical articles dealing with homeland security issues and concerns, especially pertaining to civil rights and privacy issues.

American Sociological Review

Founded in 1936, the *American Sociological Review* is the flagship, peer-reviewed academic journal of the American Sociological Association. It is a Sage-published journal of original works of interest to sociology in general, and committed to advance understanding of fundamental social processes. It is published bimonthly. It is ranked second among 143 journals of sociology. It frequently has articles on minority groups and population affected by homeland security policy, the Patriot Act, and immigration policy designed to crack down on immigration enforcement and border control.

Brookings Review

The *Brookings Review* is a quarterly magazine focused on economic, political, and foreign policy issues. It began publication in 1982. It provides provocative articles written by professionals who know the ins-and-outs of Washington, D.C., and of the international scene. It is published by the Brookings Institution. It reviews books related to homeland security, and articles dealing with the security versus civil liberties conflict.

California Law Review

The *California Law Review* is the preeminent legal publication of the University of California, Berkeley School of Law. It is ranked among the top 10 law reviews and boasts among its alumni several chief justices. It was founded in 1912. It is published six times annually and covers a variety of timely topics in legal scholarship, often related to homeland security and to civil rights and liberties issues impacted by the policy implications of homeland security concerns. It is edited and published entirely by students at Berkeley Law. Each issue has a commentary and an essay section. It has a free online access e-version of past issues.

Comparative Strategies

Comparative Strategies is an international peer-reviewed journal sponsored by the National Institute for Public Policy and the

Center for Strategic Studies, University of Reading. It is published annually. It draws on historical perspectives and strategic insights from leading international defense analysts and subject matter experts for critical security issues. It covers the rise of new, potentially hostile and dangerous regional state and non-state powers. It regularly features commentary by leading U.S. policy makers; special issue topics; and texts of U.S., foreign, and NATO documents on major defense issues. It publishes book reviews of relevant books.

Cornell Law Review

Cornell Law Review was founded in 1915. It is a student-run and student-edited journal publishing novel legal scholarship that has immediate and long-term impact on the legal community. It is published in six print issues annually, and has articles, essays, student notes, and book reviews. It has an annual symposium issue. It recently featured an article on asylum rights. It publishes an online database of past issues.

Demography

This peer-reviewed journal of the Population Association of America publishes scholarly research of interest to demographers from a multidisciplinary perspective, with emphasis on the social sciences, geography, history, biology, statistics, business, epidemiology, and public health, all of which are impacted by homeland security problems and issues. It publishes specialized research papers and historical and comparative studies.

Foreign Affairs

This bimonthly magazine publishes articles and original essays on topics related to foreign policy, including policy related to homeland security, to both legal and illegal immigration, by both scholars and practitioners in the field of foreign affairs/foreign policy. It regularly publishes related book reviews.

Forensic Examiner

Forensic Examiner is the official peer-reviewed journal of the American College of Forensic Examiners Institute. It has transitioned to an online, continuously published journal. It is the leading forensic magazine. It has recently published articles on cyber terrorism, on the cyber radicalization of American college students, on forensic accounting used to combat terrorism in the United States, and on asylum applications in federal immigration courts.

Georgetown Immigration Law Journal

This quarterly law review is the most specifically related law journal dealing with immigration law, its current developments, and reform-related matters concerning all three branches of government. It frequently focuses on illegal immigration, and occasionally on homeland security issues and concerns that impact immigration. It contains case reviews, articles, notes, and commentaries. It publishes workshop reports devoted to immigration law.

Harvard Law Review

This law review is published eight times per year. It contains original articles, case reviews, essays, commentaries, and book reviews that occasionally focus on homeland security, immigration law, and its reforms. It began publication in 1887. It is published by an independent group of students at Harvard Law School. It is ranked number one of 143 law journals.

Independent Review

The *Independent Review* is a journal of political economy that is a peer-reviewed periodical published quarterly since 1997. It is an interdisciplinary journal devoted to the study of political economy and the critical analysis of government policy. It is provocative, lucid, and engaging in style. Its articles range across the fields of economics, political science, law, history, philosophy, and sociology. It features in-depth examination of past, present, and future policy issues by leading scholars and experts. It has frequently featured articles on civil rights and civil liberties, on government secrecy and privacy rights, on immigration and race issues, and on terrorism and national crises.

Journal of Database Management

The *Journal of Database Management* publishes original research on all aspects of database management, systems analysis and design, and software engineering. It seeks to improve theory and practice related to information technology and management of information sources. It is targeted at both academic researchers and practicing IT professionals. It has been published since 1990. It has featured articles on cyber space and cyber warfare and defense.

Journal on Migration and Human Security

A publication of the Center for Migration Studies of New York, it is an online, peer-reviewed public policy academic journal focusing on the broad scope of social, political, and economic dimensions of human security. It also publishes an annual, bound volume of its articles.

Minnesota Law Review

The *Minnesota Law Review* has been published in six issues per year since 1917 by the University of Minnesota Law School. It is an entirely student-run law review with a board of editors comprised of 39 editors who govern its policies and procedures. It hosts an annual symposium, such as the 2016 symposium of balancing First Amendment Rights with an Inclusive Environment on Public University Campuses, or its 2009 symposium on cyber space and law.

Policy Studies Journal

This journal of the Policy Studies Organization is published at Iowa State University, College of Education. It is published quarterly and contains articles related to all issues of public policy, including homeland and national security issues and policies. It also publishes occasional symposium issues, and regular book reviews.

Political Science Quarterly

Political Science Quarterly is a double-blind, peer-reviewed academic journal covering government, politics, and policy. It has been published since 1886 by the Academy of Political Science. Each issue contains six articles and up to 40 book reviews. It is a journal of public and international affairs and is ranked 117th of 161 political science journals. It publishes articles and book reviews related to homeland security and to the concern for balancing security versus civil liberties policy.

Presidential Studies Quarterly

Presidential Studies Quarterly is an interdisciplinary journal of theory and research on the American presidency by the Center for the Study of the President and Congress. It is published by Blackwell Publishing. Its articles, features, review essays, and book reviews have been published since 1974 in print, and now online. It is the official journal of the Presidential Research Section of the American Political Science Association. It has published articles relating to the role of the presidency in homeland security policy, and the powers of the presidency as those powers impact security and the privacy rights and civil liberties of citizens.

The Review of Policy Research

The *Review of Policy Research* is a bimonthly peer-reviewed academic journal published by Wiley-Blackwell for the Policy Studies Organization. It has been published since 1981. It is a political science discipline journal that focuses on the politics and policy of science, technology and environmental issues, science policy, environment resource management, information networks, cultural industries, biotechnology, security and surveillance, privacy, globalization, education, research and innovation, development, intellectual property, health and demographics. It is ranked 20th of the 163 journals of "Political Science," and 20th of 47 in "Public Administration."

Security Management

Security Management is an award-winning flagship publication of ASIS International. It is published monthly. It publishes articles on national security, physical security, cyber security, strategic security, and security by industry. ASIS is the leading organization for security professionals. Founded in 1955, it advocates the role and value of the security management profession to business, the media, government entities, and the public. Its articles feature timely information on emerging threats as well as practical solutions to protect people, property, and information.

Social Justice

Social Justice is a quarterly, peer-reviewed educational journal, founded in 1974, that seeks to inform theory and practice on issues of equality and justice. It focuses on crime, police repression, social control, the penal system, human and civil rights, citizenship and immigration issues, environmental victims, health and safety concerns, welfare and education, ethnic and gender relations, and persistent global inequities. It provides social criticism as a distinctive form of knowledge and to present divergent viewpoints in a readable fashion.

Social Science Quarterly

Published for the Southwestern Social Science Association by Blackwell, this interdisciplinary quarterly has articles of original research, review essays, book reviews, and occasional symposium issues, and contains articles dealing with U.S. immigration and illegal immigration policy, with issues related to the incorporation of immigrants and their children into majority society, and occasional articles on homeland security policy as it impacts, often negatively, U.S. society.

Social Science Research

Social Science Research publishes papers devoted to quantitative social science research and methodology. It features articles to illustrate the use of quantitative methods to empirically test social science theory. Its research cuts across traditional disciplinary boundaries. It publishes special feature issues, such as *Katrina in New Orleans*. They concern current pressing issues in world society, typically with a political angle in keeping with the tradition of the New School for Social Research's politically conscious history. It organizes and publishes the proceedings of a conference series. It is published by Elsevier for the New School for Social Research and has been published since 1934.

White House Studies

White House Studies is a quarterly, peer-reviewed journal of scholarship and commentary on the politics and history of the presidency and the White House. It reviews current books and publishes original and timely scholarly articles. It has a regular feature on White House history, and regularly features profiling first couples. Though scholarly, its articles are generally shorter than most academic journals to be more suitable to a wide audience that includes scholars, libraries, presidential sites and institutions, and White House enthusiasts. It is published by Nova Science Journals for the University of Southern Mississippi.

Films

The 800-Mile Wall (2009), 90 minutes, color. An award-wining film by John Carlos Frey, it is a powerful, independent-produced film about the border fence and documents all the problems that would be involved in building Trump's border wall.

Fahrenheit 9/11 (2004), 122 minutes, color. Dog Eat Dog Films/IMDbPro. This documentary film is written by, directed by, and stars filmmaker Michael Moore. He uses archival film footage and candid interviews with politicians to dramatically presents his view on what happened to the United States after the 9/11 attacks, and how the Bush administration allegedly used the event to push forward its agenda for the War on Terror in Afghanistan and Iraq.

An Inconvenient Sequel: Truth to Power (2017), 100 minutes, color, Actual Films/Participant Media. This documentary film is directed by Bonni Cohen and Jon Shenk. It follows former vice president Al Gore as he continues his tireless fight, traveling around the world to train an army of activists and influence international climate policy. It goes behind the scenes, public and private, funny and poignant, as it follows Gore as he pursues the inspirational idea that while the stakes have never been higher, the perils of climate change can be overcome with human ingenuity and passion.

An Inconvenient Truth (2006), 95 minutes, color, Lawrence Bender Productions, IMDbPro. This documentary film by filmmaker Davis Guggenheim follows Al Gore on the lecture circuit as the former presidential candidate campaigns to raise public awareness of the dangers of global warming and calls for immediate actions to curb its destructive effects on the environment.

Inside the Terror Network (2001), 60 minutes, color, Insight Media. This PBS video examines three of the 9/11 hijackers for insight into how and why they were radicalized into international terrorism. It traces their movements in the days, month, and years leading up to the 9/11 attacks, and shows how they slipped between the cracks of U.S. law enforcement to carry out their deadly attacks.

The Kingdom (2007), 110 minutes, color, distributed by Universal Pictures, and produced by Relativity Media. This action, thriller feature film depicts the story of a team of FBI agents sent to investigate a terrorist bombing of a U.S. facility in Riyadh, Saudi Arabia. It is directed by Peter Berg and stars Jamie Foxx and Jennifer Garner. The FBI team finds all sorts of difficulties in their investigation, but is aided by Colonel Faris Al Ghazi, who advises them on how to act in the hostile environment.

Olympus Has Fallen (2013), 120 minutes, color, Millennium Films production, Film District distributors. This action thriller feature film depicts a heavily armed and highly trained group of terrorists who attack the White House, overrun the defense, and take the president and his staff hostage. His former personal security officer is on the scene and rescues the president and his son before the terrorists can unleash their ultimate plan.

Patriots Day (2016), 133 minutes, color, IMDbPro, produced by Bluegrass films and Closest to the Hole Productions, distributed by CBS Films/Lionsgate. This Peter Berg–directed crime drama feature film depicts the story of the 2013 Boston Marathon bombing and its aftermath, which includes the city-wide FBI and Boston Police manhunt to find the Tsarnev brothers, the terrorists responsible for the bombing. It stars Mark Wahlberg. It was chosen by the National Board of Review as one of the 10 best films of 2016.

United 93 (2006), 75 minutes, color, distributed by Universal Pictures, produced by Studio Canal/Sidney Kimmel Entertainment. This drama/history/thriller is a feature-film depiction, the real-time account of the events on United 93, one of the planes hijacked on 9/11, which crashed into a farm field near Shanksville, Pennsylvania. It enacts the heroic struggle of the plane's passengers with the four hijackers/terrorists to take back control of the plane, foiling the terrorist plot to crash the plane into the Capitol building. It is directed by Paul Greengrass.

War on Terror (2011), 48 minutes, color, IMDbPro, produced and distributed by Parallel Universe. This Australian documentary/history film is a special that includes a profile piece on Osama bin Laden, the Al Qaeda mastermind of the attacks on the United States. It details the bold military operation by the U.S. Seal team that found, hunted, and killed Osama bin Laden in Pakistan, just north of the capital. It shows the angry reactions from supporters of bin Laden, the denial of news of his death, and details on the mystery courier. It premiered in Australian HD theaters in 2011.

White House Down (2013), 131 minutes, color, produced by Centropolis Entertainment and Mythology Entertainment and distributed by Columbia Pictures. An American action/ thriller directed by Roland Emmerich, it depicts an assault on the White House by a paramilitary group, and the Capitol Police Officer who tries to stop them. It stars Channing Tatum as the police officer and Jamie Foxx as the president, and James Woods as the retiring head of the Secret Service who is secretly the leader of the attack.

World Trade Center (2006), 129 minutes, color, Paramount Pictures/Warner Brothers. A history/disaster drama directed by Oliver Stone, the film presents a powerful and provocative story depicting the real-life events of the 9/11 attacks. It portrays two officers of the New York City Port Authority who attempted to evacuate the World Trade Center Twin Towers building after the towers were struck by airliners piloted by terrorists. It stars Nicolas Cage, Michael Shannon, and Michael Pena.

Videos

America at a Crossroads, (2007–2009), PBS Documentary Series. This series of 20 programs each an hour in length concerns the issues facing the United States as related to the War on Terror. It won Emmy Awards for Outstanding Programming and for News and Documentary. Operation Homecoming examines the war on terrorism, the conflicts in Afghanistan and Iraq, the experiences of American troops. The series is a project created by the National Endowment for the Arts and is hosted by Robert Macneil.

Hunting Bin Laden, is a 55-minute Frontline/PBS episode that first aired on September 13, 2001. It is in color. It is available on IMDbPro. It details the long hunt for the elusive terrorist and mastermind of the attacks of 9/11.

Liberty and Security in an Age of Terrorism (2003), 23 minutes, color, Film Media Group. This video grapples with the issues of balance between homeland security in the post-9/11 world and the basic civil liberty values central to American society. Using a hypothetical scenario, a panel of persons confront the issues and wrestle with the high-stakes questions in discussing the implications of the USA Patriot Act, surveillance of suspects, closed deportation hearings, demands for student information, and just what constitutes an unaligned combatant.

9/11 Ten Years Later, 60 minutes, color, CBS Television, available on IMDbPro. This documentary video is an unprecedented and exclusive insider's account by filmmakers James Hanlon and Jules Naudet. The documentary is hosted by Robert De Niro. It examines the World Trade Center attack and contains footage of the first plane striking the World Trade Center, and footage of ground zero during the attacks, interviews with many firefighters discussing their lives, families, and how the world has changed since the tragedy, including the health issues that have plagued firefighters working at ground zero.

The Patriot Act under Fire (2003), 23 minutes, color, Film Media Group. For many, worrying about constitutional rights seems like an archaic luxury in the age of international terrorism. The need for tighter security made civil liberties seem less critical when the nation confronted terrorism by passing urgent measures such as the USA Patriot Act, designed to defend the country. Two years after its passage, ABC News and anchor Ted Koppel take a hard look at the law with representatives from the Justice Department, the ACLU, and others.

The Terrorism Alert System (2003), 23 minutes, color, Insight Media. This video explains the much-maligned five-level, color-coded terrorism alert system developed by the Department of

Homeland Security, providing recommendations to government and the private sector on responses to each level of risk.

With Us or against Us: Afghans in America (2002), 27 minutes, color, Filmmakers Library. This short documentary examines the experiences of Afghan immigrants to the United States and their plight facing discrimination and hysteria and their plight facing discrimination and hysteria after the 9/11 attacks.

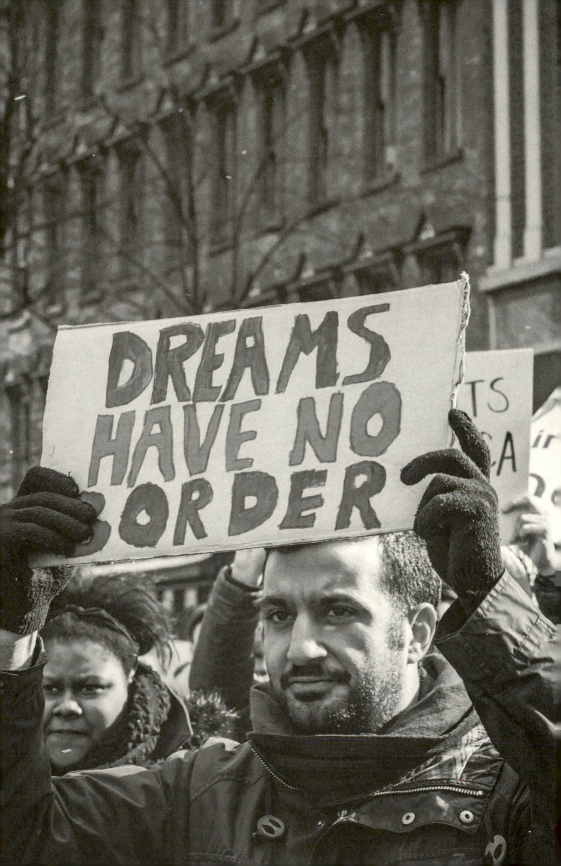

Pre-2001 "Precursor" Actions Setting Conditions That Influence Post-9/11 Actions

1965   Congress passes the Immigration and Nationality Act. It establishes a preference system for legal immigration that emphasizes family reunification and meeting certain skill goals. It standardizes admissions procedures, setting up a system of 20,000 admissions per country on a first-come, first-served basis for Eastern Hemisphere nations, with a total of 170,000. The first ceiling on Western Hemisphere immigration is set at 120,000. Annual legal immigration to the United States is 296,697.

1975   Saigon falls after the United States pulls out of Vietnam. Vietnamese, Cambodian, and Laotian refugees flee to the United States from Southeast Asia (a.k.a. the Indochina region). They are classified as refugees from communist countries and are thereby assisted in resettlement and aided by "assimilation assistance" programs, many conducted by church-based organizations that assist immigrants. President Carter establishes and the Congress funds the Indochinese Refugee Resettlement Program. Other mass refugees come from El Salvador and Jews

---

Students at Rensselaer Polytechnic Institute rally to protest the Muslim ban and to support international students on February 1, 2017. Several federal courts have ruled parts of the travel ban unconstitutional. (Sandra Foyt/Dreamstime.com)

fleeing the Soviet Union. Annual legal immigration to the United States is 386,194.

1976   Congress amends the 1965 act, extending the per-country 20,000 limit of visa applications to Western Hemisphere nations, regulated by the preference system, and setting the conditions for the unanticipated influx of tens of thousands of undocumented immigrants from Mexico and Central America. Annual legal immigration to the United States is 502,289.

1980   Congress passes the Refugee Act to systematize refugee policy, incorporating the UN definition of refugee and setting the annual number of refugees to be accepted at 50,000 persons who have a "well-founded fear" of persecution based on race, religion, nationality, or membership in a social or political movement, and provides for the additional admission of 5,000 "asylum seekers." Annual legal immigration is 530,639.

1986   Congress enacts the Immigration Reform and Control Act (IRCA), which imposes employer sanctions in a vain attempt to stop the illegal immigration of undocumented immigrants. Annual legal immigration to the United States is 601,708.

1990   Congress passes a major reform law (known as IMMACT) concerning legal immigration, setting new ceilings for worldwide immigration, redefining the preference system for family reunification and employment, and setting up a new category of preference called "the diversity immigrants." It enacts special provisions regarding Central American refugees, Filipino veterans, and persons seeking to leave Hong Kong.

Annual legal immigration to the United States is 1,536,483.

1993   Congress ratifies the North American Free Trade Agreement (NAFTA).

Annual legal immigration to the United States is 904,193.

1994   California passes Proposition 187, the "Save Our State" Initiative.

Annual legal immigration to the United States is 804,416.

1995 Osama bin Laden issues "fatwa" versus West and the United States.

Annual legal immigration to the United States is 720,461.

1996 Congress enacts the Illegal Immigration Reform and Immigrant Responsibility Act (IIRIRA) and the Anti-Terrorism and Effective Death Penalty Act. Among its many provisions, it grants to INS inspectors the authority to make "on-the-spot credible fear" determinations involving asylum. Annual legal immigration to the United States is 915,900.

1998 Osama bin Laden signs a second "fatwa" against the United States. Al Qaeda begins planning to attack the United States in what ends up as the 9/11 attacks.

U.S. Congress establishes the Hart-Rudman Commission on National Security.

Annual immigration to the United States is 654,451.

1999 Congress passes the Trafficking Victims Protection Act. Annual immigration is 646,568.

2000 October 12, Al Qaeda operatives carry out attack on USS *Cole* in the port of Yemen.

Annual legal immigration to the United States is 849,807.

The Post-9/11 Actions

2001 September 11 terrorist attack on the World Trade Center Twin Towers in New York City, the Pentagon in Washington, D.C., and a hijacked plane downed in rural Pennsylvania believed to have been targeted for the U.S. Congress Capitol Buildings. Immediate calls for a crackdown on international terrorism begin. President Bush announces the "war on terrorism." On September 18, Congress passes Authorization to Use Force against Terrorists.

October 1, 2001, the United States invades Afghanistan in "Operation Enduring Freedom." This begins the war that continues today, 16 years later and counting.

On October 8, 2001, President Bush establishes the Office of Homeland Security within the White House and the Homeland Security Council (Executive Order 13228).

On October 26, 2001, Congress enacts the USA Patriot Act granting sweeping new powers to the attorney general, the FBI, and the DOJ, and authority to detain "enemy combatants" involved in or suspected of terrorism. The DOJ rounds up about 1,200 Muslims arrested and detained for days to months as being "suspected" terrorists. No one among those swept up is ever charged with terrorist activity. In November, the DOJ breaks up terrorist cells in Portland, Oregon, Detroit, Michigan, and Buffalo, New York. The DOD begins drone attacks to kill Al Qaeda leaders.

The first Dream Act bill is introduced.

Annual legal immigration to the United States is 1,064,318.

2002   The INS issues notice to several of the (now dead) hijackers that they are given permission to enroll in United States–located (Florida) flight training programs. This results in immediate calls for restructuring the INS to remove the Border Patrol functions from the INS.

In November, Congress establishes the cabinet-level Department of Homeland Security. The attorney general is granted sweeping new powers for expedited removal. In March, the INS is abolished, and its functions are transferred to the DHS. The undersecretary for Border and Transportation Security begins oversight of Immigration Enforcement and Citizenship and Immigration Services.

The United Nations issues its Protocols on Human Trafficking and Immigrant Smuggling in Palermo, Italy, signed by 141 countries, including the United States.

NSEERS is implemented; SEVIS is implemented. The United States opens up a detention camp at Guantanamo Bay (a.k.a. "Gitmo").

Annual legal immigration to the United States is 1,059,902.

2003   In January, Congress creates the Terrorist Threat Integration Center in the CIA.

Annual legal immigration to the United States is 703,542.

2004   The 9/11 Commission issues its final report detailing the intelligence failures contributing to the success of the terrorist cells and their attacks.

Congress passes the Intelligence Reform and Terrorism Prevention Act. President Bush appoints John Negroponte, ambassador to Iraq, as the first DNI.

The National Counterterrorism Center is established, housed within the CIA.

Unauthorized immigrants within the United States reach an estimated 11 million. ICE reports 1.1 million apprehensions at the nation's borders.

Annual legal immigration to the United States is 957,883.

2005   The House passes the Border Protection, Anti-terrorism and Illegal Immigration Control Act, known as the REAL ID Act. Congress also passes the National Container Security Act. It enacts the Detainee Treatment Act, which forbids the use of waterboarding as an enhanced interrogation technique. On February 15, Michael Chertoff is appointed as the secretary of the DHS. In August, Hurricane Katrina strikes the United States, and New Orleans, Louisiana, and Mississippi are hard hit.

Nine states pass antihuman trafficking acts; and three states pass laws mandating state and local law enforcement to enforce federal immigration laws against unauthorized immigrants. The governors of Arizona and New Mexico issue "state of emergency" declarations because of the extreme adverse effects of illegal immigration on their respective states.

Ministers of the European Union approve the use of biometric cards for immigrants to EU countries. Japan begins fingerprinting all incoming immigrants. France expels several thousand illegal immigrants. Russia imposes fines for hiring illegal immigrants. Annual legal immigration to the United States is 1,122,373.

2006   Congress extends the USA Patriot Act in March, officially the Uniting and Strengthening America by Providing Appropriate Tools to Intercept and Obstruct Terrorism Act.

Congress passes the Secure Fence Act, and President Bush signs it into law. The law authorizes the construction of a 700-mile bollard-type fence along the Southwestern border.

The Border Action Network, an advocacy group, is established.

The second Dream Act bill is introduced in Congress.

Annual legal immigration to the United States is 1,266,129.

The third Dream Act bill is introduced in Congress.

2007   President Obama is elected. His administration begins a surge in the use of expedited removals to deport unauthorized immigrants. Annual legal immigration to the United States is 1,107,126. Obama appoints Janet Napolitano as secretary of DHS. She launches cyber war efforts, including establishment of the Center for Strategic and International Studies. A fourth Dream Act bill is introduced in Congress.

2008   President Obama uses executive action to mitigate certain aspects of IIRIRA.

Annual immigration to the United States is 1,120,818. The DHS creates the Cyber Security and the Cyber Traffic systems (Einstein 1, 2, 3). The U.S. Cyber Command is established.

2009   Arizona passes a law mandating state and local police to demand anyone suspected of being illegal to show documents to prove their legal status.

In *Arizona v. United States* (132 S. Ct. 2492), the Supreme Court rules the Arizona law unconstitutional. The DHS thwarts NYC. Subway system bombing attack. A fourth Dream Act bill is introduced in Congress.

Annual legal immigration to the United States is 1,042,625.

2010   A fifth Dream Act bill is introduced. Annual legal immigration is 1,042,625.

2011   Osama bin Laden is killed on May 2, in a U.S. Navy Seal team raid in Pakistan. Annual legal immigration to the United States is 1,062,040.

A sixth Dream Act bill is introduced in Congress.

2012   President Obama issues executive action order, DACA, granting temporary, conditional legal status to "Dreamer" children. Annual legal immigration to the United States is 1,031,631.

2013   Annual legal immigration to the United States is 990,553. Jeh Johnson is appointed secretary of the DHS on December 23, 2013.

2014   The Senate passes S.744, a comprehensive immigration reform bill in a bipartisan vote, but the measure is blocked in the U.S. House of Representatives. Annual legal immigration is 1,016,518.

President Obama extends the DACA order.

2015   President Obama issues the DAPA executive action order, granting temporary, conditional legal residency to unauthorized immigrant parents of U.S. citizens and legal permanent aliens. A surge in arrivals of children unaccompanied by adults from El Salvador, Guatemala, and Honduras moves President Obama to grant "Temporary Protected Status" to 5,000 such children for whom it is deemed too unsafe to return them to their country of origin. Annual legal immigration to the United States is 1,051,031.

2016   February 17, U.S. district judge, Texas, Andrew Hanen, places an injunction of the Obama administration's implementation of the DAPA order.

2017   President Trump is elected. In January, President Trump appoints John Kelly as secretary of DHS and Jim Mattis as secretary of the Department of Defense. On January 25, 2017, he issues an executive order to start a pilot program to build a wall on the U.S.-Mexico border.

On January 25, President Trump issues his executive order against "sanctuary cities" known as "Enhancing the Public Safety in the Interior of the United States." On January 27, he issues his (first) Muslim travel ban. On January 31, President Trump fires Acting Attorney General Sally Yates for refusing to defend the travel ban order in the federal court. On February 3, Federal District Judge Robart, in Seattle, Washington, rules that the travel ban order is unconstitutional. On March 6, Trump issues a second travel ban order that Judge Watson, a federal district judge in Hawaii, and Judge Chuang, of the Maryland Federal District Court, also rule it unconstitutional.

In May, President Trump orders the DHS to establish the Victims of Immigration Crime Enforcement (VOICE) program. On June 21, 2017, the U.S. Supreme Court partially upholds the second travel ban order and schedules oral arguments on the order for fall 2017.

Glossary

Accompaniment the emotional and temporal support given to an unauthorized immigrant by the new sanctuary movement.

Advocacy the support given by the sanctuary movement to unauthorized immigrants involving attendance at immigration court hearings, and accompanying individuals to mandatory check-ins with the Department of Homeland Security.

Alien a person who is not a citizen or national of a given nation-state.

Amnesty a legal pardoning of a person who entered the United States illegally or is otherwise in nonlegal status, thereby changing his or her legal status to legal resident alien.

Asymmetric threat a form of cyberattack against the United States against which there are no defenses using tactics that are morally reprehensible or restricted by legal agreement.

Axis of Evil countries Iran, Iraq, and North Korea.

Behemoth a mighty animal described in Job 40:15–24 as an example of the power of God. In current lexicon, it is used to mean something monstrous in size, power, or appearance.

Biometric identification the use of DNA, fingerprints, iris scans, facial recognition technology, and voice imprints to identify someone as an anti-terrorist screening procedure.

Biometrics use of fingerprints, facial recognition technology, and iris scans as a way of accurately identifying people in a quick and efficient manner.

Border Patrol the law enforcement arm of the Department of Homeland Security.

Botnet capturing and using a robot computer linked to a net or system.

Brain drain refers to the flow of talented migrants from lesser-developed to developed countries.

Bureaucratic culture a hierarchical and formal organization that has several layers where tasks, authority, and responsibility are delegated between departments, offices, or people. This structure is held together by a central or main administration, and it has led to the development of modern civilization.

Climate change a change in global or regional climate patterns; in particular, a change apparent from the mid- to late 20th century onward and attributed to the increased levels of atmospheric carbon dioxide produced by human use of fossil fuels.

COTS an acronym for commercial, off-the-shelf software that is less expensive but highly vulnerable to cyberattacks, for example, Windows NT.

Cyber space all of the computer networks in the world and everything they connect and control.

Cyberwarfare an unauthorized penetration by, or on the behalf of, or in support of, a government into another nation's computer or network, or any other activity affecting a computer system, in which the purpose is to add, alter, or falsify data, or cause disruption of or damage to a computer or network device, or the objects of computer control.

DACA acronym for Deferred Action for Childhood Arrivals, a program of the Obama administration's DHS that protected Dreamer children from deportation as unauthorized immigrants.

DAPA acronym for Deferred Action for Parental Accountability.

De facto a Latin phrase meaning "by action."

De jure a Latin phrase meaning something being done "by law."

Deportation a legal process by which a nation sends individuals back to their countries of origin after refusing them legal residence.

Devolution the transfer or delegation of power to a lower level, especially by a central government to local or regional administration.

Distributed denial of service a weapon of cyber warfare that uses a botnet to flood the attacked country's Internet system with an overwhelming number of demands or messages that cause the computer system to break down.

Dream Act an acronym for Development, Relief, and Education for Alien Minors, a proposed law that would provide a path to citizenship for unauthorized immigrants brought to the United States as minor children.

Due process of law the constitutional limitation on government behavior to deal with an individual according to prescribed rules and procedures.

Earned legalization a proposal to allow unauthorized immigrants to change their status to that of legal permanent resident by paying fines and satisfying stipulated conditions akin to those who came as authorized permanent resident aliens.

Earned residency a path to get a green card and the right to stay in the United States but not a path to citizenship. It involves paying taxes, learning English, and committing no substantial crime.

Emigrant a person who voluntarily leaves his or her country of birth for permanent resettlement elsewhere.

Employer sanctions a provision of the 1986 Immigration Reform and Control Act that provided legal penalties (fines and/or prison) for knowingly hiring an illegal alien.

Executive orders actions issued by a president, assigned numbers, and published in the federal register, akin to laws passed by Congress, that direct members of the executive branch to follow a new policy or directive.

Exempt an individual or class or category of individuals to whom a certain provision of the law does not apply.

Expedited removal a stipulation in law changing the procedures by which persons in the United States without legal status may be deported with fewer judicial protections to do so.

Fatwa a ruling by an Islamic imam or leader, giving legal and religious authority for a holy war or specific actions (e.g., the terrorist killing of innocent civilians) in furtherance of a holy war (a jihad).

First-responders fire, police, and emergency medical personnel; the DHS maintains a First Responders Group.

Formally used defense sites (FUDs) refers to closed military bases and facilities.

Globalization a tide of economic, technological, and intellectual forces integrating a global community.

Green card a document issued by the DHS that certifies an individual as a legal immigrant entitled to work in the United States.

Groupthink a social psychological term that refers to a phenomenon in which people strive for consensus within a group in which people set aside their personal beliefs or adopt the opinion of the rest of the group; people who oppose the overriding opinion of the group remain silent to keep peace rather than disrupt the uniformity of the group.

Guest-worker program a program enabling the legal importation of workers for temporary labor in specified occupations.

H-1B Visa a category of temporary visa issued to a nonimmigrant allowing employers who will employ guest workers temporarily in a specialty occupation or field for a stipulated period of time.

Illegal aliens   individuals who are in a territory without documentation permitting permanent residence..

Immigrant   an alien admitted to the United States as a lawful permanent resident.

Inclusion   an individual's or group's engagement with the processes or organizations that recognize the individual or group by conferring membership or by providing resources such as entitlement or protests; it provides a sense of security, stability, and predictability understood primarily as an ability to plan for the future.

Investor immigrant   an individual permitted to immigrate based on the promise to invest $1 million in an urban area or $500,000 in a rural area to create at least 10 jobs.

Jihad   an armed "holy war" issued by a Muslim leader (usually an imam) that provides a religious/legal justification for terrorist actions against the West.

Kinetic warfare   war using "active as opposed to latent" motion— such as dropping bombs, shooting bullets, killing people.

Las Posadas   a reenactment of the flight of the Holy Family (Jesus, Mary, and Joseph) to Egypt used by the sanctuary movement to project a powerful image of the plight of the undocumented seeking hospitality in the United States.

Legacy wastes   wastes remaining from nuclear and chemical processes at military facilities and bases following military base closures.

Logic bombs   a malicious program timed to cause harm at a certain point in time that is inactive until that point and is activated by a preset trigger, such as a preprogrammed date and time inserted into a computer or computer system's software.

Lone-wolf terrorist   a person perpetrating a terrorist act or plot who is inspired by but not associated with an international terrorist group or organization, such as Al Qaeda or ISIS.

L-Visa   one of two types of visas issued for persons employed at a management or executive level and issued for a specified time of up to three years and renewable for a maximum of seven years that is used for intracompany transferees who have specialized knowledge in the field; L-2 visas are issued to spouses or minor children of L-1 visa holders.

Malware   an abbreviated term meaning "malicious software" designed to gain access to or damage a computer without the knowledge of the owner, including spyware, keyloggers, true viruses, worms, or malicious codes that infiltrate a computer.

Naturalization   the legal act of making an individual a citizen who is not born a citizen.

Nonimmigrant   an alien seeking temporary entry into the United States for a specific purpose other than permanent settlement—such as a foreign government official, tourist, student, temporary workers, or cultural exchange visitor.

Overstayers   persons who enter the United States on a temporary visa who then stay beyond the time specified in their visa at which time they are to voluntarily depart the United States and by which such overstaying their status becomes unauthorized/illegal.

Passport   a legal identification document issued by a sovereign nation-state attesting to the nationality of an individual for the purpose of international travel.

Patriotic assimilation   the adoption, by the newcomer, of American civic values and the American heritage as one's own.

Permanent resident   a noncitizen who is allowed to live permanently in the United States and who can travel in and out of the country without a visa and can work without restriction; such a person is allowed to accumulate time toward becoming a naturalized citizen.

Political incorporation a model that holds for a minority community to witness an effective response to its needs; minority leaders must come to occupy positions of government authority.

Prosecutorial discretion a privilege given to the prosecuting attorney in deciding whether to prosecute or to plea bargain, recommend parole, and so on.

Protocol an international agreement governing the understanding and procedures that member-states who are parties to a treaty agreed upon for a given purpose, as in the UN protocols regarding the status and treatment of refugees.

Pull factor an aspect of the receiving nation that draws immigrants for resettlement.

Push factor an event that compels large numbers of persons to emigrate—leave their country of origin for permanent resettlement elsewhere.

Racial profiling a pattern of behavior of police officers based on racial appearance.

Refugee a qualified applicant for conditional entry into the United States whose application could not be approved because of an adequate number of preference visas.

Remediation technologies processes for dealing with the cleanup of contaminated soils, water, and similar legacy wastes.

Requests for detention requests that an agency hold an individual beyond the point at which he or she would otherwise be released.

Requests for notification requests that state or local law enforcement notify ICE of a pending release during the time that a person is otherwise in custody under state or local authority.

Rogue nations nation-states that refuse to abide by international law and norms and continue to develop or use banned nuclear and chemical weapons.

Salafis a fundamentalist Islamic group associated with Wahhabism.

Sanctuary city   a city in the United States that follows certain procedures that shelter illegal immigrants that may be by "de jure" or "de facto" action. The designation has no legal meaning and is most commonly used for cities that do not permit municipal funds or resources to be applied in furtherance of enforcement of federal immigration laws; that is, they do not allow police or municipal employees to inquire about one's immigrant status.

Stakeholder   a person or organization with an interest or concern in something, especially a business; or one who is involved or is affected by a policy or course of action.

STEM   an acronym for science, technology, engineering, and mathematics.

Stovepiping   a pathway for transmitting information directly through levels of a hierarchy by bypassing intervening levels that remain uninformed about the information.

Sunsetting provisions   provisions written into a law that provides for an automatic expiration of the law after a specified time period.

Torture   an irreversible, permanent, and negative change in a person's well-being.

Unauthorized immigrants   those who come undocumented or break or overstay the conditions of their visas and become illegal immigrants without the status of permanent resident alien.

Undocumented immigrants   individuals who enter the United States without inspection or paper documentation, allowing them to enter and to reside in the United States and to legally work while doing so.

Unfunded mandates   are requirements by the federal government on state and local governments without offsetting funding for their implementation.

Virtual fencing   aerial surveillance, increased border staffing, and giving DHS authority to take security actions in the 50 national parks within 100 miles of U.S. borders.

Visa   a legal document issued by a consular or similar state department official allowing a person to travel to the United States for either permanent or temporary reasons—such as immigrant, student, tourist, government representative, business, or cultural exchange.

Walling   an "enhanced interrogation" technique in which interrogators slam detainees against a wall using an improvised collar, such as a rolled-up towel.

Waterboarding   an enhanced interrogation technique in which detainees are secured to a board with a towel covering their mouths, and water is poured over the towel simulating drowning.

Withdrawal   an alien's voluntary removal of an application for admission in lieu of an exclusion hearing before an immigration judge.

Xenophobia   an unfounded fear of foreigners.

Zero-day malware   a type of malware that has only recently been discovered and had not been anticipated; such malware is ferreted out using a deep-pocket inspection system and is resolved with security upgrades or software patches.

Index

About the Author

Dr. Michael C. LeMay is professor emeritus from California State University-San Bernardino, where he served as director of the National Security Studies program, an interdisciplinary master's degree program, and as chair of the Department of Political Science, and assistant dean for student affairs of the College of Social and Behavioral Sciences. He has frequently written and presented papers at professional conferences on the topic of immigration. He has also written numerous journal articles, book chapters, published essays, and book reviews. He has published in *The International Migration Review, In Defense of the Alien, Journal of American Ethnic History, Southeastern Political Science Review, Teaching Political Science,* and the *National Civic Review.* He is author of more than a dozen academic volumes dealing with immigration history and policy. His prior books on the subject are *Illegal Immigration: A Reference Handbook,* 2e (2015, ABC-CLIO) and *Doctors at the Borders: Immigration and the Rise of Public Health* (2015, Praeger); he is series editor and contributing author of the three-volume series, *Transforming America: Perspectives on Immigration* (2013, ABC-CLIO); *Illegal Immigration: A Reference Handbook,* 1e (2007, ABC-CLIO); *Guarding the Gates: Immigration and National Security* (2006, Praeger Security International); *U.S. Immigration: A Reference Handbook* (2004, ABC-CLIO); *U.S. Immigration and Naturalization Laws and Issues: A Documentary History,* edited with Elliott Barkan (1999, Greenwood); *Anatomy of a Public Policy: The Reform of Contemporary Immigration Law* (1994, Praeger); *The Gatekeepers: Comparative*

Immigration Policy (1989, Praeger); *From Open Door to Dutch Door: An Analysis of U.S. Immigration Policy since 1820* (1987, Praeger); and *The Struggle for Influence* (1985, University Press of America). Professor LeMay has written two textbooks that have considerable material related to these topics: *Public Administration: Clashing Values in the Administration of Public Policy,* 2e (2006, Wadsworth), and *The Perennial Struggle: Race, Ethnicity and Minority Group Relations in the United States,* 3e (2009, Prentice-Hall). He frequently lecturers on topics related to immigration history and policy. He loves to travel and has lectured around the world and visited more than 100 cities in 40 countries. He has two works in progress: *Winning Office and Making a Nation: Immigration and the American Political Party System* (under review, coauthored with Scot Zentner) and *U.S. Immigration Policy, Ethnicity and Religion in American History.* (forthcoming, Praeger Press, 2018).